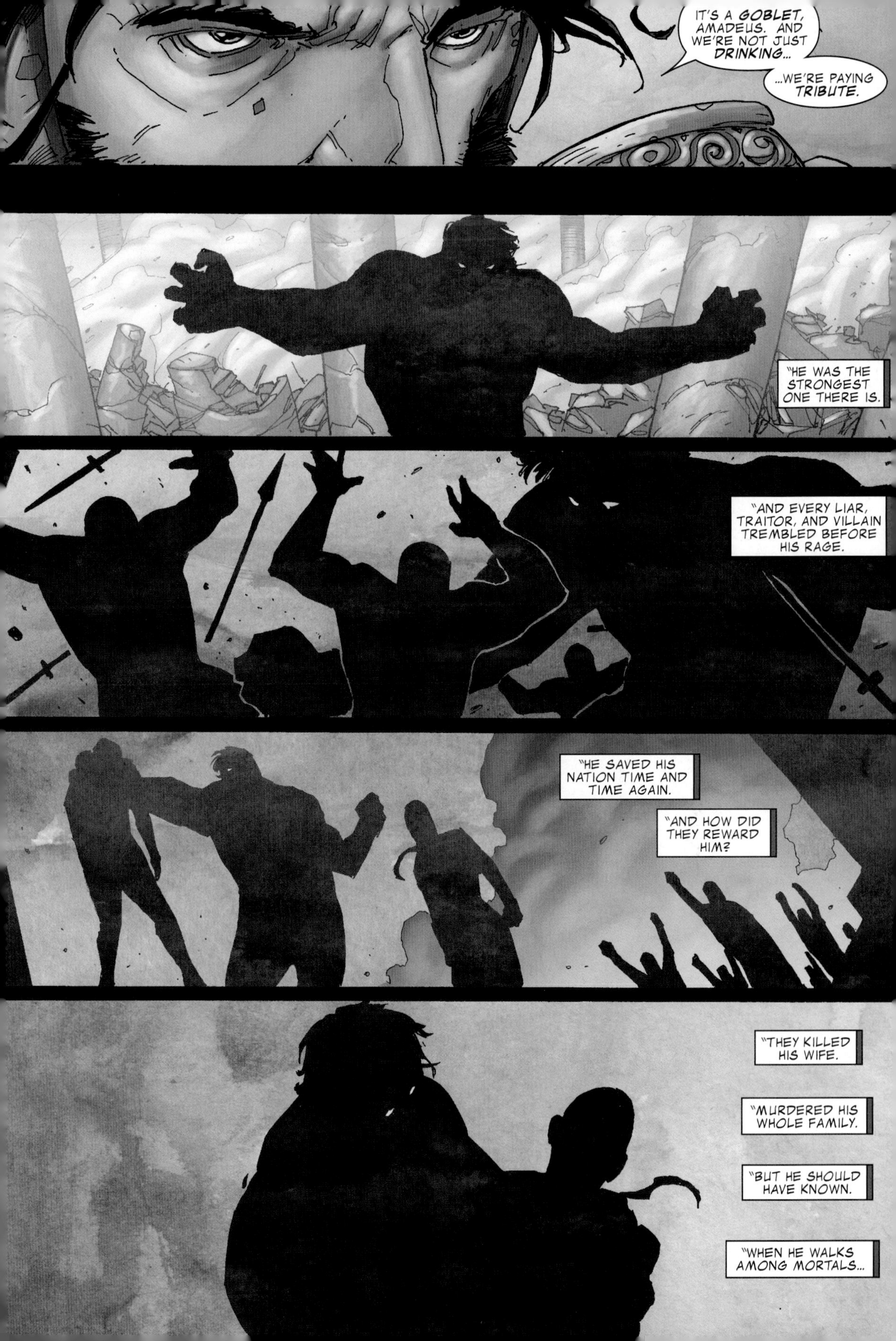
IT'S A GOBLET, AMADEUS. AND WE'RE NOT JUST DRINKING...
...WE'RE PAYING TRIBUTE.
"HE WAS THE STRONGEST ONE THERE IS.
"AND EVERY LIAR, TRAITOR, AND VILLAIN TREMBLED BEFORE HIS RAGE.
"HE SAVED HIS NATION TIME AND TIME AGAIN.
"AND HOW DID THEY REWARD HIM?
"THEY KILLED HIS WIFE.
"MURDERED HIS WHOLE FAMILY.
"BUT HE SHOULD HAVE KNOWN.
"WHEN HE WALKS AMONG MORTALS...

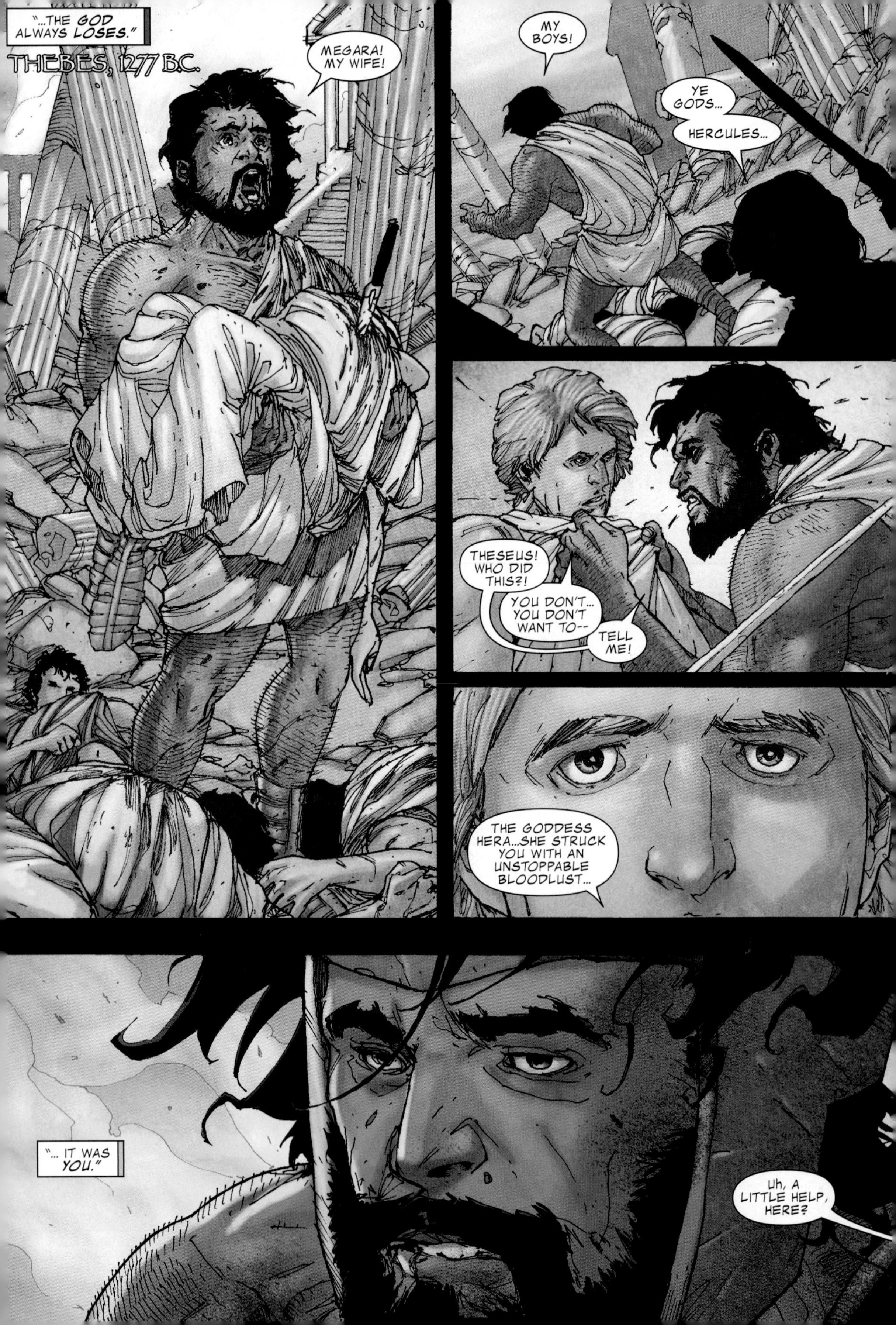

"...THE GOD ALWAYS LOSES."
THEBES, 1277 B.C.
MEGARA! MY WIFE!
MY BOYS!
YE GODS...
HERCULES...
THESEUS! WHO DID THIS?!
YOU DON'T... YOU DON'T WANT TO--
TELL ME!
THE GODDESS HERA...SHE STRUCK YOU WITH AN UNSTOPPABLE BLOODLUST...
"... IT WAS YOU."
UH, A LITTLE HELP, HERE?

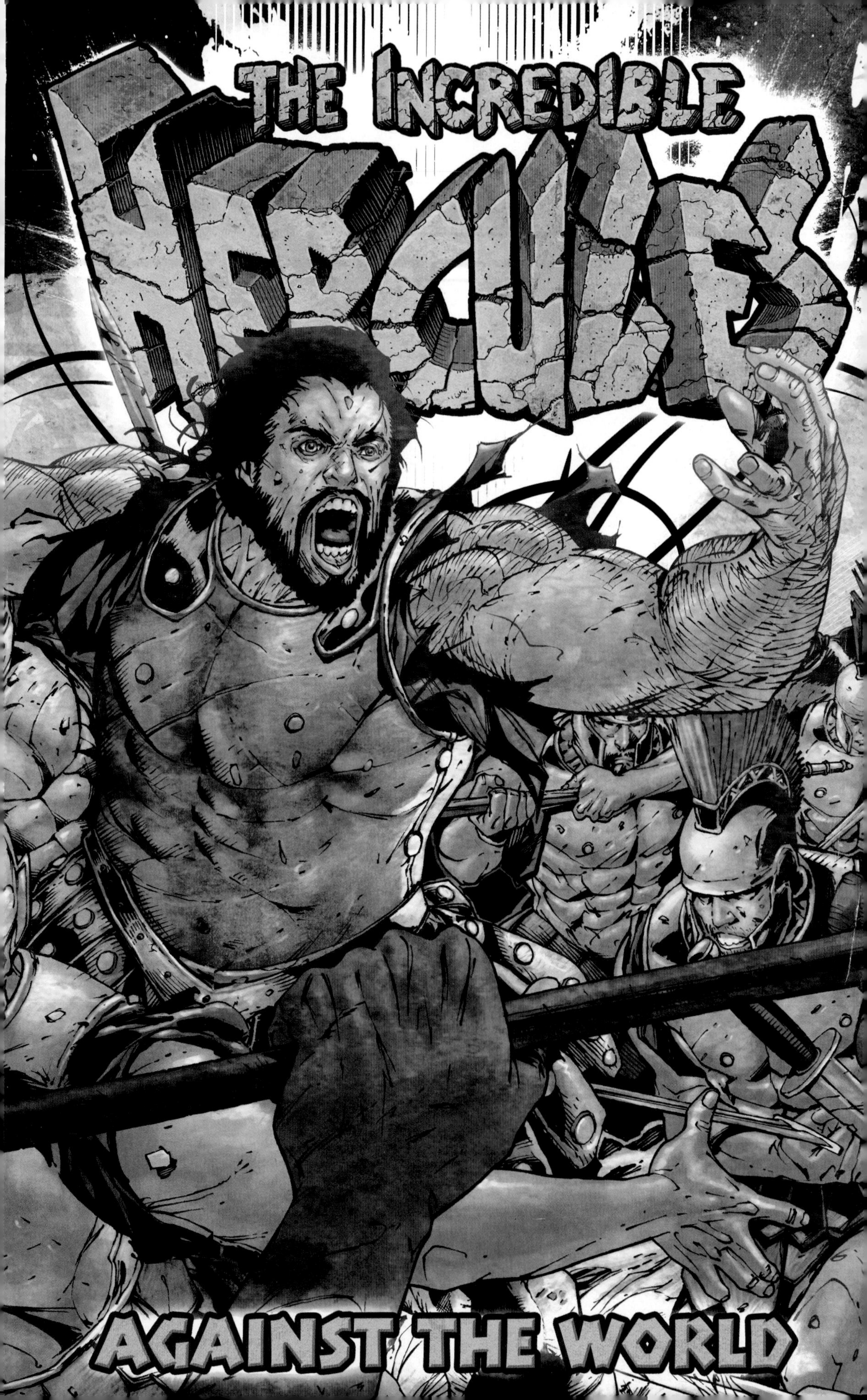
THE INCREDIBLE
HERCULES
AGAINST THE WORLD

THE INCREDIBLE HERCULES

Writers: **GREG PAK** & **FRED VAN LENTE**

INCREDIBLE HULK #112 & INCREDIBLE HERCULES #113-115

Penciler: **KHOI PHAM**

Inkers: **KHOI PHAM** (Issue #112) • **PAUL NEARY** (Issue # 113-114)

PAUL NEARY with **DANNY MIKI** (Issue #115)

Colorists: **STEPHANE PERU** (Issue #112-114) & **DENNIS CALERO** (Issue #115)

Letterers: **CHRIS ELIOPOULOS** & **VC'S JOE CARAMAGNA**

Cover Artists: **ARTHUR ADAMS** & **LAURA MARTIN** (Issue #112)

ARTHUR ADAMS & **GURU EFX** (Issue #113-115)

HULK VS. HERCULES: WHEN TITANS COLLIDE

Artists: **KHOI PHAM, PAUL NEARY** & **DENNIS CALERO** (Pages 1-2, 31)

ERIC NGUYEN (Pages 3-7) • **REILLY BROWN, CARLOS CUEVAS,**

TERRY PALLOT & **CHRIS SOTOMAYOR** (Pages 8, 11-30)

BOB LAYTON & **GURU EFX** (Pages 9-10)

Letterer: **VC'S JOE CARAMAGNA**

Cover Artist: **MARKO DJURDJEVIC**

Assistant Editor: **NATHAN COSBY**

Editor: **MARK PANICCIA**

Collection Editor: **CORY LEVINE**

Editorial Assistant: **JODY LEHEUP** • Assistant Editor: **JOHN DENNING**

Editors, Special Projects: **JENNIFER GRÜNWALD** & **MARK D. BEAZLEY**

Senior Editor, Special Projects: **JEFF YOUNGQUIST**

Senior Vice President of Sales: **DAVID GABRIEL**

Book Design: **RODOLFO MURAGUCHI**

Editor in Chief: **JOE QUESADA** • Publisher: **DAN BUCKLEY**

INCREDIBLE HERCULES: AGAINST THE WORLD. Contains material originally published in magazine form as INCREDIBLE HULK #112, INCREDIBLE HERCULES #113-115 and HULK VS. HERCULES: WHEN TITANS COLLIDE. First printing 2008. ISBN# 978-0-7851-3312-4. Published by MARVEL PUBLISHING, INC., a subsidiary of MARVEL ENTERTAINMENT, INC. OFFICE OF PUBLICATION: 417 5th Avenue, New York, NY 10016. Copyright © 2007 and 2008 Marvel Characters, Inc. All rights reserved. $19.99 per copy in the U.S. and $21.00 in Canada (GST #R127032852); Canadian Agreement #40668537. All characters featured in this issue and the distinctive names and likenesses thereof, and all related indicia are trademarks of Marvel Characters, Inc. No similarity between any of the names, characters, persons, and/or institutions in this magazine with those of any living or dead person or institution is intended, and any such similarity which may exist is purely coincidental. **Printed in the U.S.A.** ALAN FINE, CEO Marvel Toys & Publishing Divisions and CMO Marvel Entertainment, Inc.; DAVID GABRIEL, SVP of Publishing Sales & Circulation; DAVID BOGART, SVP of Business Affairs & Talent Management; MICHAEL PASCIULLO, VP of Merchandising & Communications; JIM O'KEEFE, VP of Operations & Logistics; DAN CARR, Executive Director of Publishing Technology; JUSTIN F. GABRIE, Director of Editorial Operations; SUSAN CRESPI, Editorial Operations Manager; OMAR OTIEKU, Production Manager; STAN LEE, Chairman Emeritus. For information regarding advertising in Marvel Comics or on Marvel.com, please contact Mitch Dane, Advertising Director, at mdane@marvel.com. For Marvel subscription inquiries, please call 800-217-9158.

10 9 8 7 6 5 4 3 2 1

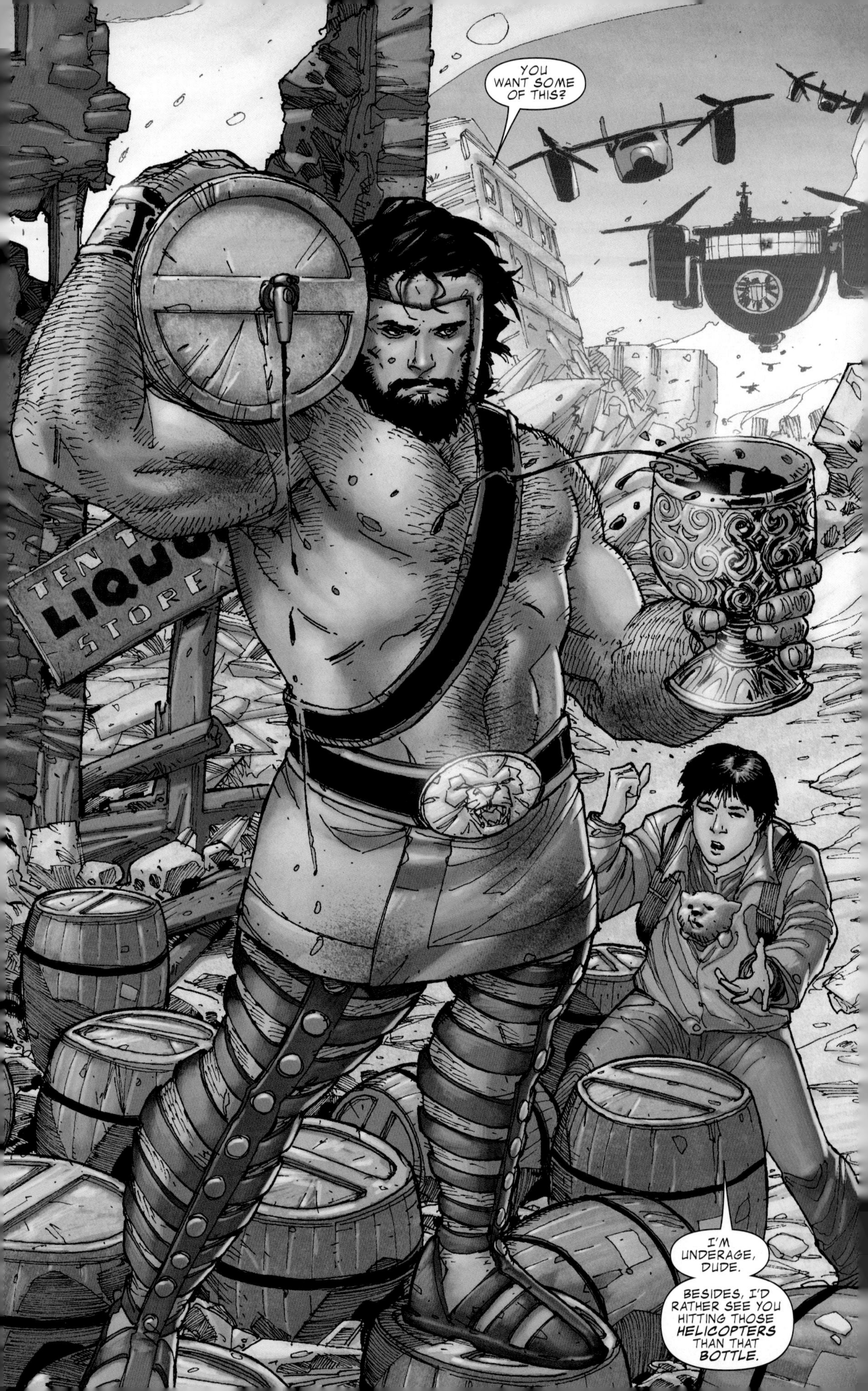
YOU WANT SOME OF THIS?
TEN T LIQU STORE
I'M UNDERAGE, DUDE.
BESIDES, I'D RATHER SEE YOU HITTING THOSE HELICOPTERS THAN THAT BOTTLE.

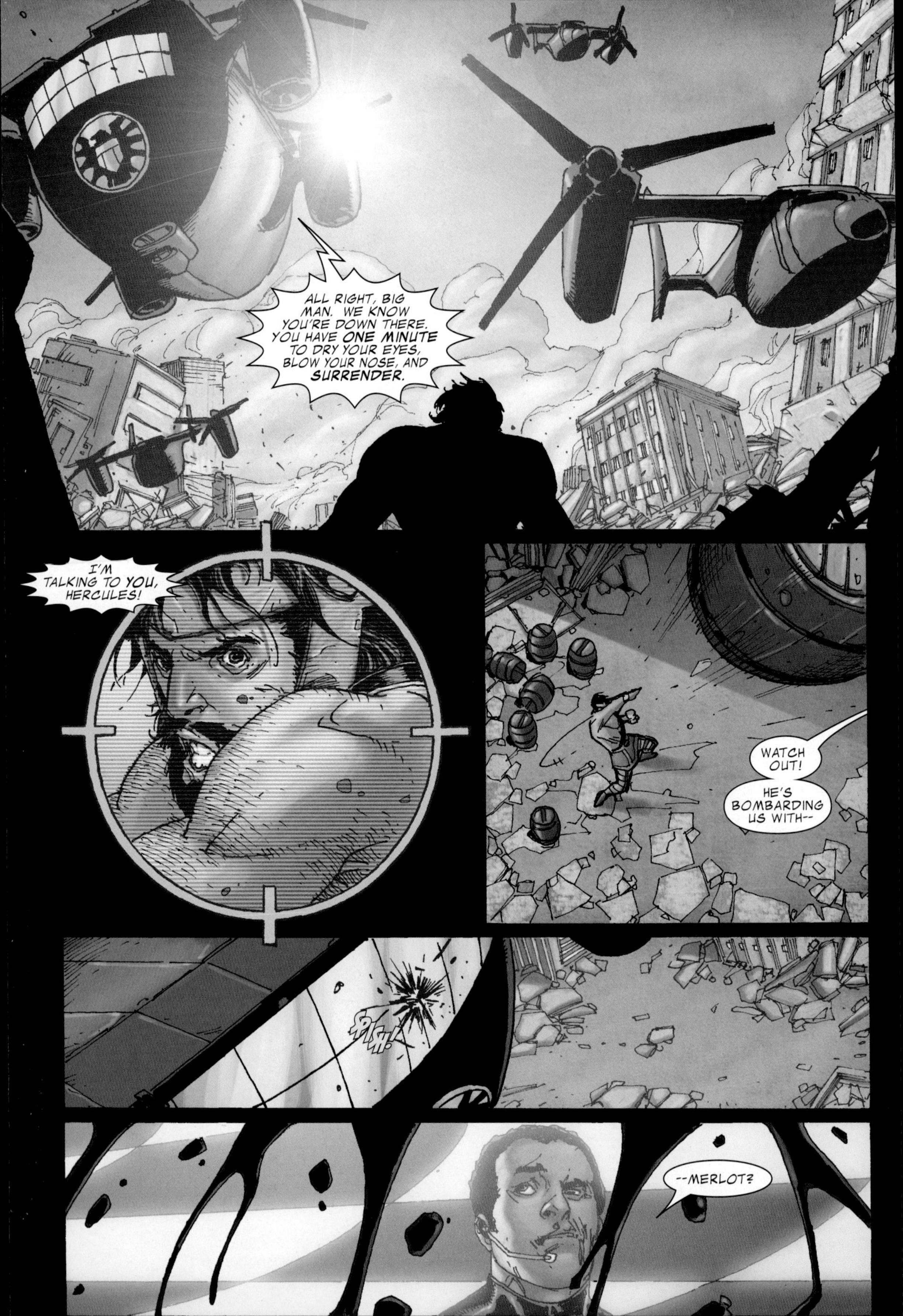
ALL RIGHT, BIG MAN. WE KNOW YOU'RE DOWN THERE. YOU HAVE **ONE MINUTE** TO DRY YOUR EYES, BLOW YOUR NOSE, AND **SURRENDER.**
I'M TALKING TO **YOU,** HERCULES!
WATCH OUT!
HE'S BOMBARDING US WITH--
SPISH!
--MERLOT?

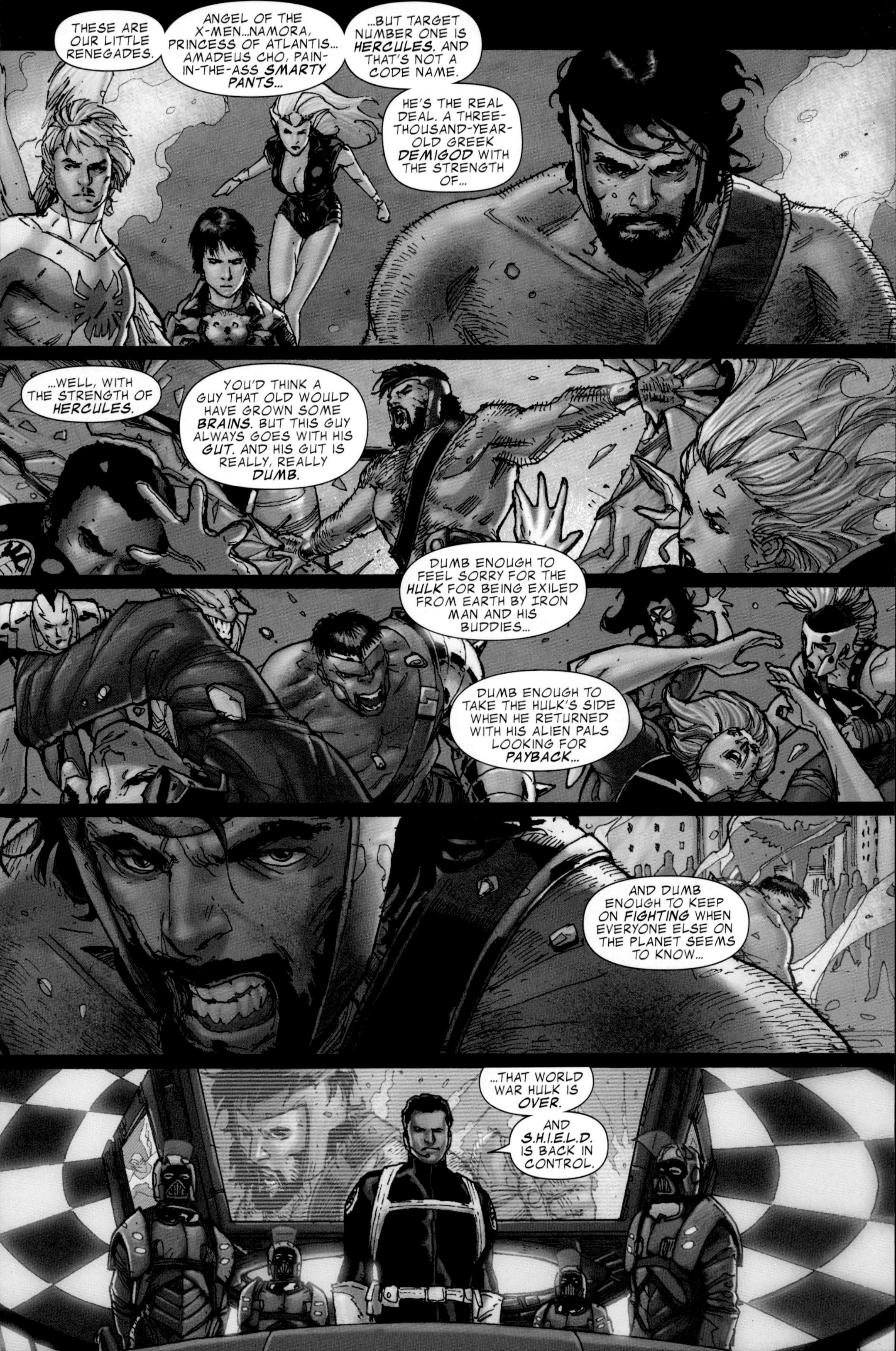
THESE ARE OUR LITTLE RENEGADES.
ANGEL OF THE X-MEN...NAMORA, PRINCESS OF ATLANTIS... AMADEUS CHO, PAIN-IN-THE-ASS SMARTY PANTS...
...BUT TARGET NUMBER ONE IS HERCULES. AND THAT'S NOT A CODE NAME.
HE'S THE REAL DEAL. A THREE-THOUSAND-YEAR-OLD GREEK DEMIGOD WITH THE STRENGTH OF...
...WELL, WITH THE STRENGTH OF HERCULES.
YOU'D THINK A GUY THAT OLD WOULD HAVE GROWN SOME BRAINS. BUT THIS GUY ALWAYS GOES WITH HIS GUT. AND HIS GUT IS REALLY, REALLY DUMB.
DUMB ENOUGH TO FEEL SORRY FOR THE HULK FOR BEING EXILED FROM EARTH BY IRON MAN AND HIS BUDDIES...
DUMB ENOUGH TO TAKE THE HULK'S SIDE WHEN HE RETURNED WITH HIS ALIEN PALS LOOKING FOR PAYBACK...
AND DUMB ENOUGH TO KEEP ON FIGHTING WHEN EVERYONE ELSE ON THE PLANET SEEMS TO KNOW...
...THAT WORLD WAR HULK IS OVER.
AND S.H.I.E.L.D. IS BACK IN CONTROL.

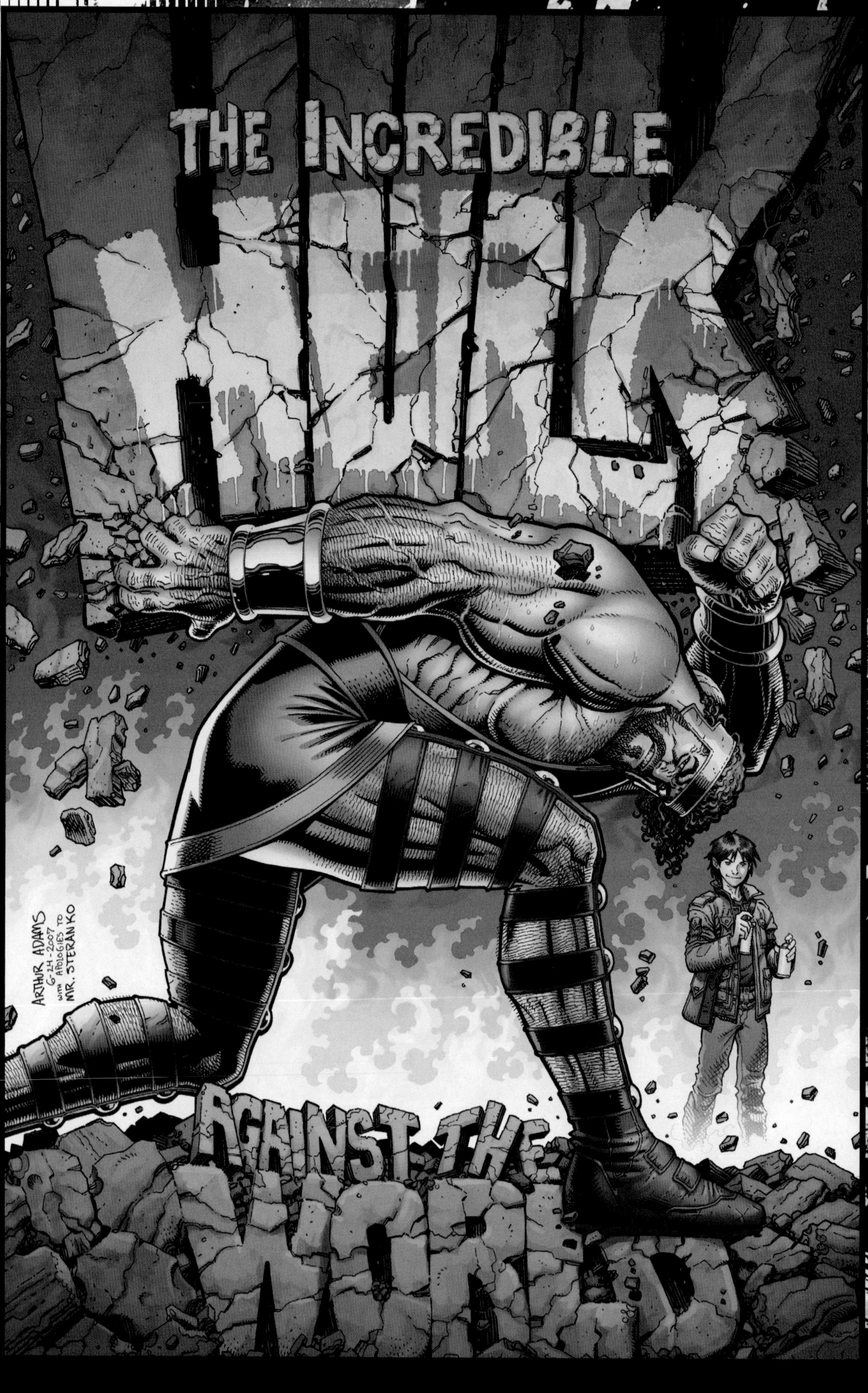
THE INCREDIBLE
AGAINST THE
ARTHUR ADAMS
6-24-2007
with APOLOGIES TO
MR. STERANKO

INCREDIBLE HULK #112

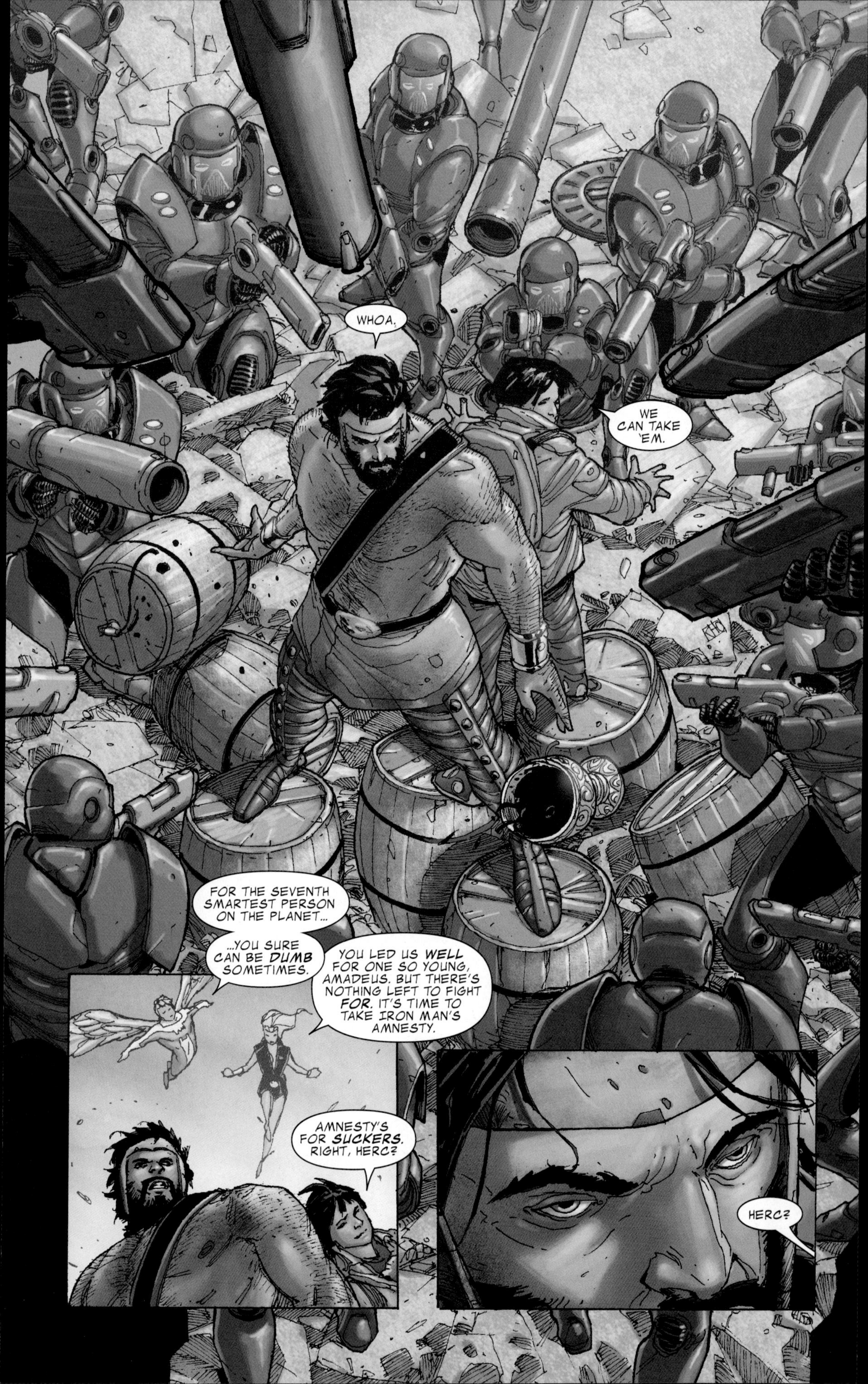
WHOA.
WE CAN TAKE 'EM.
FOR THE SEVENTH SMARTEST PERSON ON THE PLANET...
...YOU SURE CAN BE DUMB SOMETIMES.
YOU LED US WELL FOR ONE SO YOUNG, AMADEUS. BUT THERE'S NOTHING LEFT TO FIGHT FOR. IT'S TIME TO TAKE IRON MAN'S AMNESTY.
AMNESTY'S FOR SUCKERS. RIGHT, HERC?
HERC?

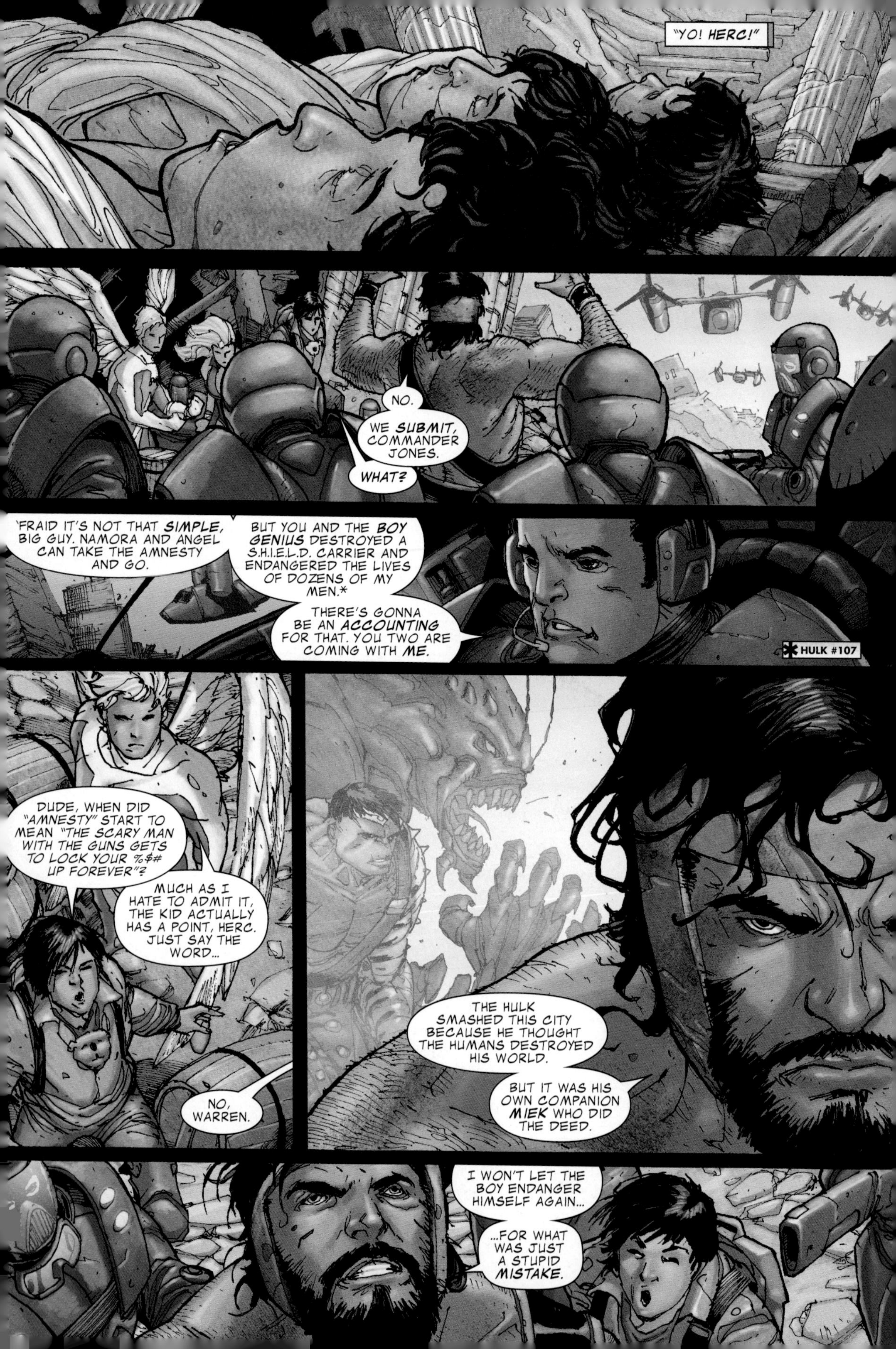

"YO! HERC!"
NO.
WE SUBMIT, COMMANDER JONES.
WHAT?
'FRAID IT'S NOT THAT SIMPLE, BIG GUY. NAMORA AND ANGEL CAN TAKE THE AMNESTY AND GO.
BUT YOU AND THE BOY GENIUS DESTROYED A S.H.I.E.L.D. CARRIER AND ENDANGERED THE LIVES OF DOZENS OF MY MEN.*
THERE'S GONNA BE AN ACCOUNTING FOR THAT. YOU TWO ARE COMING WITH ME.
* HULK #107
DUDE, WHEN DID "AMNESTY" START TO MEAN "THE SCARY MAN WITH THE GUNS GETS TO LOCK YOUR %$# UP FOREVER"?
MUCH AS I HATE TO ADMIT IT, THE KID ACTUALLY HAS A POINT, HERC. JUST SAY THE WORD...
NO, WARREN.
THE HULK SMASHED THIS CITY BECAUSE HE THOUGHT THE HUMANS DESTROYED HIS WORLD.
BUT IT WAS HIS OWN COMPANION MIEK WHO DID THE DEED.
I WON'T LET THE BOY ENDANGER HIMSELF AGAIN...
...FOR WHAT WAS JUST A STUPID MISTAKE.

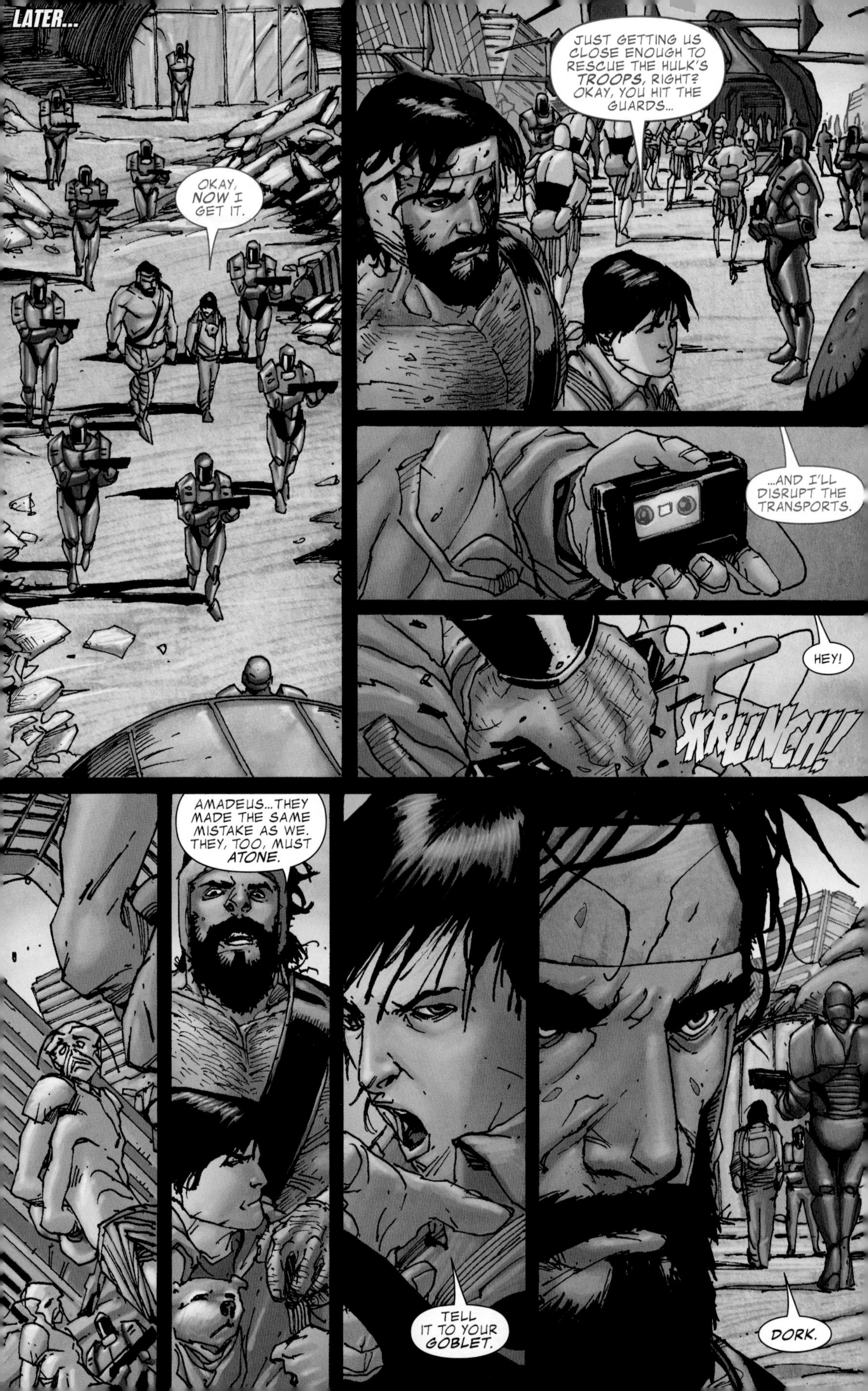
LATER...
OKAY, NOW I GET IT.
JUST GETTING US CLOSE ENOUGH TO RESCUE THE HULK'S TROOPS, RIGHT? OKAY, YOU HIT THE GUARDS...
...AND I'LL DISRUPT THE TRANSPORTS.
HEY!
SKRUNCH!
AMADEUS...THEY MADE THE SAME MISTAKE AS WE. THEY, TOO, MUST ATONE.
TELL IT TO YOUR GOBLET.
DORK.

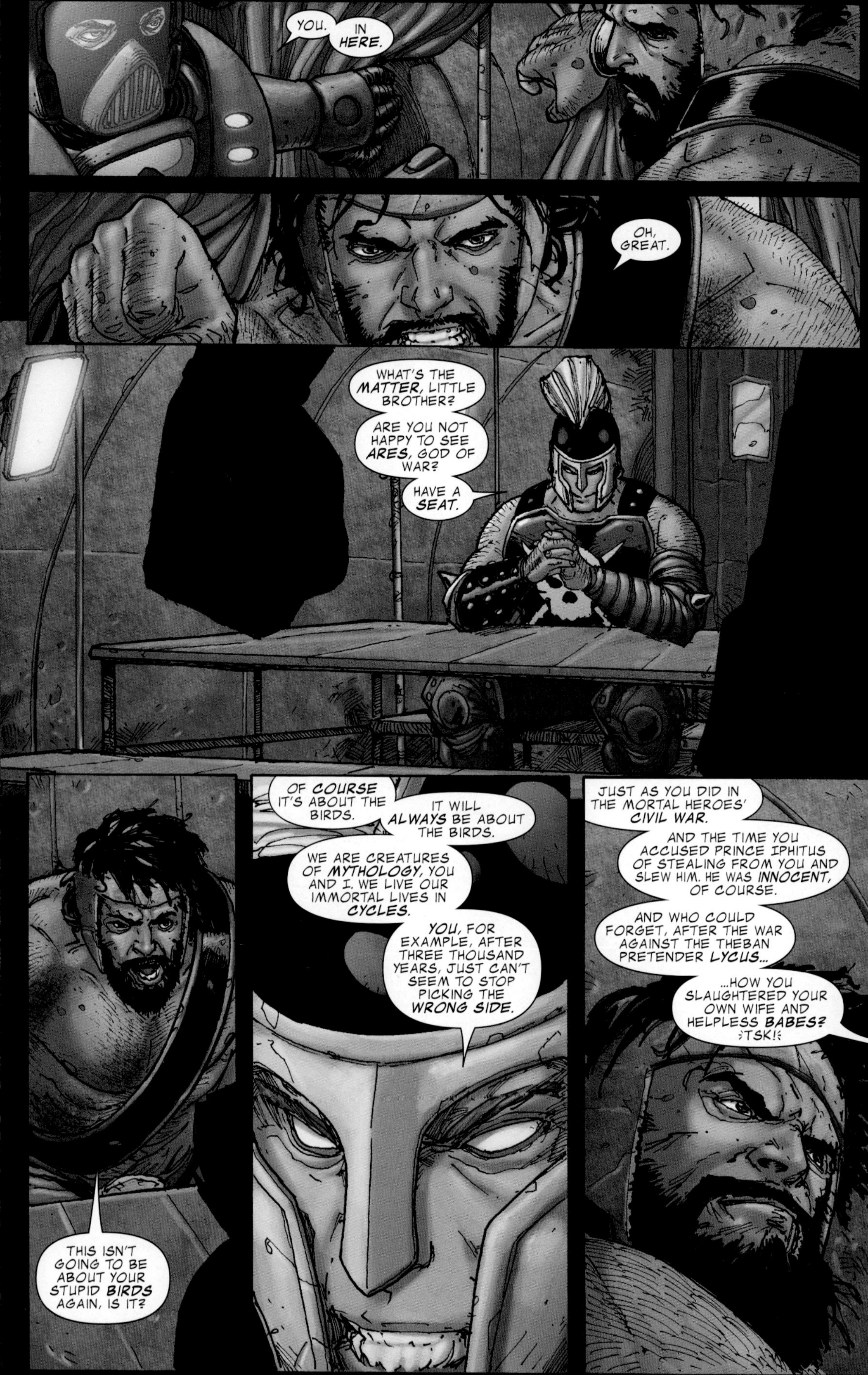
YOU. IN HERE.
OH, GREAT.
WHAT'S THE MATTER, LITTLE BROTHER?
ARE YOU NOT HAPPY TO SEE ARES, GOD OF WAR?
HAVE A SEAT.
THIS ISN'T GOING TO BE ABOUT YOUR STUPID BIRDS AGAIN, IS IT?
OF COURSE IT'S ABOUT THE BIRDS.
IT WILL ALWAYS BE ABOUT THE BIRDS.
WE ARE CREATURES OF MYTHOLOGY, YOU AND I. WE LIVE OUR IMMORTAL LIVES IN CYCLES.
YOU, FOR EXAMPLE, AFTER THREE THOUSAND YEARS, JUST CAN'T SEEM TO STOP PICKING THE WRONG SIDE.
JUST AS YOU DID IN THE MORTAL HEROES' CIVIL WAR.
AND THE TIME YOU ACCUSED PRINCE IPHITUS OF STEALING FROM YOU AND SLEW HIM. HE WAS INNOCENT, OF COURSE.
AND WHO COULD FORGET, AFTER THE WAR AGAINST THE THEBAN PRETENDER LYCUS...
...HOW YOU SLAUGHTERED YOUR OWN WIFE AND HELPLESS BABES? TSK!

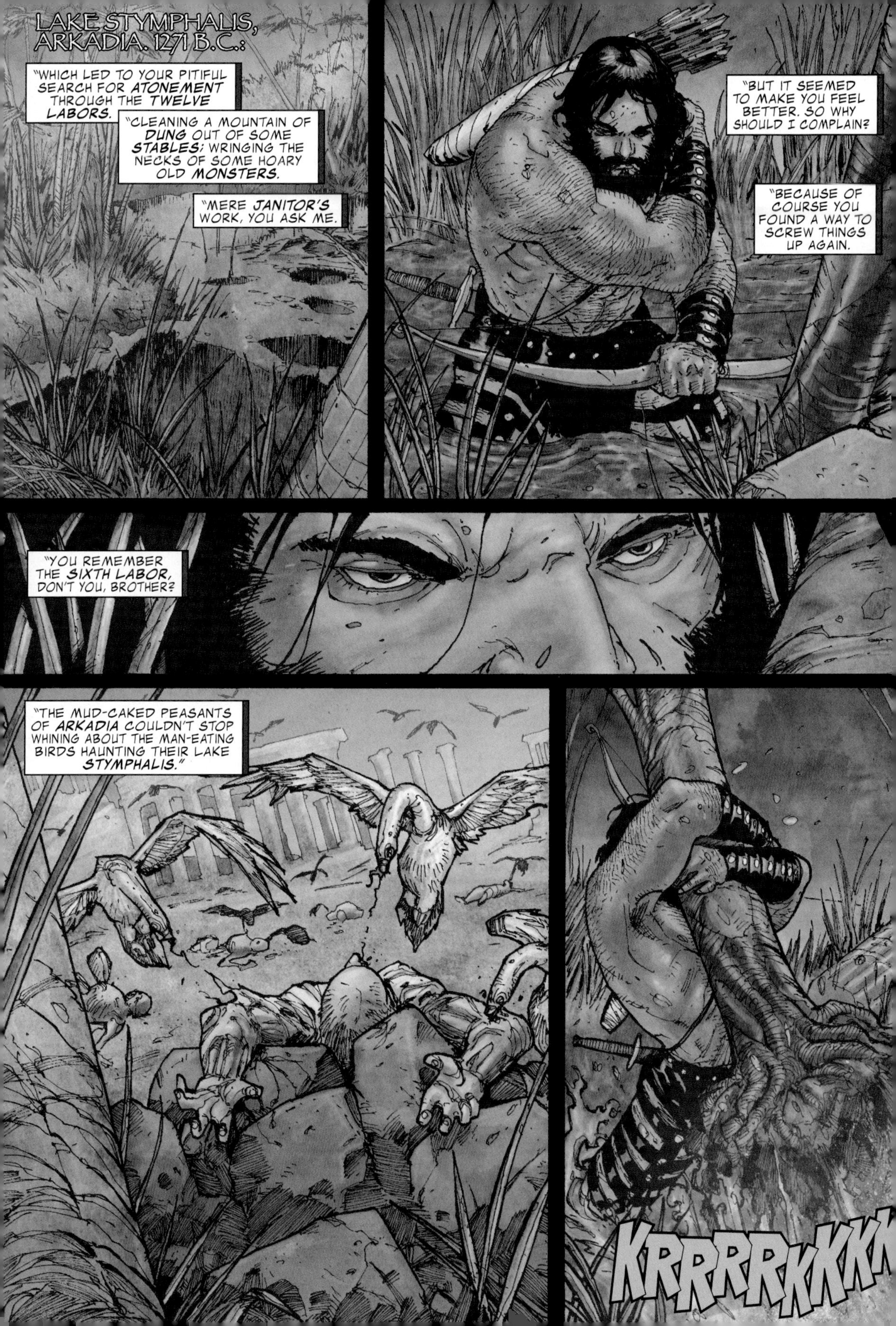
LAKE STYMPHALIS, ARKADIA. 1271 B.C.:
"WHICH LED TO YOUR PITIFUL SEARCH FOR ATONEMENT THROUGH THE TWELVE LABORS.
"CLEANING A MOUNTAIN OF DUNG OUT OF SOME STABLES; WRINGING THE NECKS OF SOME HOARY OLD MONSTERS.
"MERE JANITOR'S WORK, YOU ASK ME.
"BUT IT SEEMED TO MAKE YOU FEEL BETTER. SO WHY SHOULD I COMPLAIN?
"BECAUSE OF COURSE YOU FOUND A WAY TO SCREW THINGS UP AGAIN.
"YOU REMEMBER THE SIXTH LABOR, DON'T YOU, BROTHER?
"THE MUD-CAKED PEASANTS OF ARKADIA COULDN'T STOP WHINING ABOUT THE MAN-EATING BIRDS HAUNTING THEIR LAKE STYMPHALIS."
KRRRRKKKK

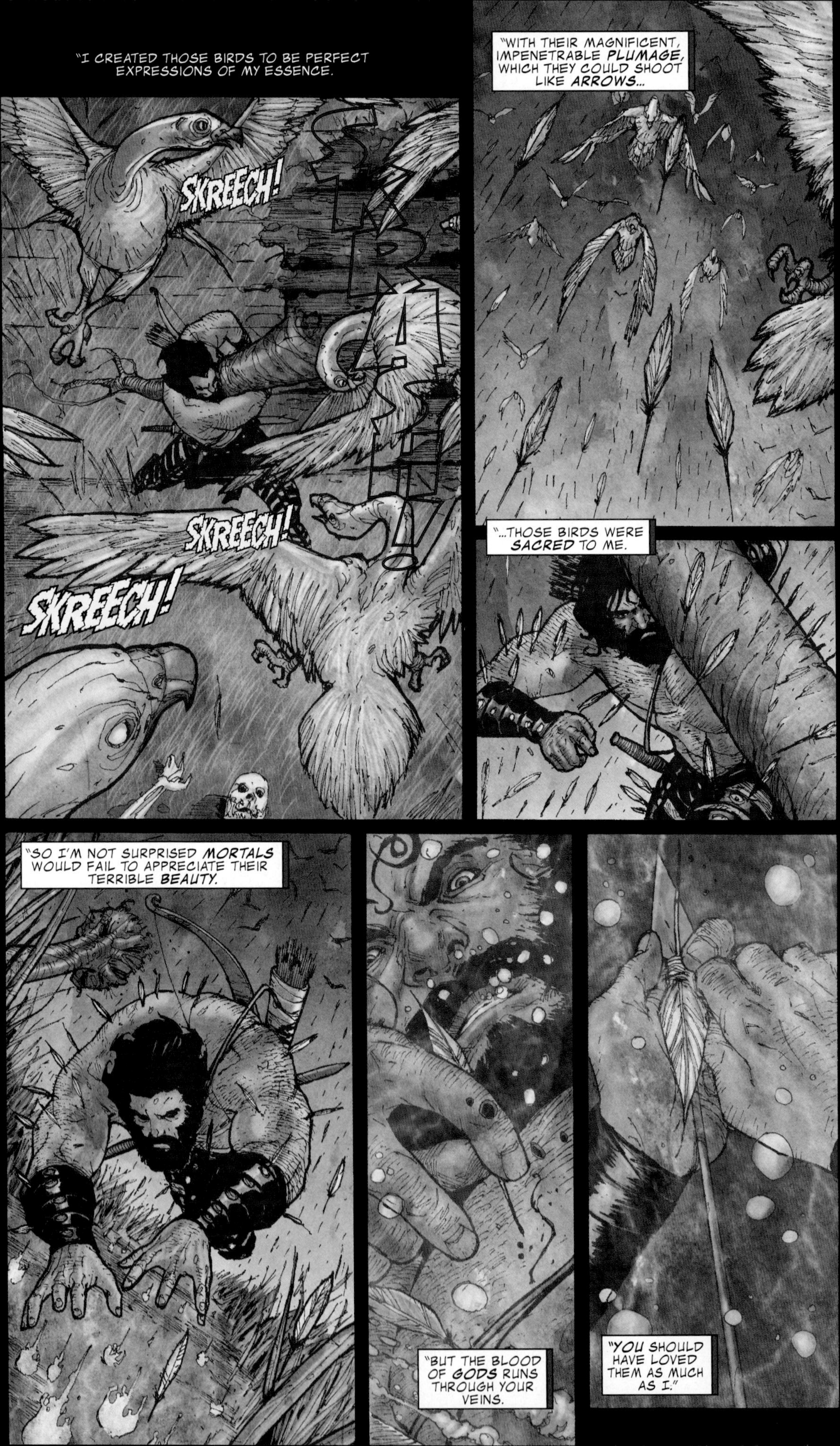
"I CREATED THOSE BIRDS TO BE PERFECT EXPRESSIONS OF MY ESSENCE.
SKREECH!
SKREECH!
SKREECH!
"WITH THEIR MAGNIFICENT, IMPENETRABLE PLUMAGE, WHICH THEY COULD SHOOT LIKE ARROWS...
"...THOSE BIRDS WERE SACRED TO ME.
"SO I'M NOT SURPRISED MORTALS WOULD FAIL TO APPRECIATE THEIR TERRIBLE BEAUTY.
"BUT THE BLOOD OF GODS RUNS THROUGH YOUR VEINS.
"YOU SHOULD HAVE LOVED THEM AS MUCH AS I."

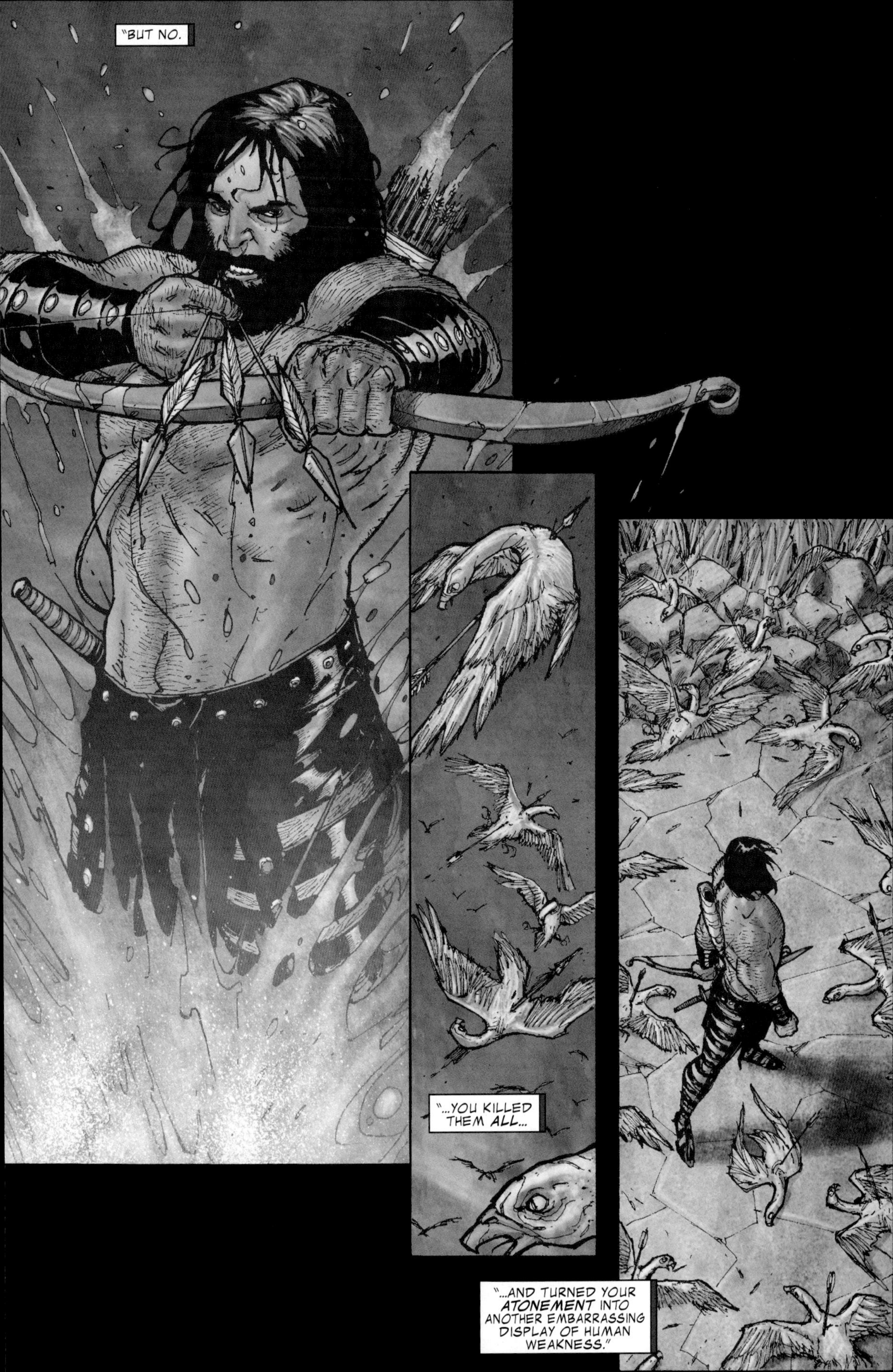
"BUT NO.
"...YOU KILLED THEM ALL...
"...AND TURNED YOUR ATONEMENT INTO ANOTHER EMBARRASSING DISPLAY OF HUMAN WEAKNESS."

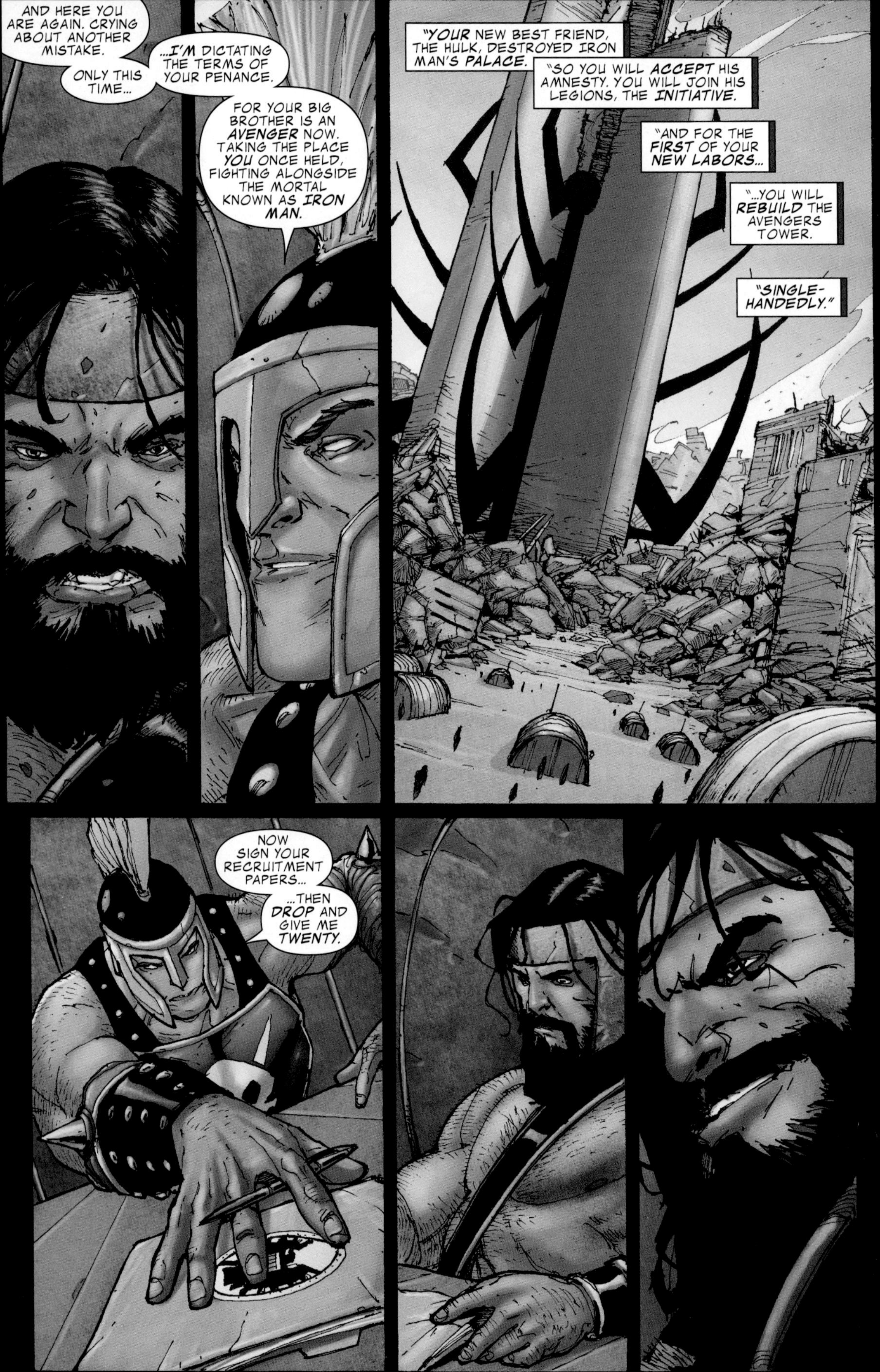
AND HERE YOU ARE AGAIN. CRYING ABOUT ANOTHER MISTAKE.
ONLY THIS TIME...
...I'M DICTATING THE TERMS OF YOUR PENANCE.
FOR YOUR BIG BROTHER IS AN AVENGER NOW. TAKING THE PLACE YOU ONCE HELD, FIGHTING ALONGSIDE THE MORTAL KNOWN AS IRON MAN.
"YOUR NEW BEST FRIEND, THE HULK, DESTROYED IRON MAN'S PALACE.
"SO YOU WILL ACCEPT HIS AMNESTY. YOU WILL JOIN HIS LEGIONS, THE INITIATIVE.
"AND FOR THE FIRST OF YOUR NEW LABORS...
"...YOU WILL REBUILD THE AVENGERS TOWER.
"SINGLE-HANDEDLY."
NOW SIGN YOUR RECRUITMENT PAPERS...
...THEN DROP AND GIVE ME TWENTY.

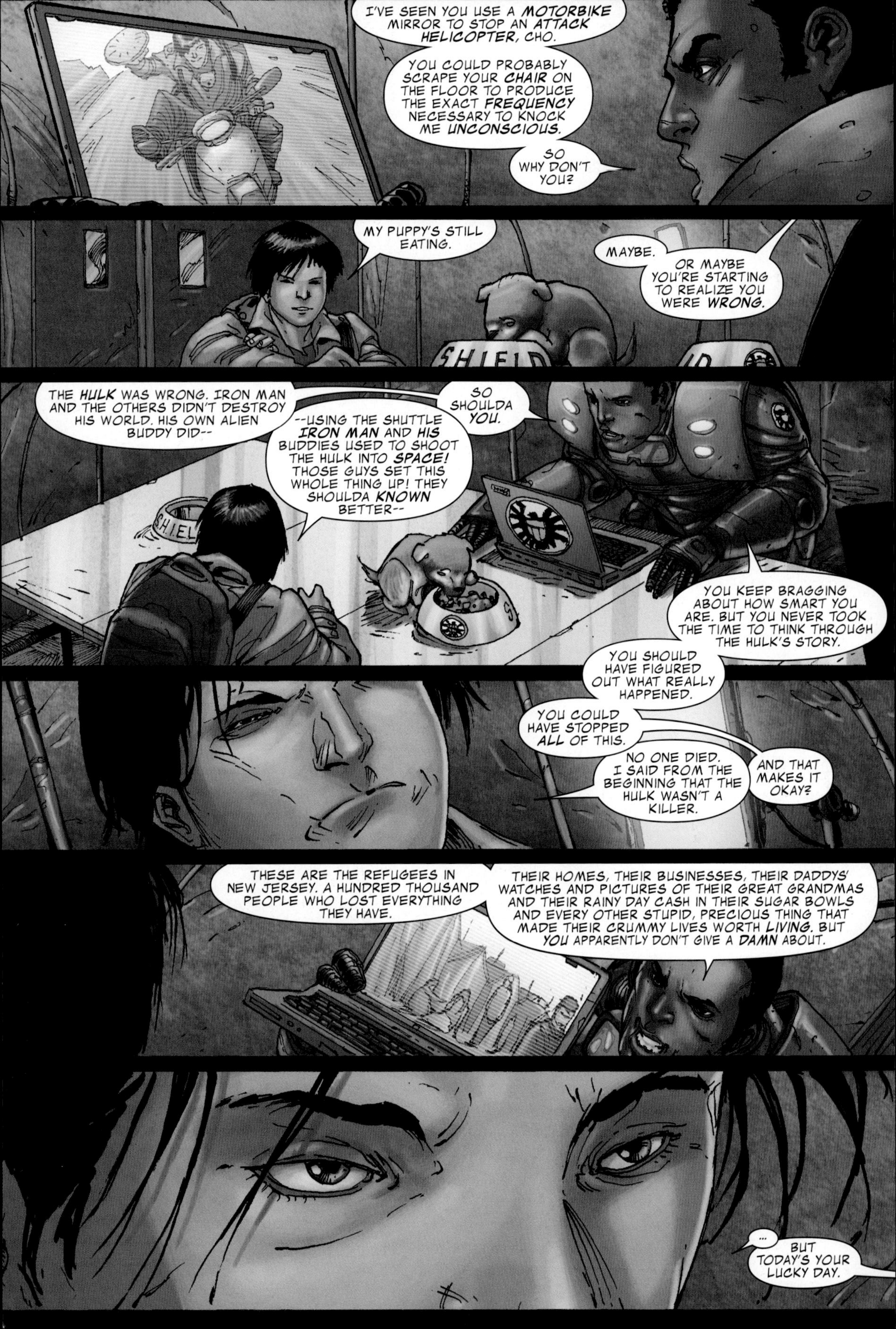
I'VE SEEN YOU USE A MOTORBIKE MIRROR TO STOP AN ATTACK HELICOPTER, CHO.
YOU COULD PROBABLY SCRAPE YOUR CHAIR ON THE FLOOR TO PRODUCE THE EXACT FREQUENCY NECESSARY TO KNOCK ME UNCONSCIOUS.
SO WHY DON'T YOU?
MY PUPPY'S STILL EATING.
MAYBE.
OR MAYBE YOU'RE STARTING TO REALIZE YOU WERE WRONG.
THE HULK WAS WRONG. IRON MAN AND THE OTHERS DIDN'T DESTROY HIS WORLD. HIS OWN ALIEN BUDDY DID--
SO SHOULDA YOU.
--USING THE SHUTTLE IRON MAN AND HIS BUDDIES USED TO SHOOT THE HULK INTO SPACE! THOSE GUYS SET THIS WHOLE THING UP! THEY SHOULDA KNOWN BETTER--
YOU KEEP BRAGGING ABOUT HOW SMART YOU ARE. BUT YOU NEVER TOOK THE TIME TO THINK THROUGH THE HULK'S STORY.
YOU SHOULD HAVE FIGURED OUT WHAT REALLY HAPPENED.
YOU COULD HAVE STOPPED ALL OF THIS.
NO ONE DIED. I SAID FROM THE BEGINNING THAT THE HULK WASN'T A KILLER.
AND THAT MAKES IT OKAY?
THESE ARE THE REFUGEES IN NEW JERSEY. A HUNDRED THOUSAND PEOPLE WHO LOST EVERYTHING THEY HAVE.
THEIR HOMES, THEIR BUSINESSES, THEIR DADDYS' WATCHES AND PICTURES OF THEIR GREAT GRANDMAS AND THEIR RAINY DAY CASH IN THEIR SUGAR BOWLS AND EVERY OTHER STUPID, PRECIOUS THING THAT MADE THEIR CRUMMY LIVES WORTH LIVING. BUT YOU APPARENTLY DON'T GIVE A DAMN ABOUT.
...
BUT TODAY'S YOUR LUCKY DAY.

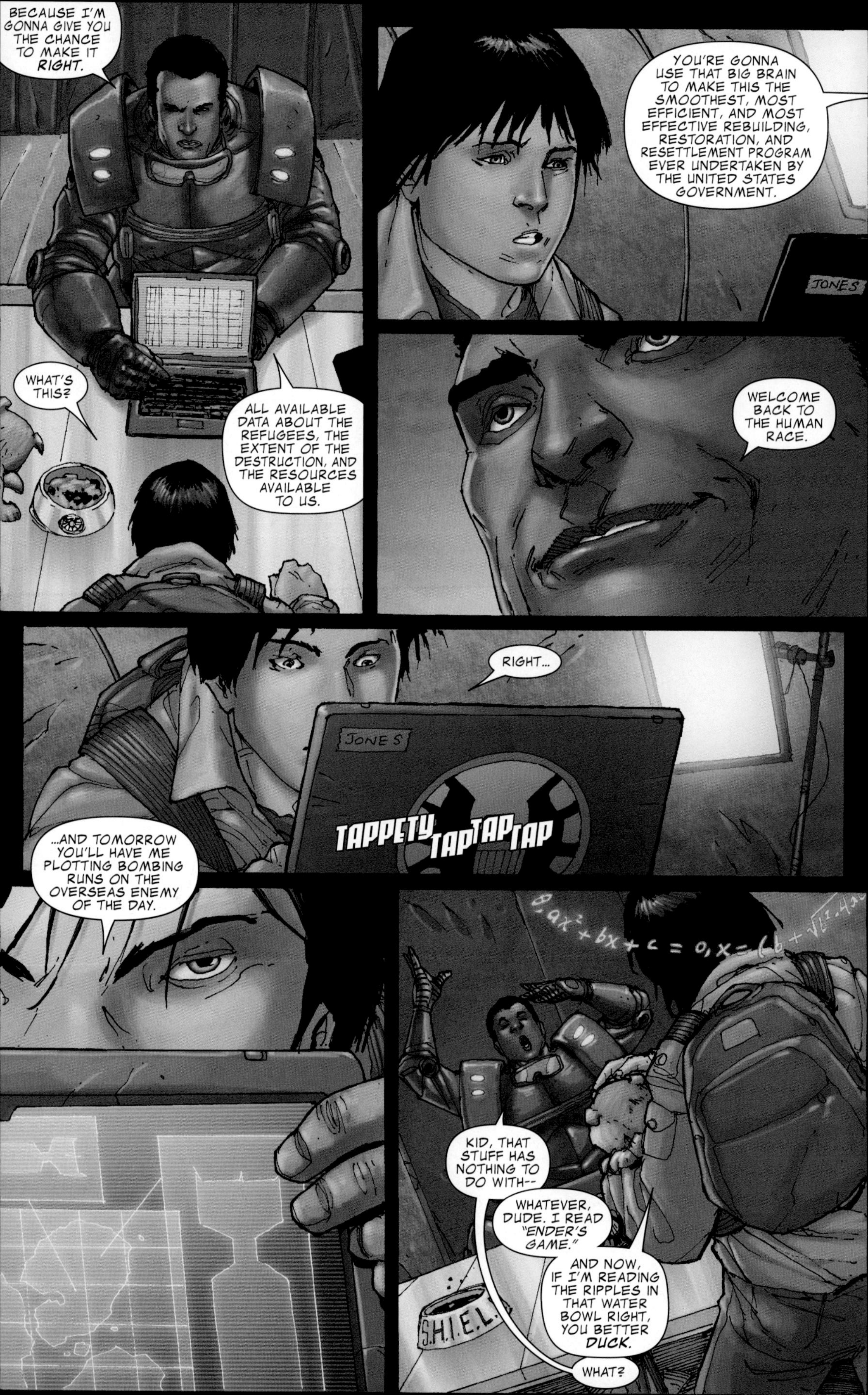
BECAUSE I'M GONNA GIVE YOU THE CHANCE TO MAKE IT RIGHT.
YOU'RE GONNA USE THAT BIG BRAIN TO MAKE THIS THE SMOOTHEST, MOST EFFICIENT, AND MOST EFFECTIVE REBUILDING, RESTORATION, AND RESETTLEMENT PROGRAM EVER UNDERTAKEN BY THE UNITED STATES GOVERNMENT.
JONES
WHAT'S THIS?
ALL AVAILABLE DATA ABOUT THE REFUGEES, THE EXTENT OF THE DESTRUCTION, AND THE RESOURCES AVAILABLE TO US.
WELCOME BACK TO THE HUMAN RACE.
RIGHT...
JONES
TAPPETY TAPTAPTAP
...AND TOMORROW YOU'LL HAVE ME PLOTTING BOMBING RUNS ON THE OVERSEAS ENEMY OF THE DAY.
KID, THAT STUFF HAS NOTHING TO DO WITH--
WHATEVER, DUDE. I READ "ENDER'S GAME."
AND NOW, IF I'M READING THE RIPPLES IN THAT WATER BOWL RIGHT, YOU BETTER DUCK.
WHAT?
S.H.I.E.L.

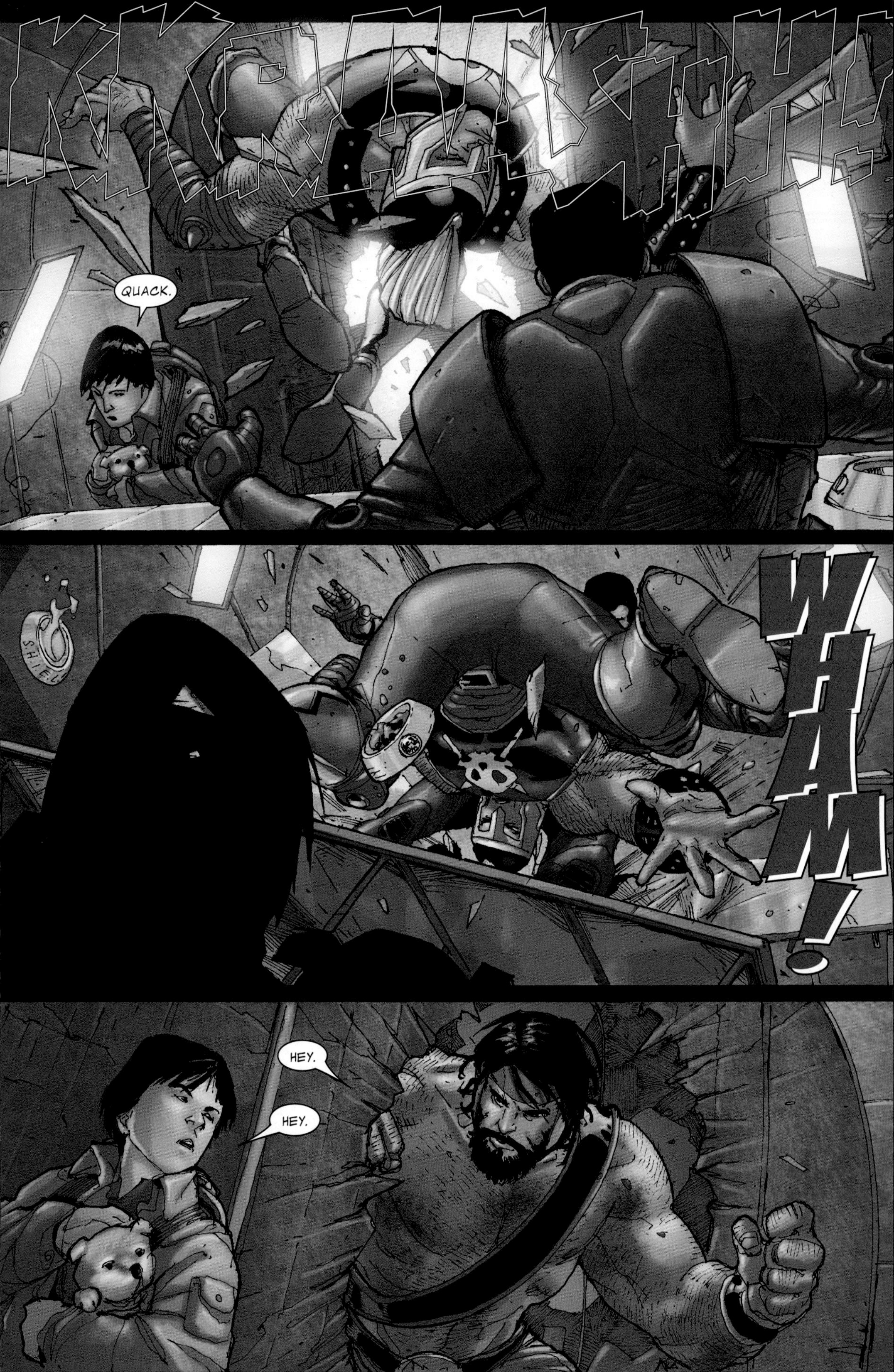
QUACK.
WHAM!
HEY.
HEY.

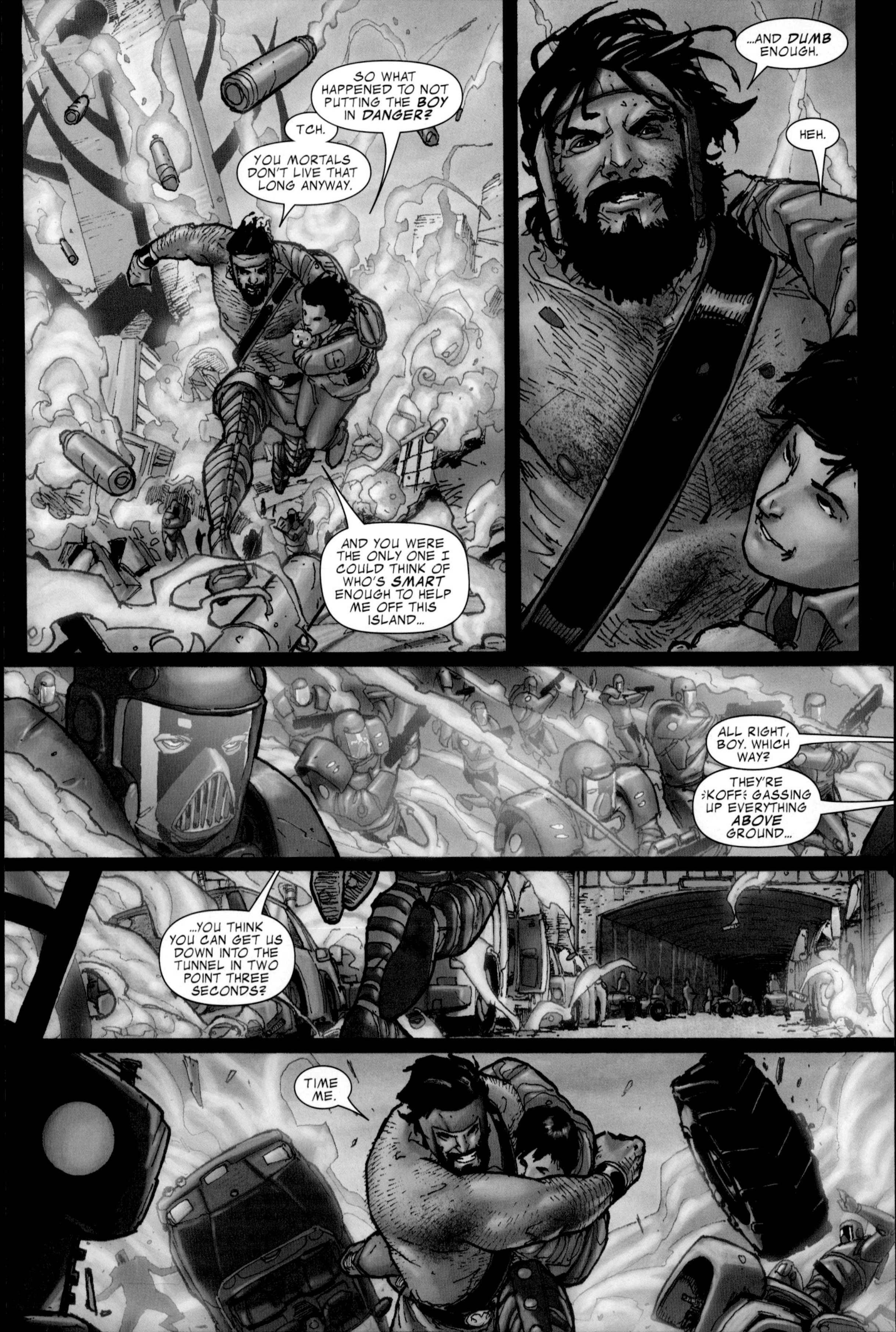
TCH.
YOU MORTALS DON'T LIVE THAT LONG ANYWAY.
SO WHAT HAPPENED TO NOT PUTTING THE BOY IN DANGER?
AND YOU WERE THE ONLY ONE I COULD THINK OF WHO'S SMART ENOUGH TO HELP ME OFF THIS ISLAND...
...AND DUMB ENOUGH.
HEH.
ALL RIGHT, BOY. WHICH WAY?
THEY'RE *KOFF* GASSING UP EVERYTHING ABOVE GROUND...
...YOU THINK YOU CAN GET US DOWN INTO THE TUNNEL IN TWO POINT THREE SECONDS?
TIME ME.

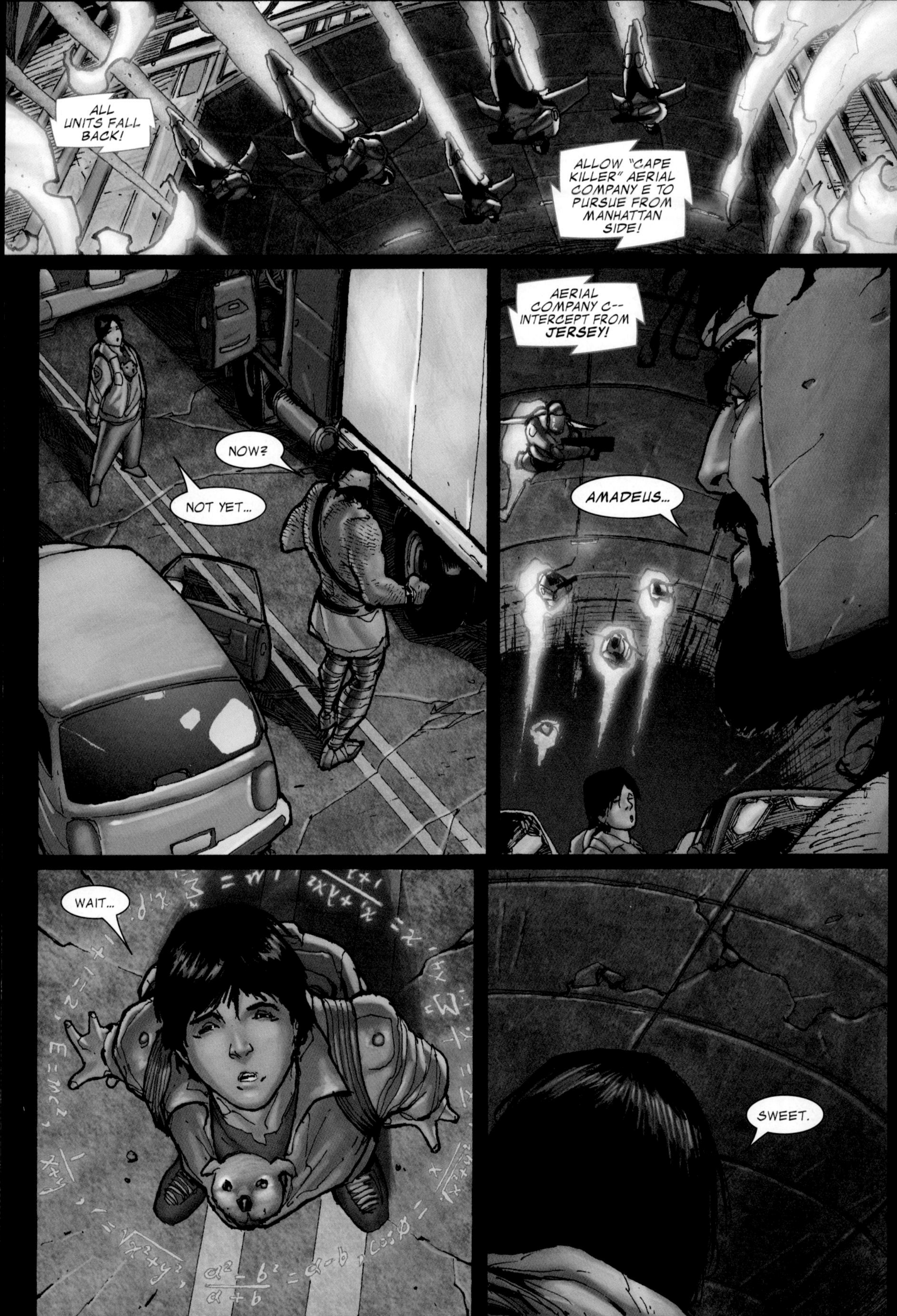
ALL UNITS FALL BACK!
ALLOW "CAPE KILLER" AERIAL COMPANY E TO PURSUE FROM MANHATTAN SIDE!
NOW?
NOT YET...
AERIAL COMPANY C-- INTERCEPT FROM JERSEY!
AMADEUS...
WAIT...
SWEET.

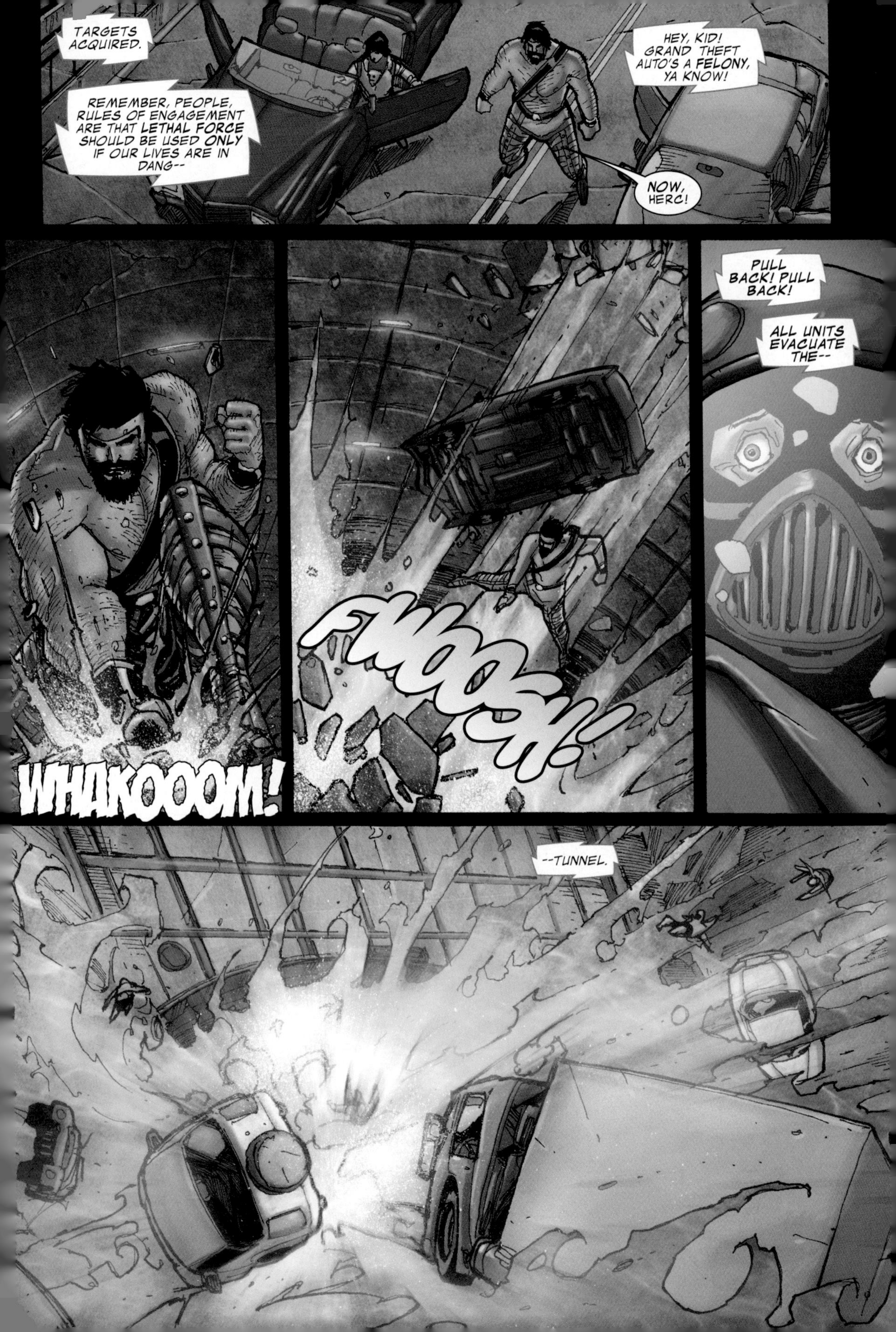
TARGETS ACQUIRED.
REMEMBER, PEOPLE, RULES OF ENGAGEMENT ARE THAT LETHAL FORCE SHOULD BE USED ONLY IF OUR LIVES ARE IN DANG--
HEY, KID! GRAND THEFT AUTO'S A FELONY, YA KNOW!
NOW, HERC!
WHAKOOOM!
FWOOSH!
PULL BACK! PULL BACK!
ALL UNITS EVACUATE THE--
--TUNNEL.

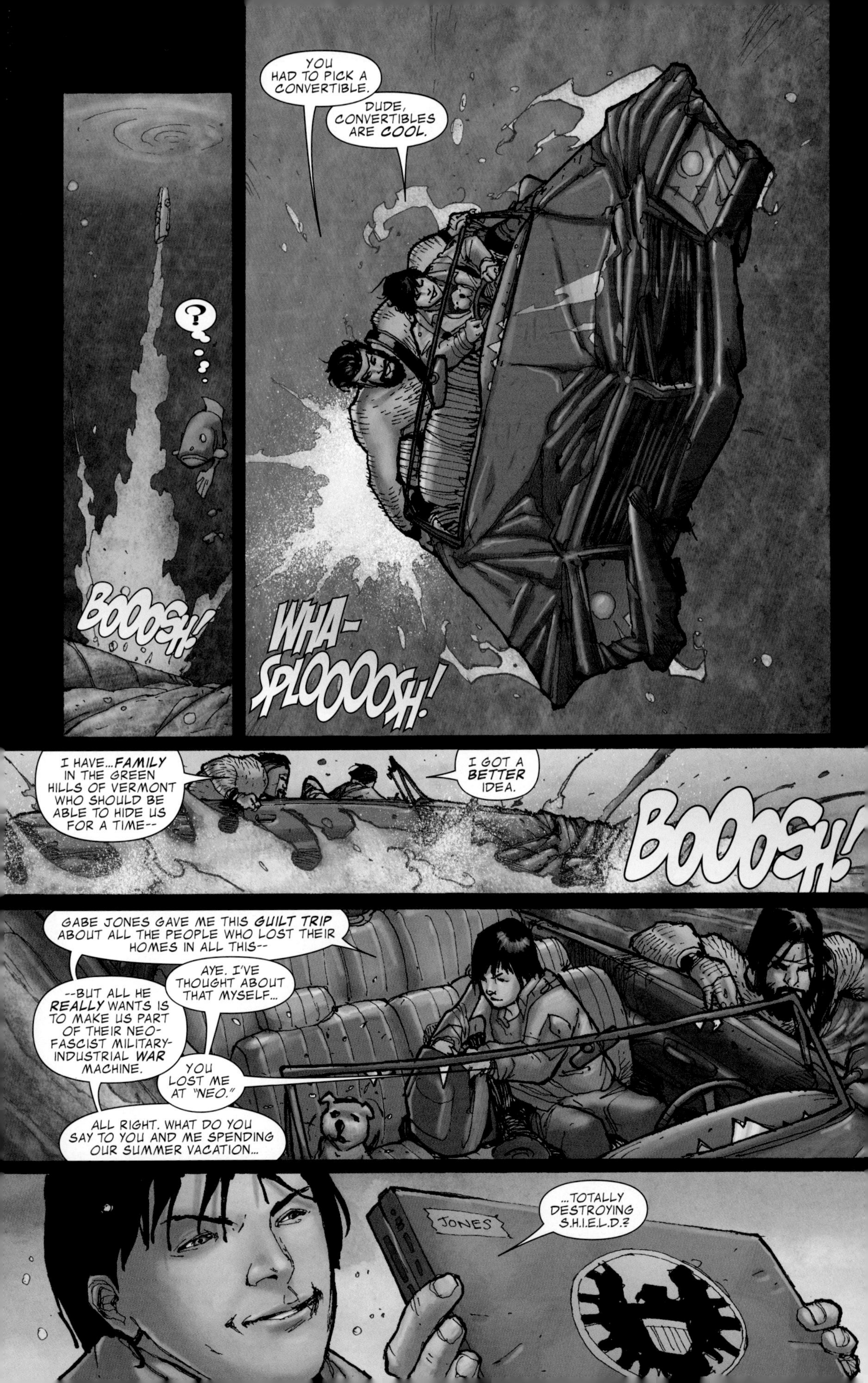
?
BOOOSH!
YOU HAD TO PICK A CONVERTIBLE.
DUDE, CONVERTIBLES ARE COOL.
WHA-SPLOOOOSH!
I HAVE...FAMILY IN THE GREEN HILLS OF VERMONT WHO SHOULD BE ABLE TO HIDE US FOR A TIME--
I GOT A BETTER IDEA.
BOOOSH!
GABE JONES GAVE ME THIS GUILT TRIP ABOUT ALL THE PEOPLE WHO LOST THEIR HOMES IN ALL THIS--
--BUT ALL HE REALLY WANTS IS TO MAKE US PART OF THEIR NEO-FASCIST MILITARY-INDUSTRIAL WAR MACHINE.
AYE. I'VE THOUGHT ABOUT THAT MYSELF...
YOU LOST ME AT "NEO."
ALL RIGHT. WHAT DO YOU SAY TO YOU AND ME SPENDING OUR SUMMER VACATION...
JONES
...TOTALLY DESTROYING S.H.I.E.L.D.?

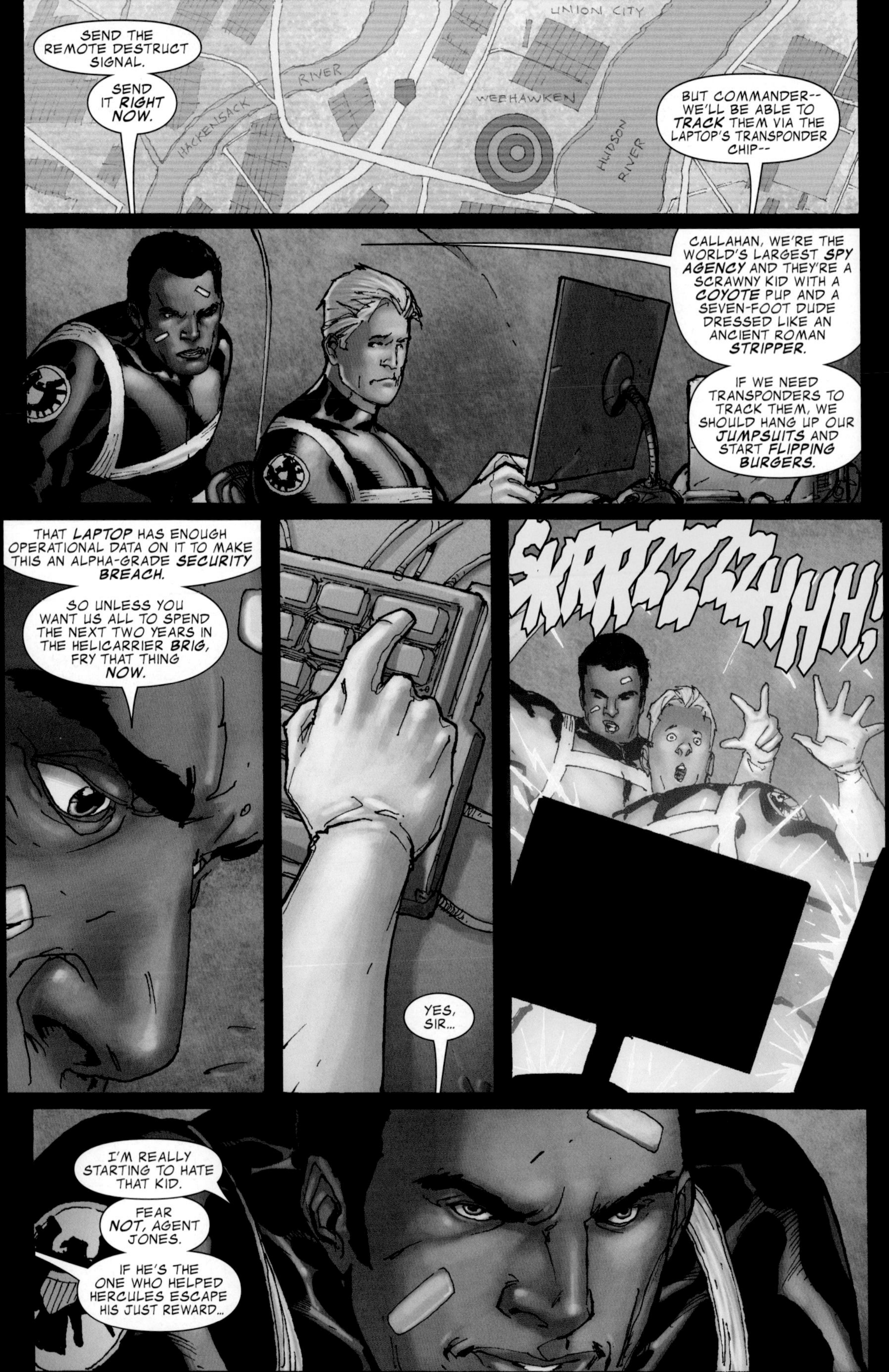

UNION CITY
RIVER
HACKENSACK
WEEHAWKEN
HUDSON RIVER
SEND THE REMOTE DESTRUCT SIGNAL.
SEND IT RIGHT NOW.
BUT COMMANDER-- WE'LL BE ABLE TO TRACK THEM VIA THE LAPTOP'S TRANSPONDER CHIP--
CALLAHAN, WE'RE THE WORLD'S LARGEST SPY AGENCY AND THEY'RE A SCRAWNY KID WITH A COYOTE PUP AND A SEVEN-FOOT DUDE DRESSED LIKE AN ANCIENT ROMAN STRIPPER.
IF WE NEED TRANSPONDERS TO TRACK THEM, WE SHOULD HANG UP OUR JUMPSUITS AND START FLIPPING BURGERS.
THAT LAPTOP HAS ENOUGH OPERATIONAL DATA ON IT TO MAKE THIS AN ALPHA-GRADE SECURITY BREACH.
SO UNLESS YOU WANT US ALL TO SPEND THE NEXT TWO YEARS IN THE HELICARRIER BRIG, FRY THAT THING NOW.
YES, SIR...
SKRRZZZZHHH!
I'M REALLY STARTING TO HATE THAT KID.
FEAR NOT, AGENT JONES.
IF HE'S THE ONE WHO HELPED HERCULES ESCAPE HIS JUST REWARD...

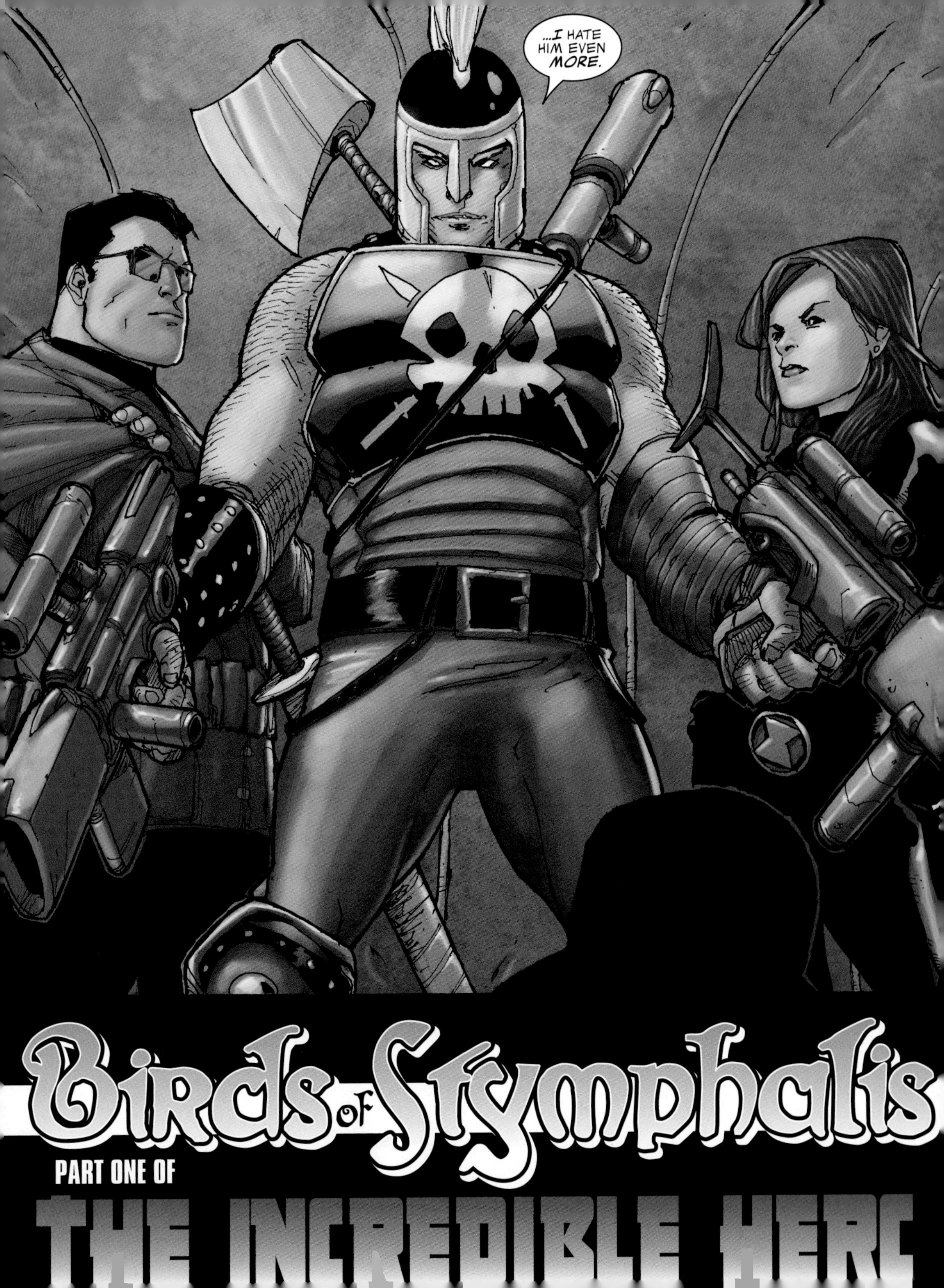
...I HATE HIM EVEN MORE.
Birds of Stymphalis
PART ONE OF
THE INCREDIBLE HERC

Yo. This is Amadeus. Mr. Cho if you're nasty.

And this...is a quiz. I'm waaaaaaaaaay smarter than you, so it'll take you longer to answer than the 26 seconds it took me to come up with the questions.

1) WHAT WAS AMADEUS' SCORE ON THE "BRAIN FIGHT" GAME SHOW?

2) WHAT'D HERCULES KILL GERYON WITH? BE SPECIFIC, YO.

3) HOW MANY WORDS ARE ON THE THIRTY-EIGHTH PAGE OF AMADEUS' SECOND COMIC BOOK APPEARANCE?

4) WHAT DID HERCULES CREATE AFTER HE REROUTED THE ALPHEUS AND PENEUS RIVERS?

5) NAME THREE OF THE SATELLITES THAT SHOT HULK AT THE END OF...AH, SHOOT...WHATEVER THAT RECENT MINISERIES WITH HULK IN IT WAS CALLED.

6) WHO TAUGHT HERCULES TO WRESTLE?

7) AFTER HERC BEAT THE CRAP OUT OF ARES THE SECOND TIME, WHO THREW ARES IN A CHARIOT AND TOOK HIM TO OLYMPUS?

8) WHAT'S THE NAME OF THE CRAFT THAT I BOUGHT WITH WORTHINGTON'S MONEY?

9) HOW MANY DAUGHTERS DID HERC HAVE WITH DEÏANEIRA? NAMES, PLEASE.

10) WHO WROTE A SONG ABOUT THE STRAIT THAT HERCULES CREATED?

1. 7839
2. OLIVE-WOOD CLUB
3. 296 (297 GIVES YOU A BONUS POINT)
4. THE OLYMPIC GAMES
5. CHINESE FIRESTARS, SHI'AR, RUSSIAN
6. AUTOLYCUS
7. DEIMUS (FEAR) AND PHOBUS (PANIC)
8. M-43 COSBY AMPHIBIOUS FLYER
9. ONE (MACARIA)
10. ALEXANDER GORODNITSKY

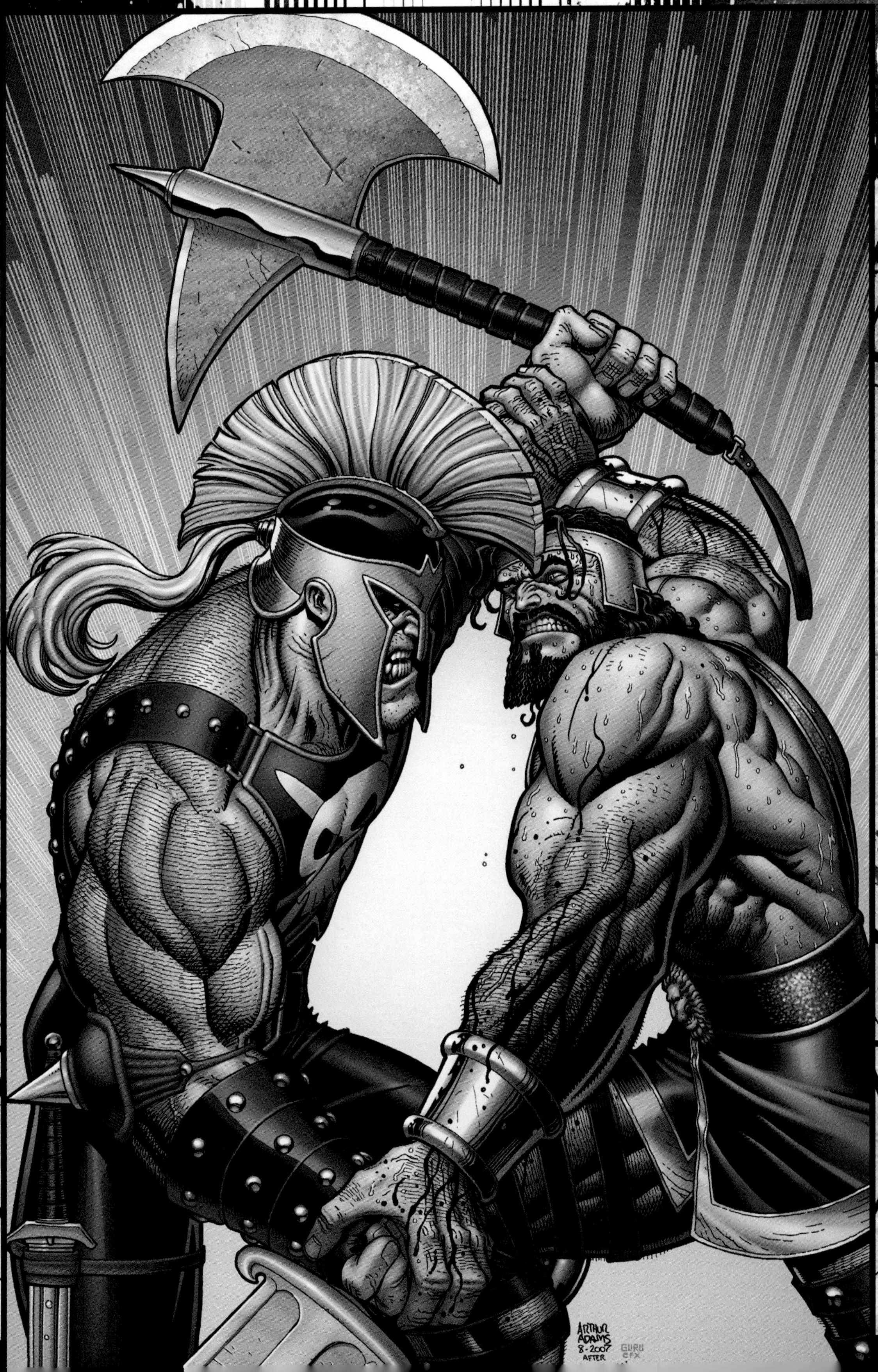
ARTHUR ADAMS 8-2007 AFTER
GURU eFX

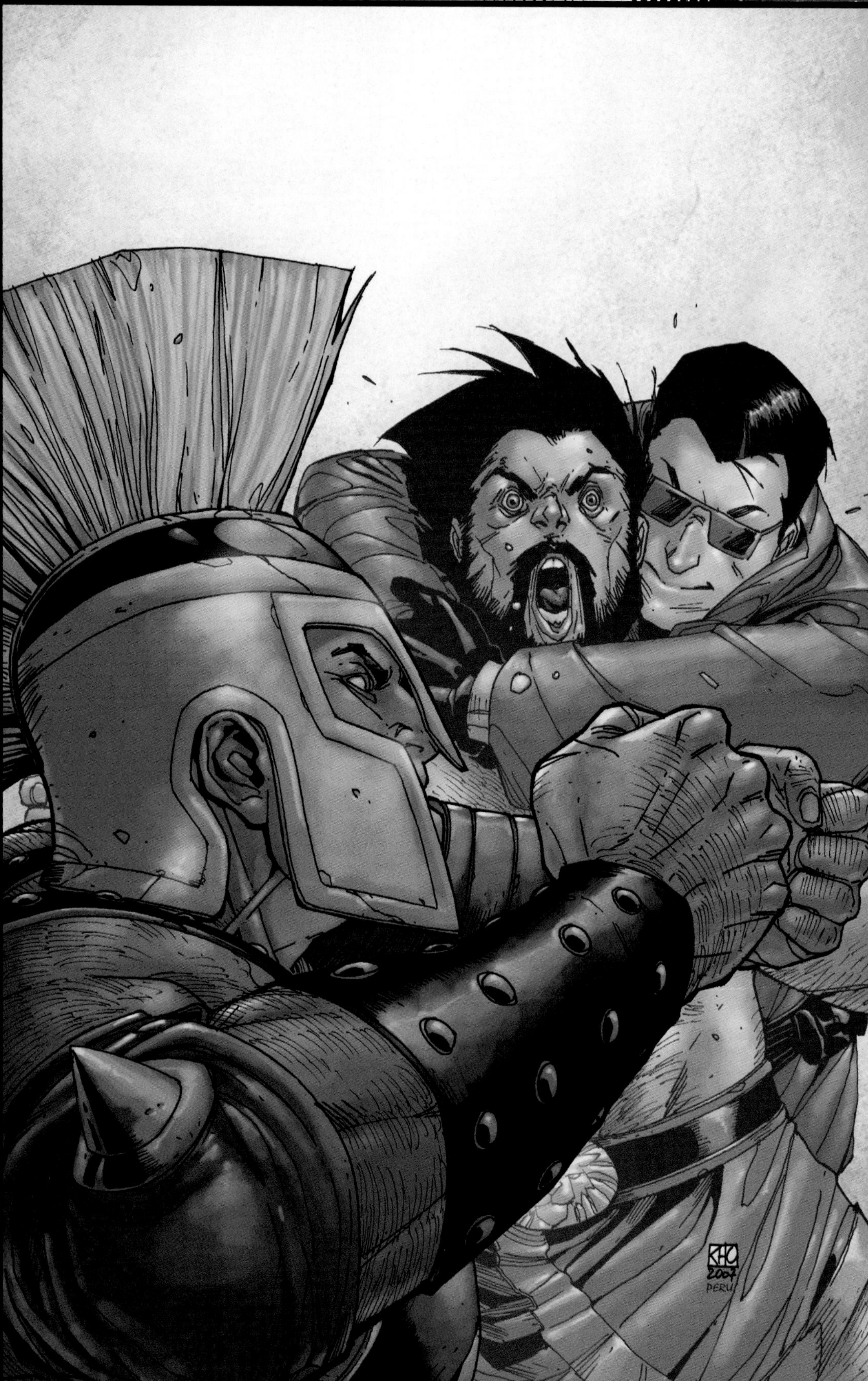
2007
PERU

INCREDIBLE HERCULES #113 VARIANT

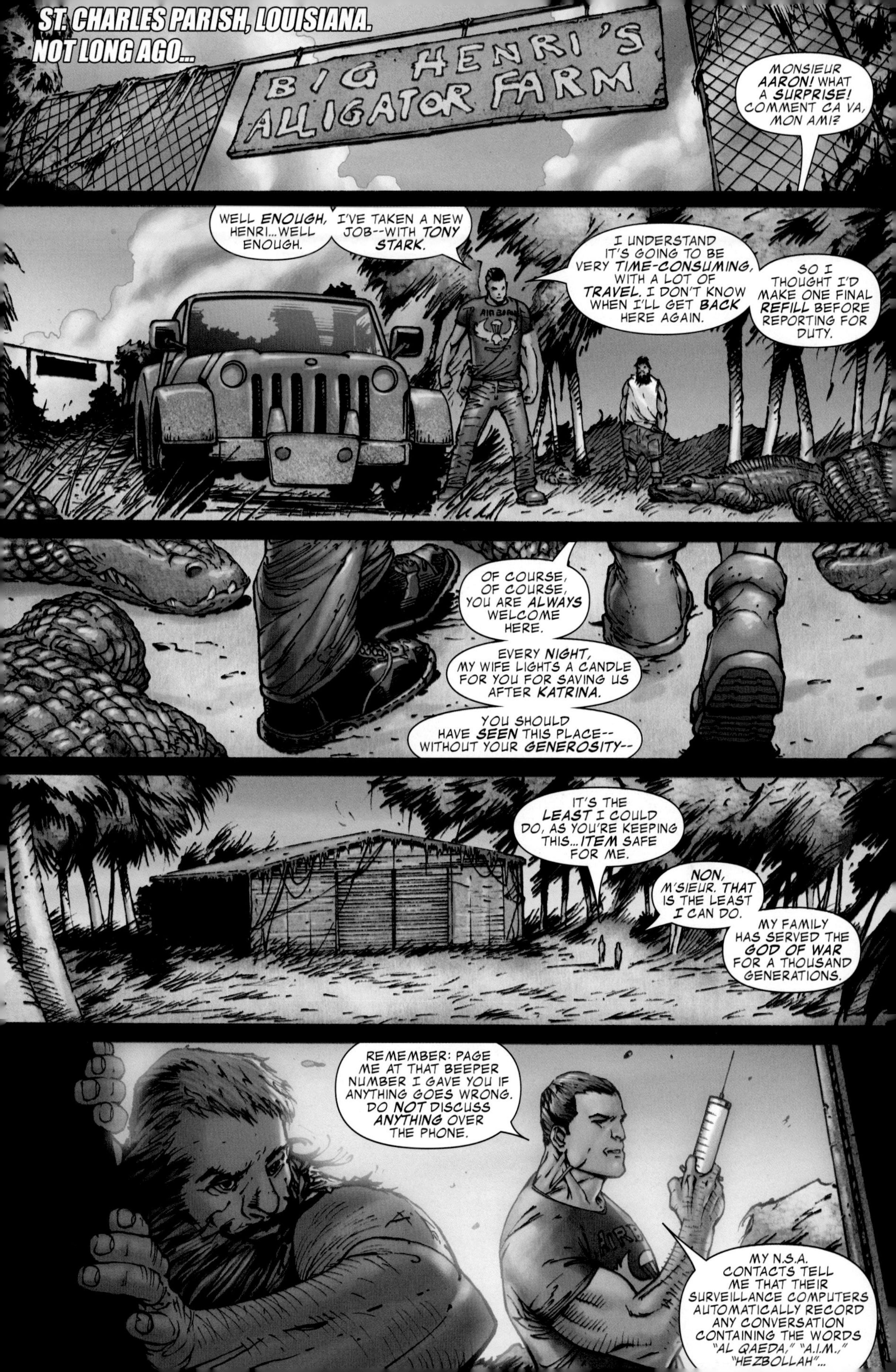

ST. CHARLES PARISH, LOUISIANA. NOT LONG AGO...
BIG HENRI'S ALLIGATOR FARM
MONSIEUR AARON! WHAT A SURPRISE! COMMENT CA VA, MON AMI?
WELL ENOUGH, HENRI...WELL ENOUGH.
I'VE TAKEN A NEW JOB--WITH TONY STARK.
I UNDERSTAND IT'S GOING TO BE VERY TIME-CONSUMING, WITH A LOT OF TRAVEL. I DON'T KNOW WHEN I'LL GET BACK HERE AGAIN.
SO I THOUGHT I'D MAKE ONE FINAL REFILL BEFORE REPORTING FOR DUTY.
OF COURSE, OF COURSE, YOU ARE ALWAYS WELCOME HERE.
EVERY NIGHT, MY WIFE LIGHTS A CANDLE FOR YOU FOR SAVING US AFTER KATRINA.
YOU SHOULD HAVE SEEN THIS PLACE-- WITHOUT YOUR GENEROSITY--
IT'S THE LEAST I COULD DO, AS YOU'RE KEEPING THIS...ITEM SAFE FOR ME.
NON, M'SIEUR. THAT IS THE LEAST I CAN DO.
MY FAMILY HAS SERVED THE GOD OF WAR FOR A THOUSAND GENERATIONS.
REMEMBER: PAGE ME AT THAT BEEPER NUMBER I GAVE YOU IF ANYTHING GOES WRONG. DO NOT DISCUSS ANYTHING OVER THE PHONE.
MY N.S.A. CONTACTS TELL ME THAT THEIR SURVEILLANCE COMPUTERS AUTOMATICALLY RECORD ANY CONVERSATION CONTAINING THE WORDS "AL QAEDA," "A.I.M.," "HEZBOLLAH"...

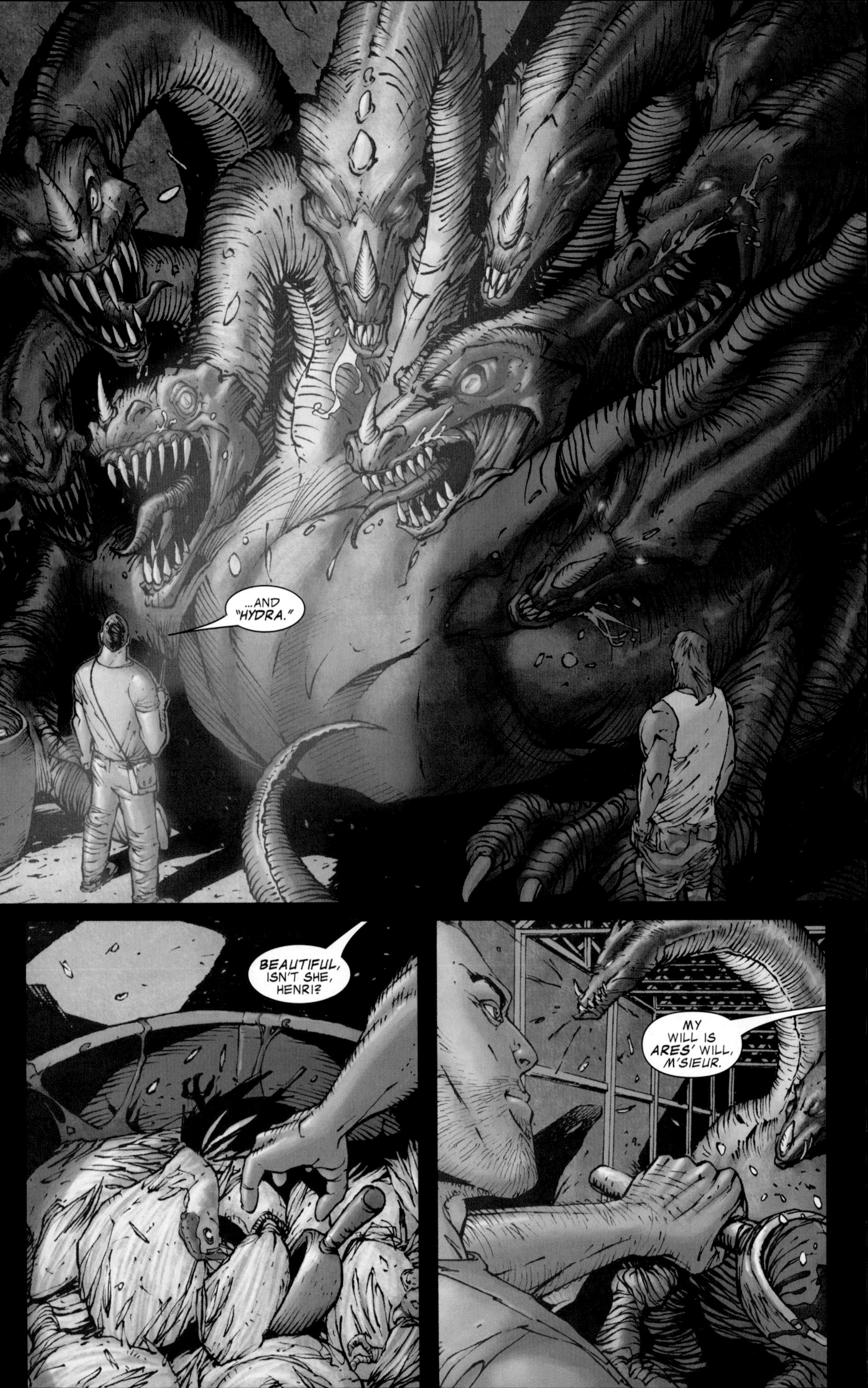
...AND "HYDRA."
BEAUTIFUL, ISN'T SHE, HENRI?
MY WILL IS ARES' WILL, M'SIEUR.

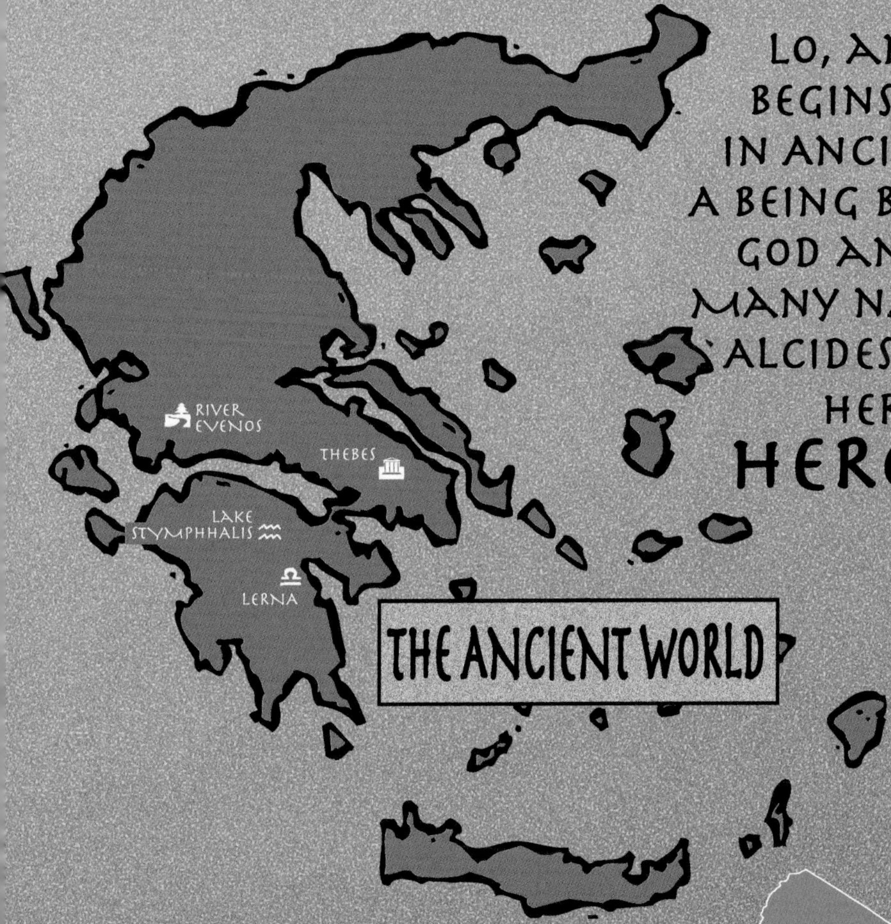
RIVER EVENOS
THEBES
LAKE STYMPHHALIS
LERNA
THE ANCIENT WORLD

LO, AND A TALE BEGINS LONG AGO IN ANCIENT GREECE. A BEING BORN OF BOTH GOD AND HUMAN. MANY NAMES HAS HE. ALCIDES. HERACLES. HERAKLES.

HERCULES.

CLEVER IS HIS COMPANION. A LAD OF GREAT RESOURCE AND RESOLVE. AMADEUS CHO. WITH PUP IN TOW.

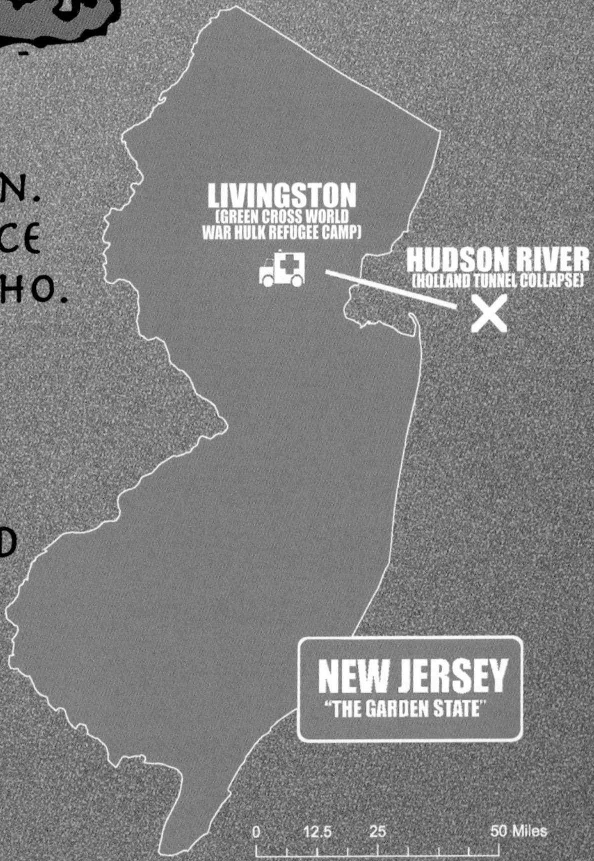
LIVINGSTON
(GREEN CROSS WORLD WAR HULK REFUGEE CAMP)
HUDSON RIVER
(HOLLAND TUNNEL COLLAPSE)
NEW JERSEY
"THE GARDEN STATE"
0 12.5 25 50 Miles

THEY FLEE FROM THE GOD OF WAR AND THE GOVERNANCE OF MAN.

THEIR JOURNEYS PERSIST...

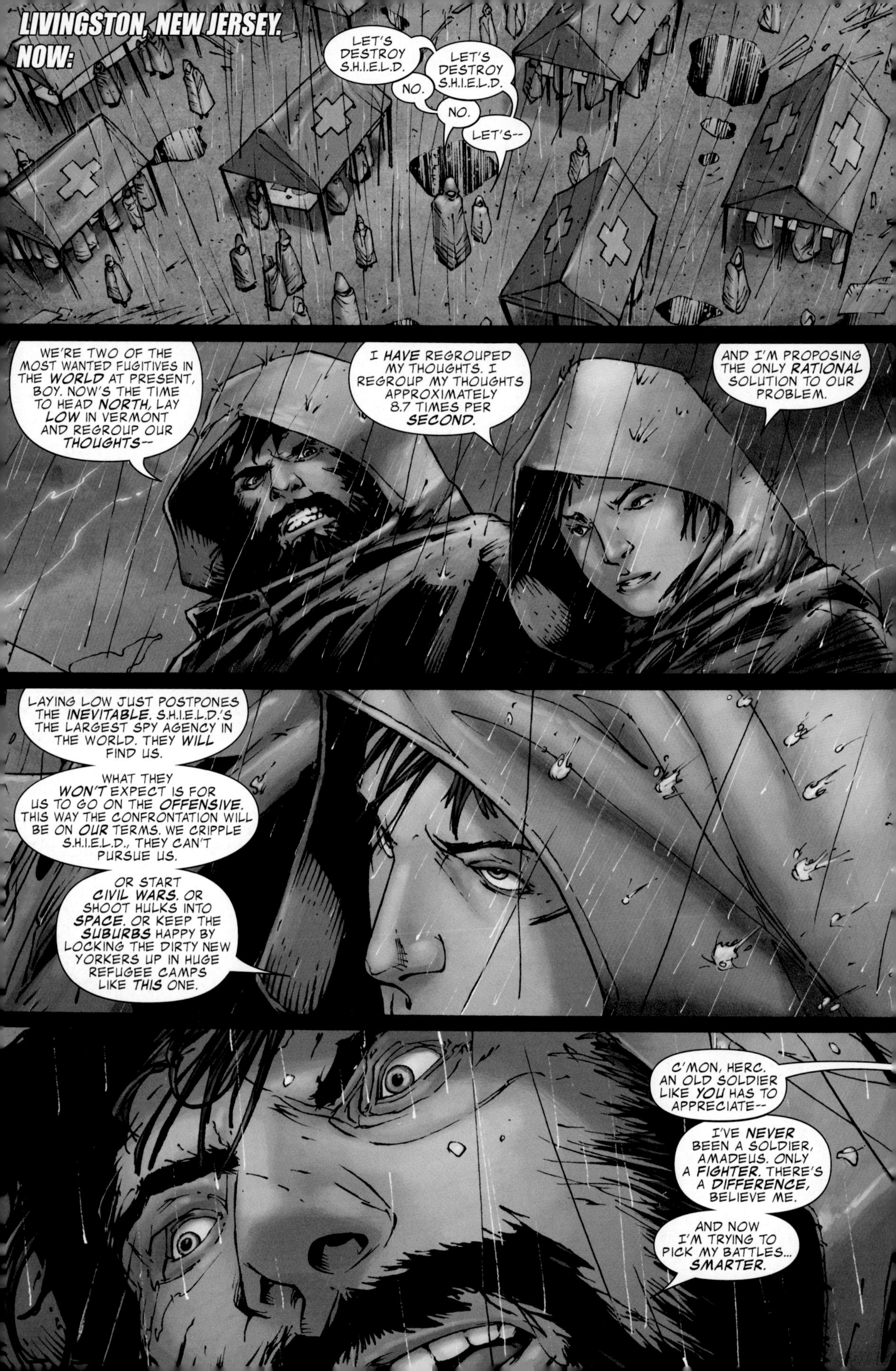

LIVINGSTON, NEW JERSEY. NOW:
LET'S DESTROY S.H.I.E.L.D.
LET'S DESTROY S.H.I.E.L.D.
NO.
NO.
LET'S--
WE'RE TWO OF THE MOST WANTED FUGITIVES IN THE WORLD AT PRESENT, BOY. NOW'S THE TIME TO HEAD NORTH, LAY LOW IN VERMONT AND REGROUP OUR THOUGHTS--
I HAVE REGROUPED MY THOUGHTS. I REGROUP MY THOUGHTS APPROXIMATELY 8.7 TIMES PER SECOND.
AND I'M PROPOSING THE ONLY RATIONAL SOLUTION TO OUR PROBLEM.
LAYING LOW JUST POSTPONES THE INEVITABLE. S.H.I.E.L.D.'S THE LARGEST SPY AGENCY IN THE WORLD. THEY WILL FIND US.
WHAT THEY WON'T EXPECT IS FOR US TO GO ON THE OFFENSIVE. THIS WAY THE CONFRONTATION WILL BE ON OUR TERMS. WE CRIPPLE S.H.I.E.L.D., THEY CAN'T PURSUE US.
OR START CIVIL WARS. OR SHOOT HULKS INTO SPACE. OR KEEP THE SUBURBS HAPPY BY LOCKING THE DIRTY NEW YORKERS UP IN HUGE REFUGEE CAMPS LIKE THIS ONE.
C'MON, HERC. AN OLD SOLDIER LIKE YOU HAS TO APPRECIATE--
I'VE NEVER BEEN A SOLDIER, AMADEUS. ONLY A FIGHTER. THERE'S A DIFFERENCE, BELIEVE ME.
AND NOW I'M TRYING TO PICK MY BATTLES... SMARTER.

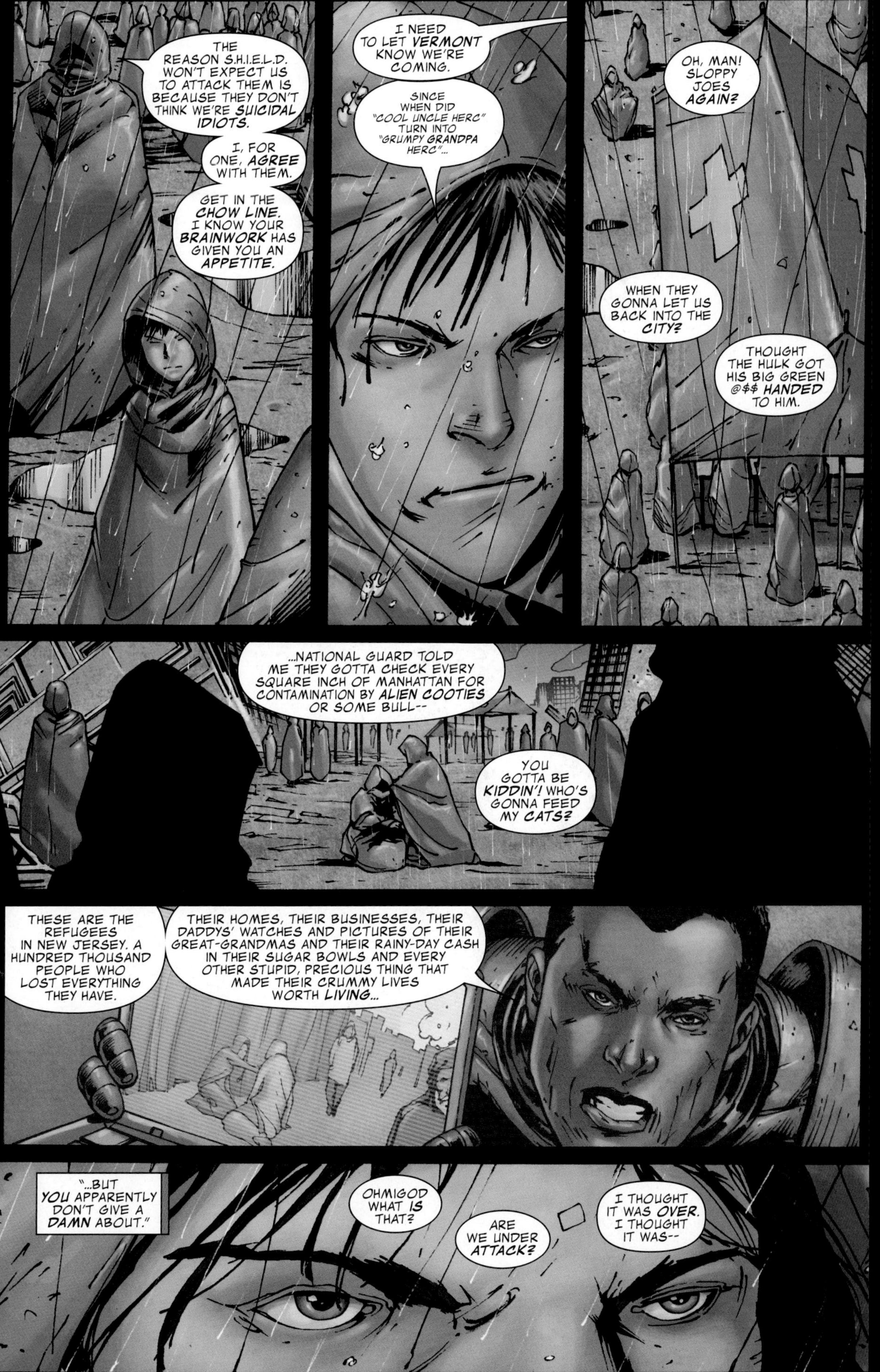
THE REASON S.H.I.E.L.D. WON'T EXPECT US TO ATTACK THEM IS BECAUSE THEY DON'T THINK WE'RE SUICIDAL IDIOTS.
I, FOR ONE, AGREE WITH THEM.
GET IN THE CHOW LINE. I KNOW YOUR BRAINWORK HAS GIVEN YOU AN APPETITE.
I NEED TO LET VERMONT KNOW WE'RE COMING.
SINCE WHEN DID "COOL UNCLE HERC" TURN INTO "GRUMPY GRANDPA HERC"...
OH, MAN! SLOPPY JOES AGAIN?
WHEN THEY GONNA LET US BACK INTO THE CITY?
THOUGHT THE HULK GOT HIS BIG GREEN @$$ HANDED TO HIM.
...NATIONAL GUARD TOLD ME THEY GOTTA CHECK EVERY SQUARE INCH OF MANHATTAN FOR CONTAMINATION BY ALIEN COOTIES OR SOME BULL--
YOU GOTTA BE KIDDIN'! WHO'S GONNA FEED MY CATS?
THESE ARE THE REFUGEES IN NEW JERSEY. A HUNDRED THOUSAND PEOPLE WHO LOST EVERYTHING THEY HAVE.
THEIR HOMES, THEIR BUSINESSES, THEIR DADDYS' WATCHES AND PICTURES OF THEIR GREAT-GRANDMAS AND THEIR RAINY-DAY CASH IN THEIR SUGAR BOWLS AND EVERY OTHER STUPID, PRECIOUS THING THAT MADE THEIR CRUMMY LIVES WORTH LIVING...
"...BUT YOU APPARENTLY DON'T GIVE A DAMN ABOUT."
OHMIGOD WHAT IS THAT?
ARE WE UNDER ATTACK?
I THOUGHT IT WAS OVER. I THOUGHT IT WAS--

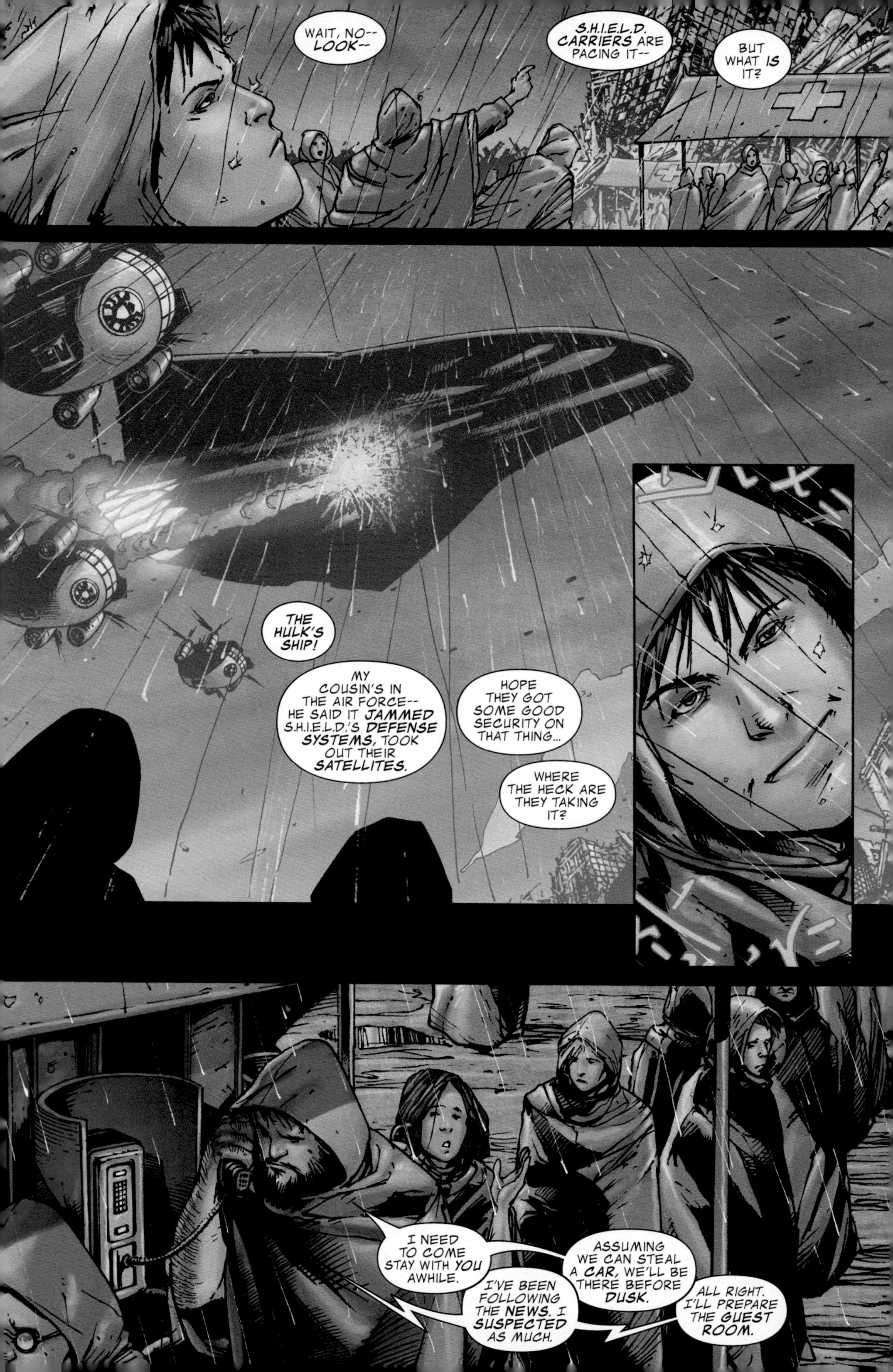
WAIT, NO-- LOOK--
S.H.I.E.L.D. CARRIERS ARE PACING IT--
BUT WHAT IS IT?
THE HULK'S SHIP!
MY COUSIN'S IN THE AIR FORCE-- HE SAID IT JAMMED S.H.I.E.L.D.'S DEFENSE SYSTEMS, TOOK OUT THEIR SATELLITES.
HOPE THEY GOT SOME GOOD SECURITY ON THAT THING...
WHERE THE HECK ARE THEY TAKING IT?
I NEED TO COME STAY WITH YOU AWHILE.
I'VE BEEN FOLLOWING THE NEWS. I SUSPECTED AS MUCH.
ASSUMING WE CAN STEAL A CAR, WE'LL BE THERE BEFORE DUSK.
ALL RIGHT. I'LL PREPARE THE GUEST ROOM.

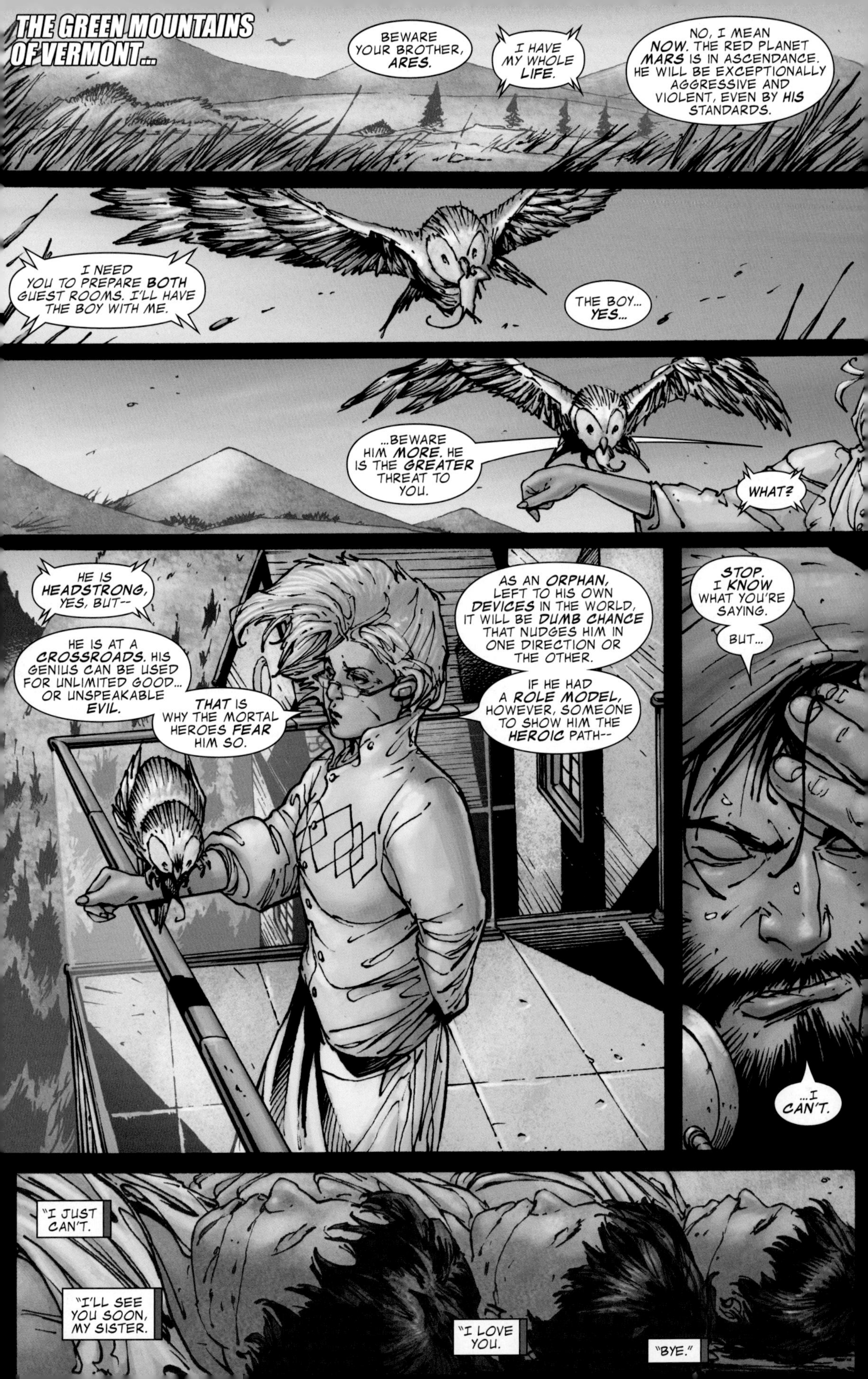
THE GREEN MOUNTAINS OF VERMONT...
BEWARE YOUR BROTHER, ARES.
I HAVE MY WHOLE LIFE.
NO, I MEAN NOW. THE RED PLANET MARS IS IN ASCENDANCE. HE WILL BE EXCEPTIONALLY AGGRESSIVE AND VIOLENT, EVEN BY HIS STANDARDS.
I NEED YOU TO PREPARE BOTH GUEST ROOMS. I'LL HAVE THE BOY WITH ME.
THE BOY... YES...
...BEWARE HIM MORE. HE IS THE GREATER THREAT TO YOU.
WHAT?
HE IS HEADSTRONG, YES, BUT--
HE IS AT A CROSSROADS. HIS GENIUS CAN BE USED FOR UNLIMITED GOOD... OR UNSPEAKABLE EVIL.
THAT IS WHY THE MORTAL HEROES FEAR HIM SO.
AS AN ORPHAN, LEFT TO HIS OWN DEVICES IN THE WORLD, IT WILL BE DUMB CHANCE THAT NUDGES HIM IN ONE DIRECTION OR THE OTHER.
IF HE HAD A ROLE MODEL, HOWEVER, SOMEONE TO SHOW HIM THE HEROIC PATH--
STOP. I KNOW WHAT YOU'RE SAYING.
BUT...
...I CAN'T.
"I JUST CAN'T.
"I'LL SEE YOU SOON, MY SISTER.
"I LOVE YOU.
"BYE."

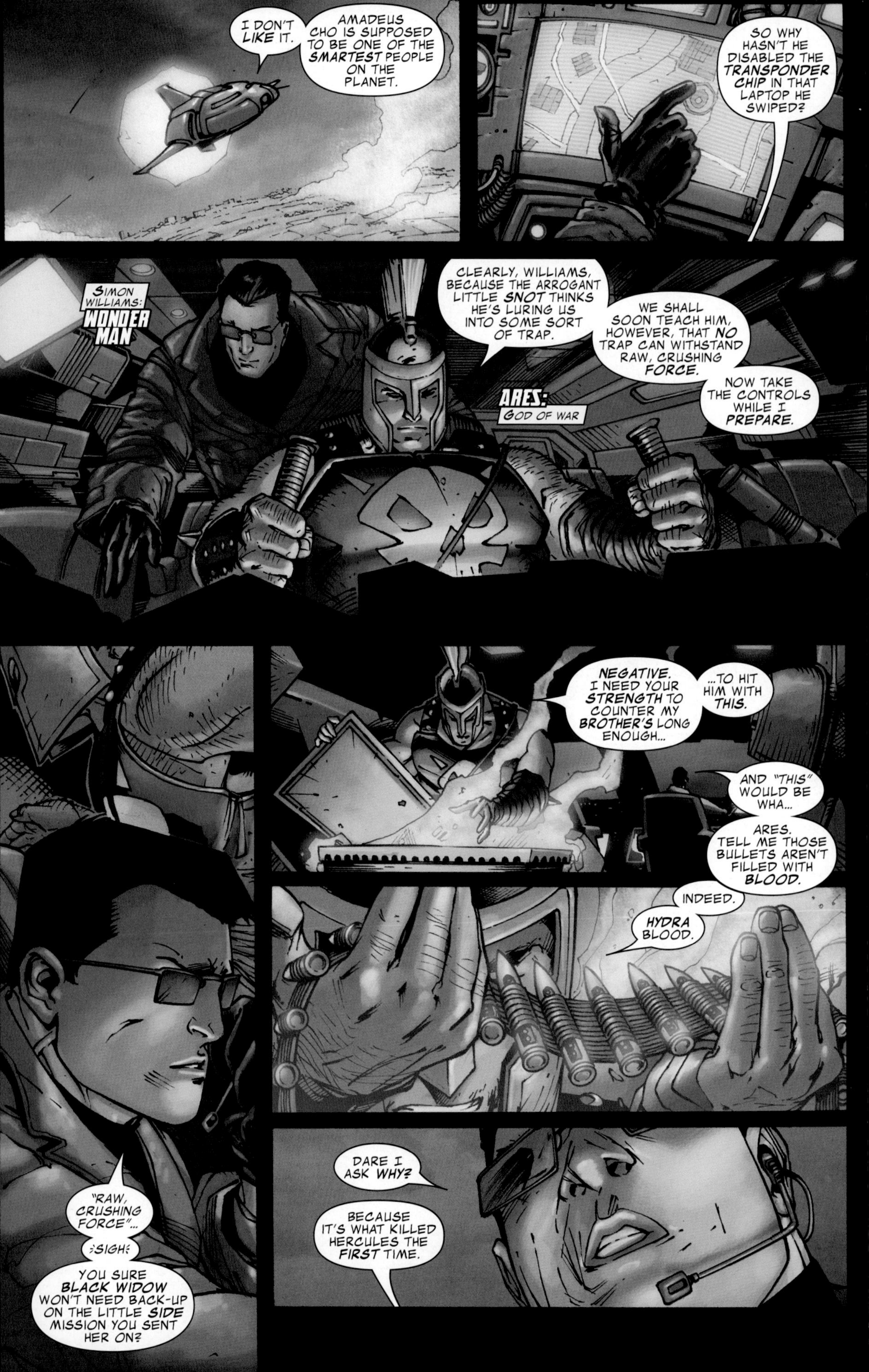
I DON'T LIKE IT.
AMADEUS CHO IS SUPPOSED TO BE ONE OF THE SMARTEST PEOPLE ON THE PLANET.
SO WHY HASN'T HE DISABLED THE TRANSPONDER CHIP IN THAT LAPTOP HE SWIPED?
SIMON WILLIAMS: WONDER MAN
CLEARLY, WILLIAMS, BECAUSE THE ARROGANT LITTLE SNOT THINKS HE'S LURING US INTO SOME SORT OF TRAP.
WE SHALL SOON TEACH HIM, HOWEVER, THAT NO TRAP CAN WITHSTAND RAW, CRUSHING FORCE.
NOW TAKE THE CONTROLS WHILE I PREPARE.
ARES: GOD OF WAR
"RAW, CRUSHING FORCE"...
SIGH
YOU SURE BLACK WIDOW WON'T NEED BACK-UP ON THE LITTLE SIDE MISSION YOU SENT HER ON?
NEGATIVE. I NEED YOUR STRENGTH TO COUNTER MY BROTHER'S LONG ENOUGH...
...TO HIT HIM WITH THIS.
AND "THIS" WOULD BE WHA...
ARES. TELL ME THOSE BULLETS AREN'T FILLED WITH BLOOD.
INDEED.
HYDRA BLOOD.
DARE I ASK WHY?
BECAUSE IT'S WHAT KILLED HERCULES THE FIRST TIME.

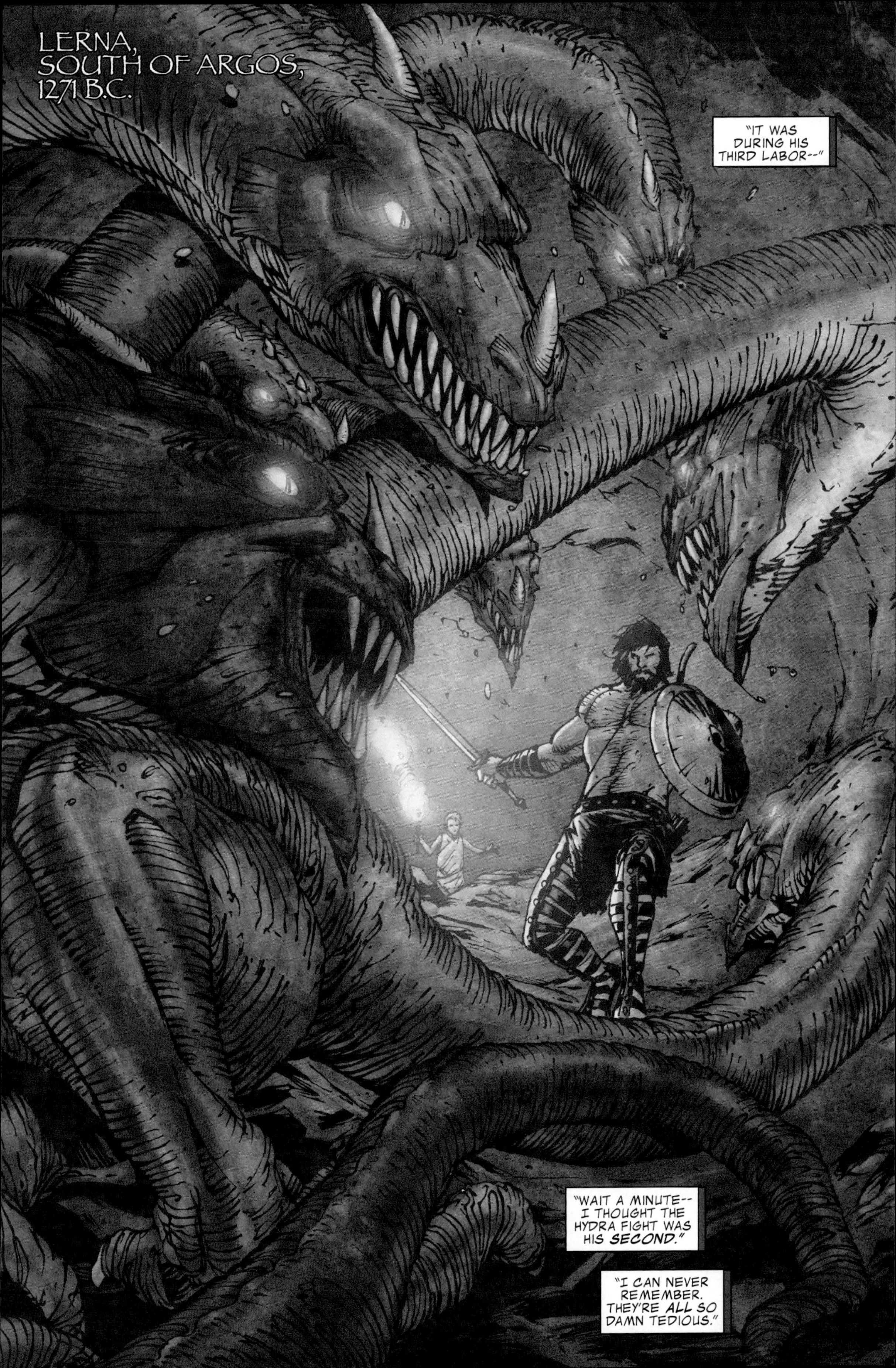
LERNA, SOUTH OF ARGOS, 1271 B.C.
"IT WAS DURING HIS THIRD LABOR--"
"WAIT A MINUTE-- I THOUGHT THE HYDRA FIGHT WAS HIS SECOND."
"I CAN NEVER REMEMBER. THEY'RE ALL SO DAMN TEDIOUS."

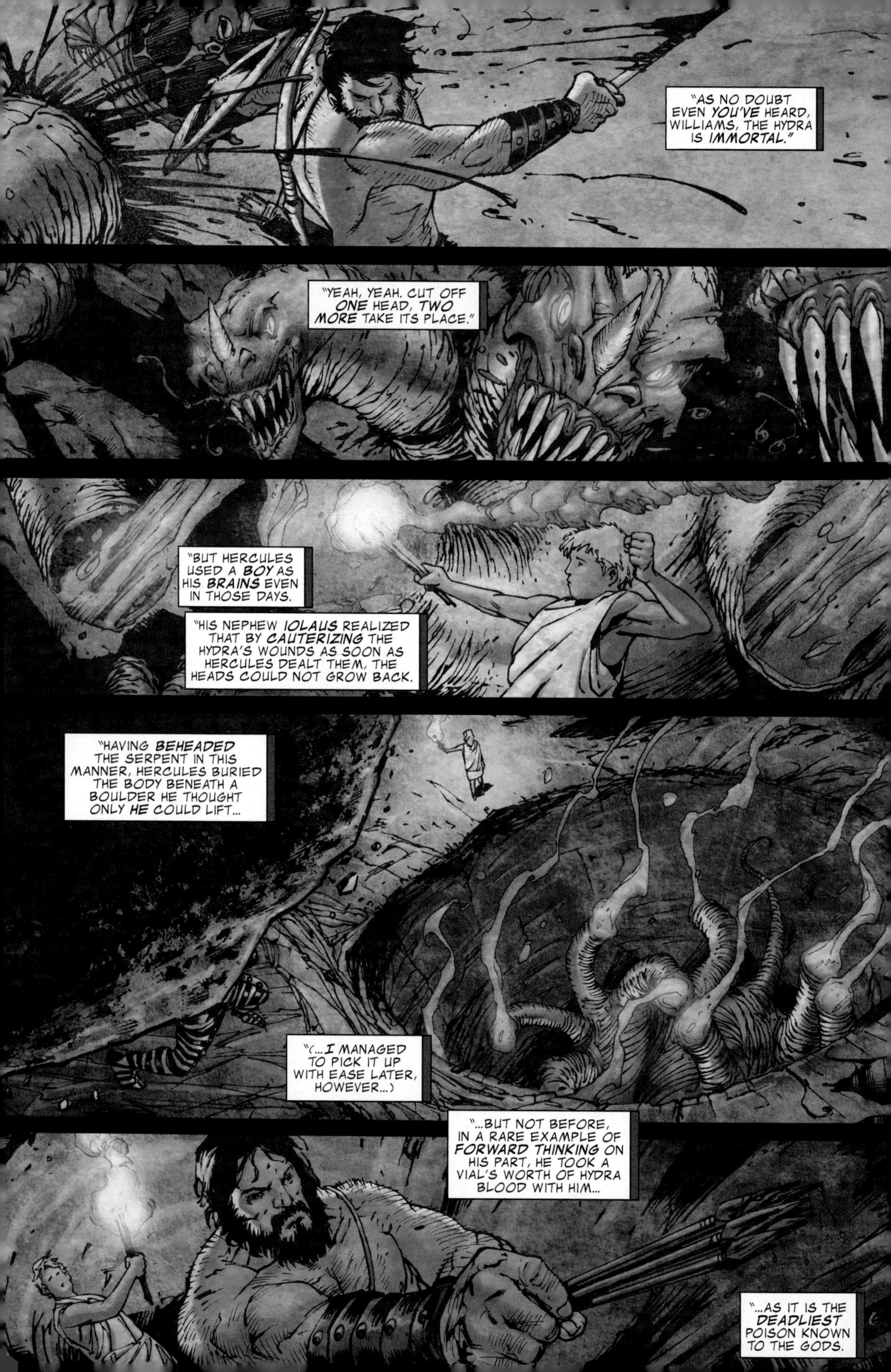
"AS NO DOUBT EVEN YOU'VE HEARD, WILLIAMS, THE HYDRA IS IMMORTAL."
"YEAH, YEAH. CUT OFF ONE HEAD, TWO MORE TAKE ITS PLACE."
"BUT HERCULES USED A BOY AS HIS BRAINS EVEN IN THOSE DAYS.
"HIS NEPHEW IOLAUS REALIZED THAT BY CAUTERIZING THE HYDRA'S WOUNDS AS SOON AS HERCULES DEALT THEM, THE HEADS COULD NOT GROW BACK.
"HAVING BEHEADED THE SERPENT IN THIS MANNER, HERCULES BURIED THE BODY BENEATH A BOULDER HE THOUGHT ONLY HE COULD LIFT...
"(...I MANAGED TO PICK IT UP WITH EASE LATER, HOWEVER...)
"...BUT NOT BEFORE, IN A RARE EXAMPLE OF FORWARD THINKING ON HIS PART, HE TOOK A VIAL'S WORTH OF HYDRA BLOOD WITH HIM...
"...AS IT IS THE DEADLIEST POISON KNOWN TO THE GODS.

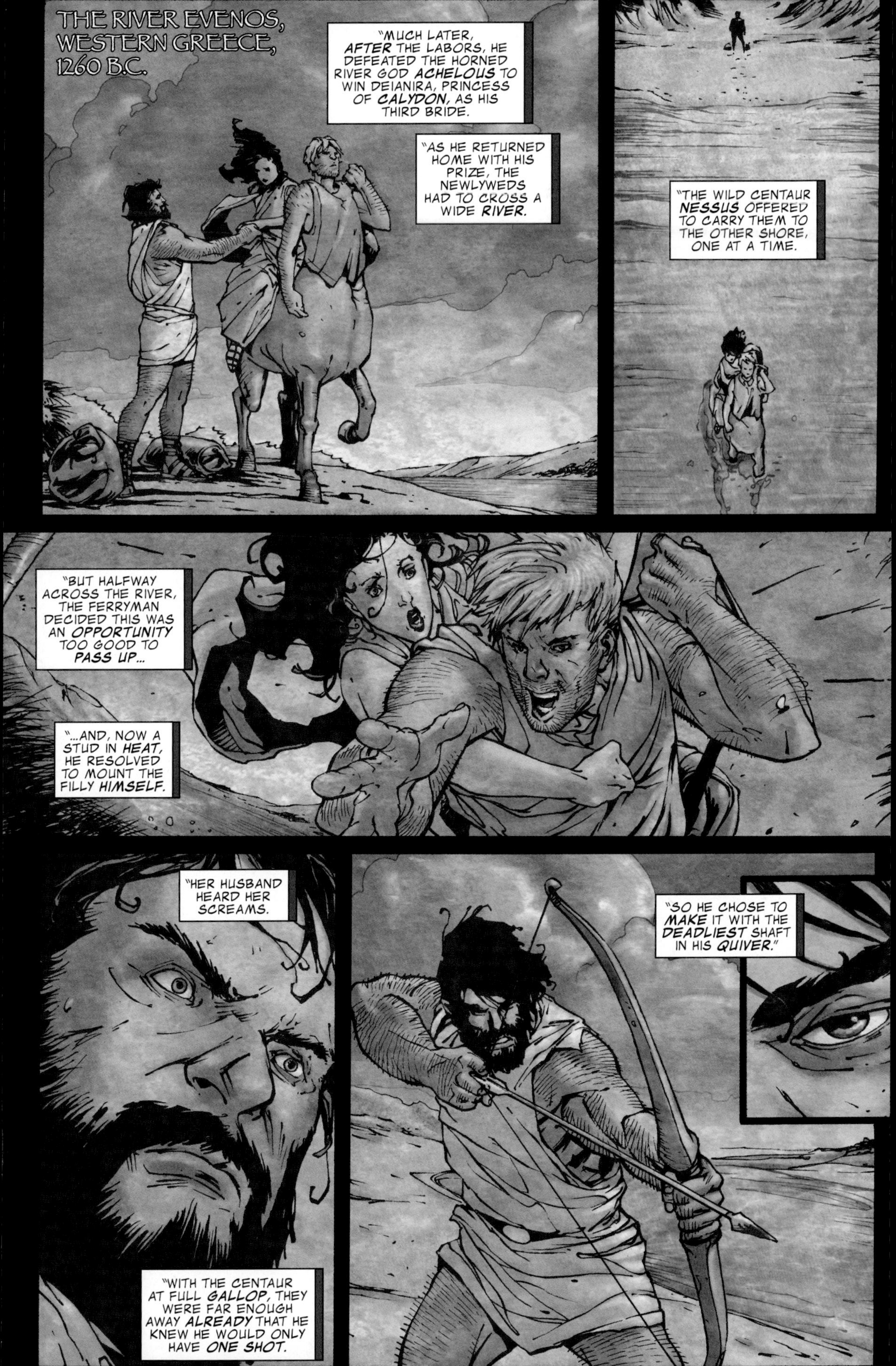
THE RIVER EVENOS, WESTERN GREECE, 1260 B.C.
"MUCH LATER, AFTER THE LABORS, HE DEFEATED THE HORNED RIVER GOD ACHELOUS TO WIN DEIANIRA, PRINCESS OF CALYDON, AS HIS THIRD BRIDE.
"AS HE RETURNED HOME WITH HIS PRIZE, THE NEWLYWEDS HAD TO CROSS A WIDE RIVER.
"THE WILD CENTAUR NESSUS OFFERED TO CARRY THEM TO THE OTHER SHORE, ONE AT A TIME.
"BUT HALFWAY ACROSS THE RIVER, THE FERRYMAN DECIDED THIS WAS AN OPPORTUNITY TOO GOOD TO PASS UP...
"...AND, NOW A STUD IN HEAT, HE RESOLVED TO MOUNT THE FILLY HIMSELF.
"HER HUSBAND HEARD HER SCREAMS.
"WITH THE CENTAUR AT FULL GALLOP, THEY WERE FAR ENOUGH AWAY ALREADY THAT HE KNEW HE WOULD ONLY HAVE ONE SHOT.
"SO HE CHOSE TO MAKE IT WITH THE DEADLIEST SHAFT IN HIS QUIVER."

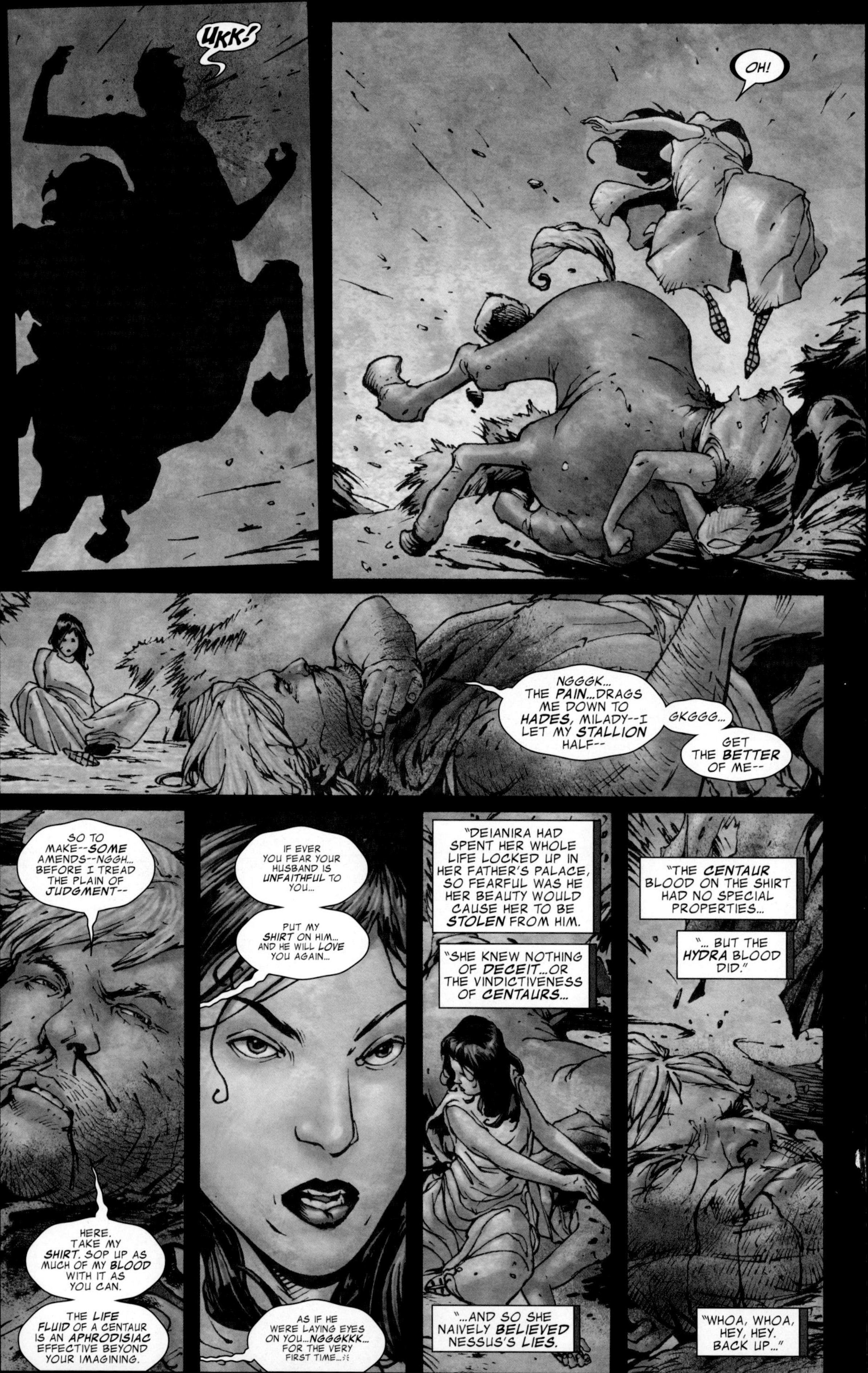
UKK!
OH!
NGGGK... THE PAIN...DRAGS ME DOWN TO HADES, MILADY--I LET MY STALLION HALF--
GKGGG...
GET THE BETTER OF ME--
SO TO MAKE--SOME AMENDS--NGGH... BEFORE I TREAD THE PLAIN OF JUDGMENT--
HERE. TAKE MY SHIRT. SOP UP AS MUCH OF MY BLOOD WITH IT AS YOU CAN.
THE LIFE FLUID OF A CENTAUR IS AN APHRODISIAC EFFECTIVE BEYOND YOUR IMAGINING.
IF EVER YOU FEAR YOUR HUSBAND IS UNFAITHFUL TO YOU...
PUT MY SHIRT ON HIM... AND HE WILL LOVE YOU AGAIN...
AS IF HE WERE LAYING EYES ON YOU...NGGGKKK... FOR THE VERY FIRST TIME...
"DEIANIRA HAD SPENT HER WHOLE LIFE LOCKED UP IN HER FATHER'S PALACE, SO FEARFUL WAS HE HER BEAUTY WOULD CAUSE HER TO BE STOLEN FROM HIM.
"SHE KNEW NOTHING OF DECEIT...OR THE VINDICTIVENESS OF CENTAURS...
"...AND SO SHE NAIVELY BELIEVED NESSUS'S LIES.
"THE CENTAUR BLOOD ON THE SHIRT HAD NO SPECIAL PROPERTIES...
"... BUT THE HYDRA BLOOD DID."
"WHOA, WHOA, HEY, HEY. BACK UP..."

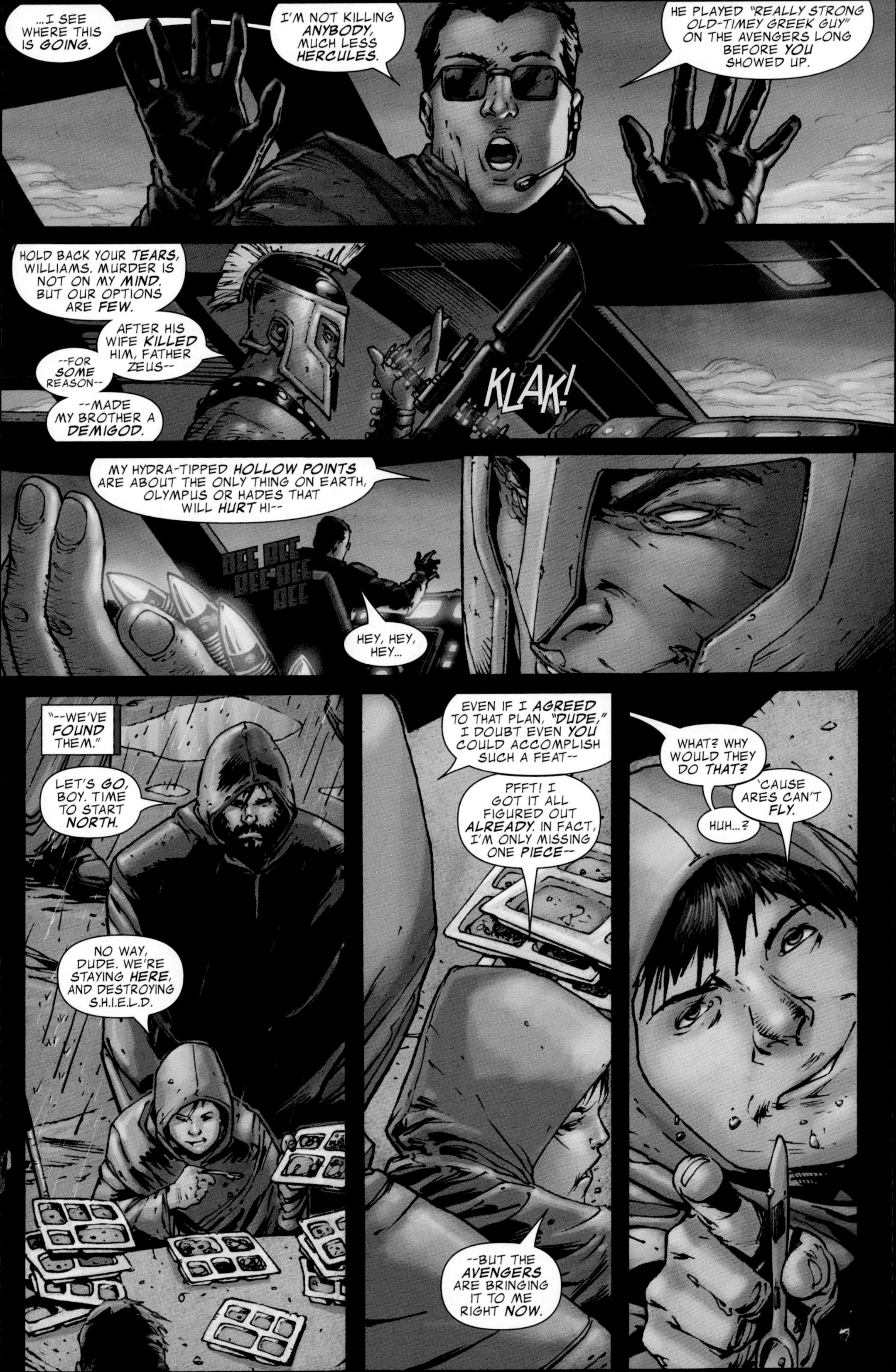

...I SEE WHERE THIS IS GOING.
I'M NOT KILLING ANYBODY, MUCH LESS HERCULES.
HE PLAYED "REALLY STRONG OLD-TIMEY GREEK GUY" ON THE AVENGERS LONG BEFORE YOU SHOWED UP.
HOLD BACK YOUR TEARS, WILLIAMS. MURDER IS NOT ON MY MIND. BUT OUR OPTIONS ARE FEW.
AFTER HIS WIFE KILLED HIM, FATHER ZEUS--
--FOR SOME REASON--
--MADE MY BROTHER A DEMIGOD.
KLAK!
MY HYDRA-TIPPED HOLLOW POINTS ARE ABOUT THE ONLY THING ON EARTH, OLYMPUS OR HADES THAT WILL HURT HI--
HEY, HEY, HEY...
"--WE'VE FOUND THEM."
LET'S GO, BOY. TIME TO START NORTH.
NO WAY, DUDE. WE'RE STAYING HERE, AND DESTROYING S.H.I.E.L.D.
EVEN IF I AGREED TO THAT PLAN, "DUDE," I DOUBT EVEN YOU COULD ACCOMPLISH SUCH A FEAT--
PFFT! I GOT IT ALL FIGURED OUT ALREADY. IN FACT, I'M ONLY MISSING ONE PIECE--
--BUT THE AVENGERS ARE BRINGING IT TO ME RIGHT NOW.
WHAT? WHY WOULD THEY DO THAT?
HUH...?
'CAUSE ARES CAN'T FLY.

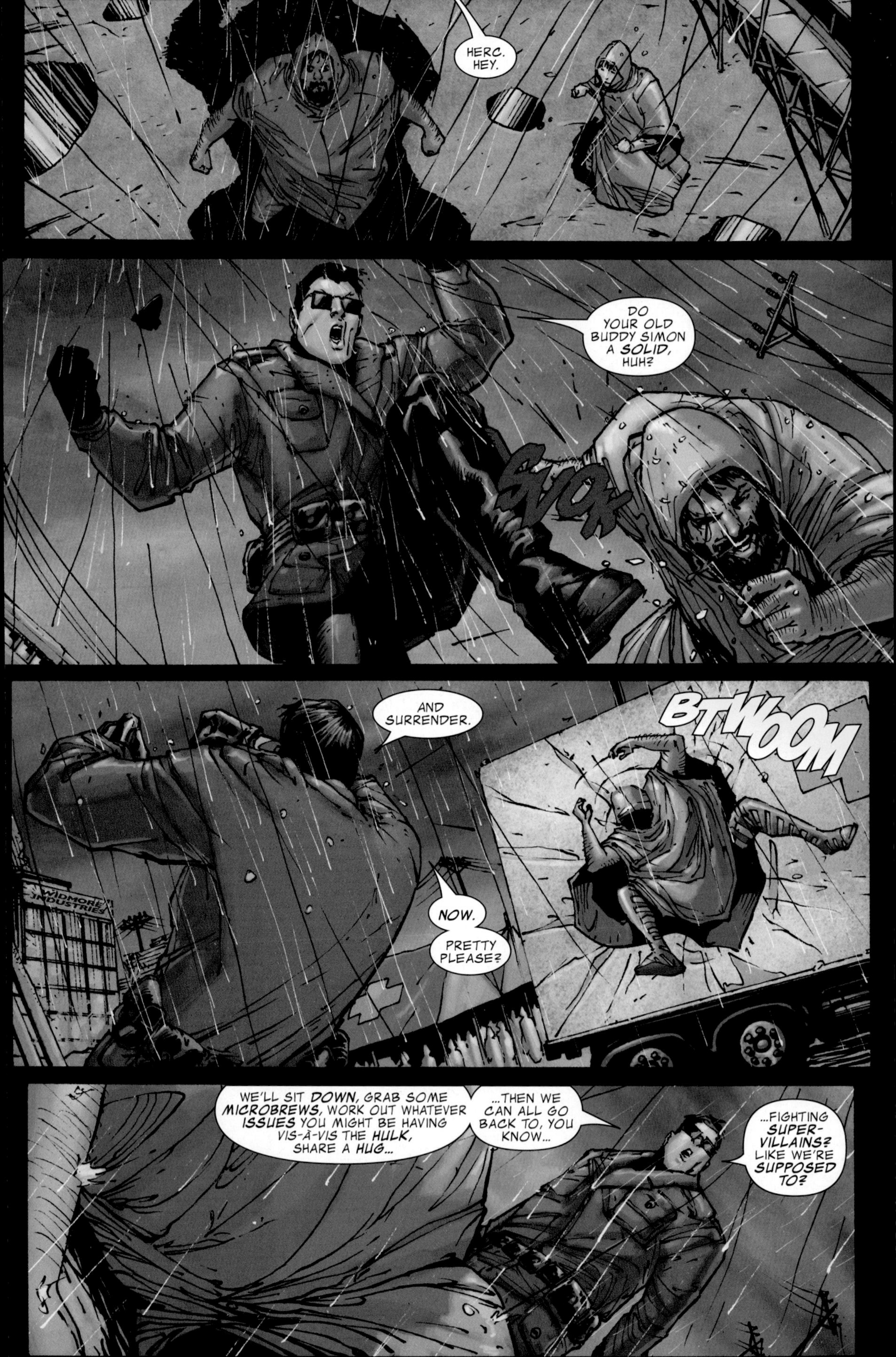
HERC. HEY.
DO YOUR OLD BUDDY SIMON A SOLID, HUH?
SVOK
AND SURRENDER.
BTWOOM
NOW.
PRETTY PLEASE?
WIDMORE INDUSTRIES
WE'LL SIT DOWN, GRAB SOME MICROBREWS, WORK OUT WHATEVER ISSUES YOU MIGHT BE HAVING VIS-À-VIS THE HULK, SHARE A HUG...
...THEN WE CAN ALL GO BACK TO, YOU KNOW...
...FIGHTING SUPER-VILLAINS? LIKE WE'RE SUPPOSED TO?

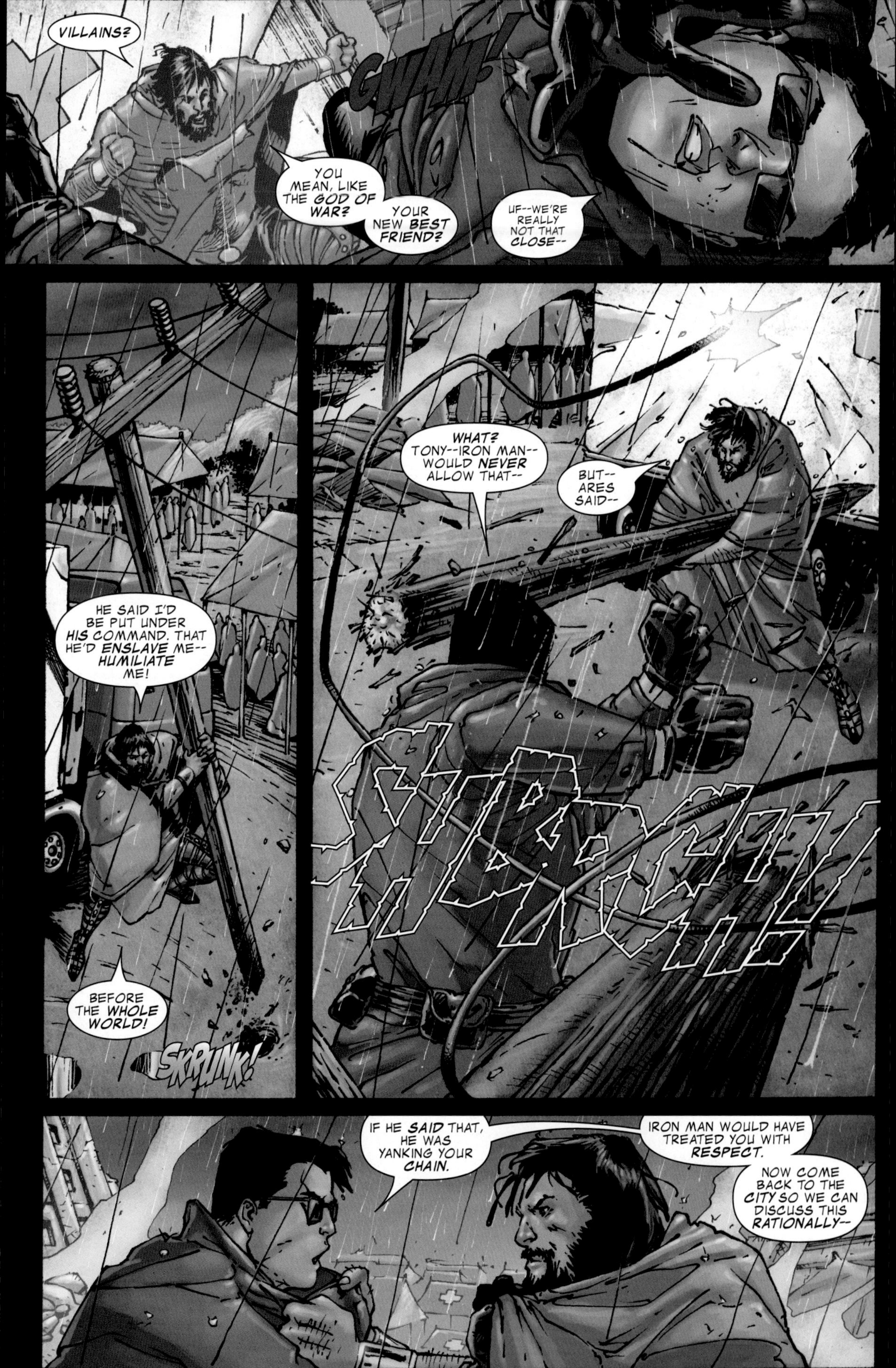

VILLAINS?
GWAM!
YOU MEAN, LIKE THE GOD OF WAR?
YOUR NEW BEST FRIEND?
UF--WE'RE REALLY NOT THAT CLOSE--
HE SAID I'D BE PUT UNDER HIS COMMAND. THAT HE'D ENSLAVE ME--HUMILIATE ME!
BEFORE THE WHOLE WORLD!
SKRUNK!
WHAT? TONY--IRON MAN--WOULD NEVER ALLOW THAT--
BUT--ARES SAID--
IF HE SAID THAT, HE WAS YANKING YOUR CHAIN.
IRON MAN WOULD HAVE TREATED YOU WITH RESPECT.
NOW COME BACK TO THE CITY SO WE CAN DISCUSS THIS RATIONALLY--

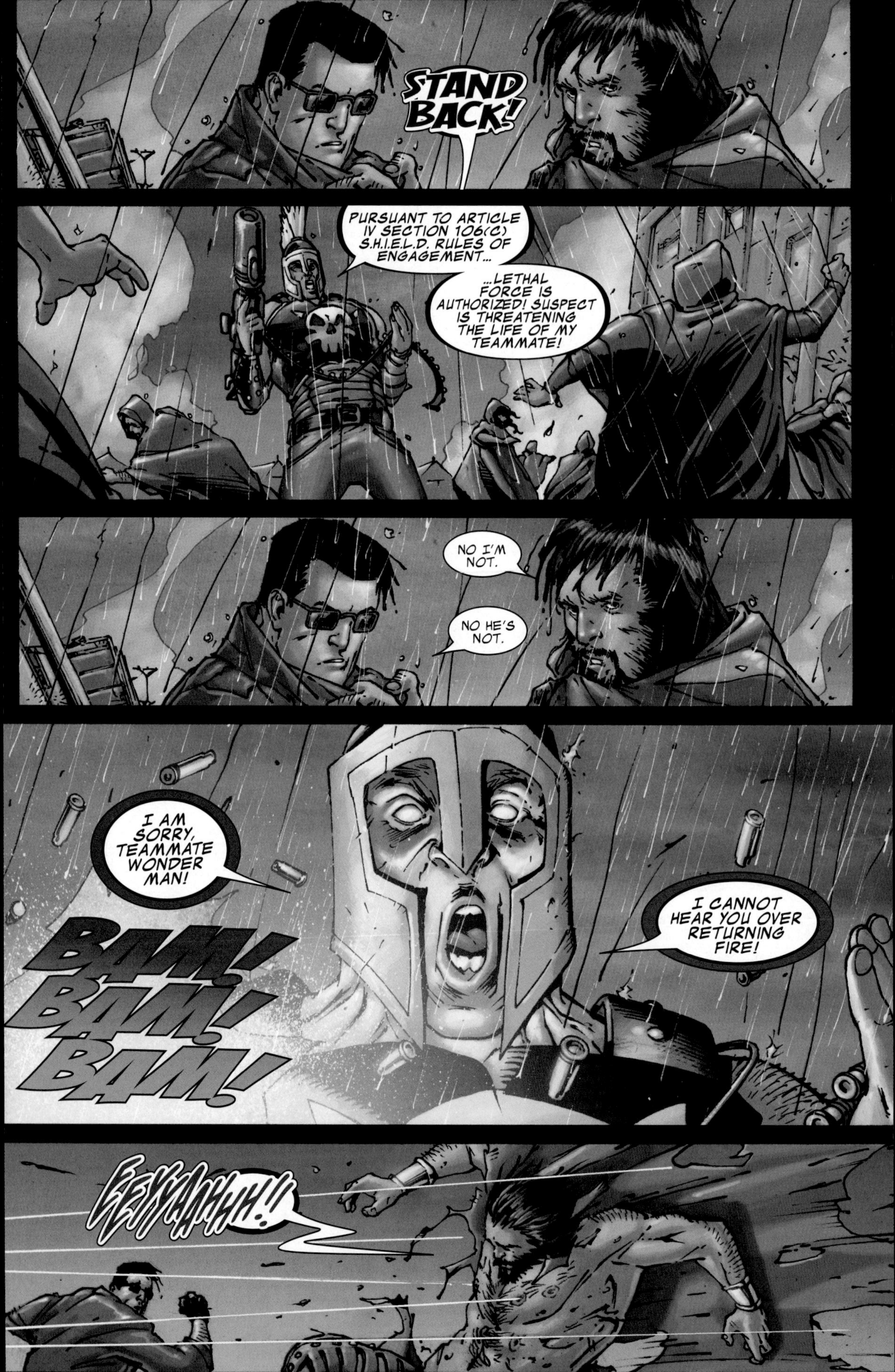
STAND BACK!
PURSUANT TO ARTICLE IV SECTION 106(C) S.H.I.E.L.D. RULES OF ENGAGEMENT...
...LETHAL FORCE IS AUTHORIZED! SUSPECT IS THREATENING THE LIFE OF MY TEAMMATE!
NO I'M NOT.
NO HE'S NOT.
I AM SORRY, TEAMMATE WONDER MAN!
I CANNOT HEAR YOU OVER RETURNING FIRE!
BAM! BAM! BAM!
EEYYAAHHH!!

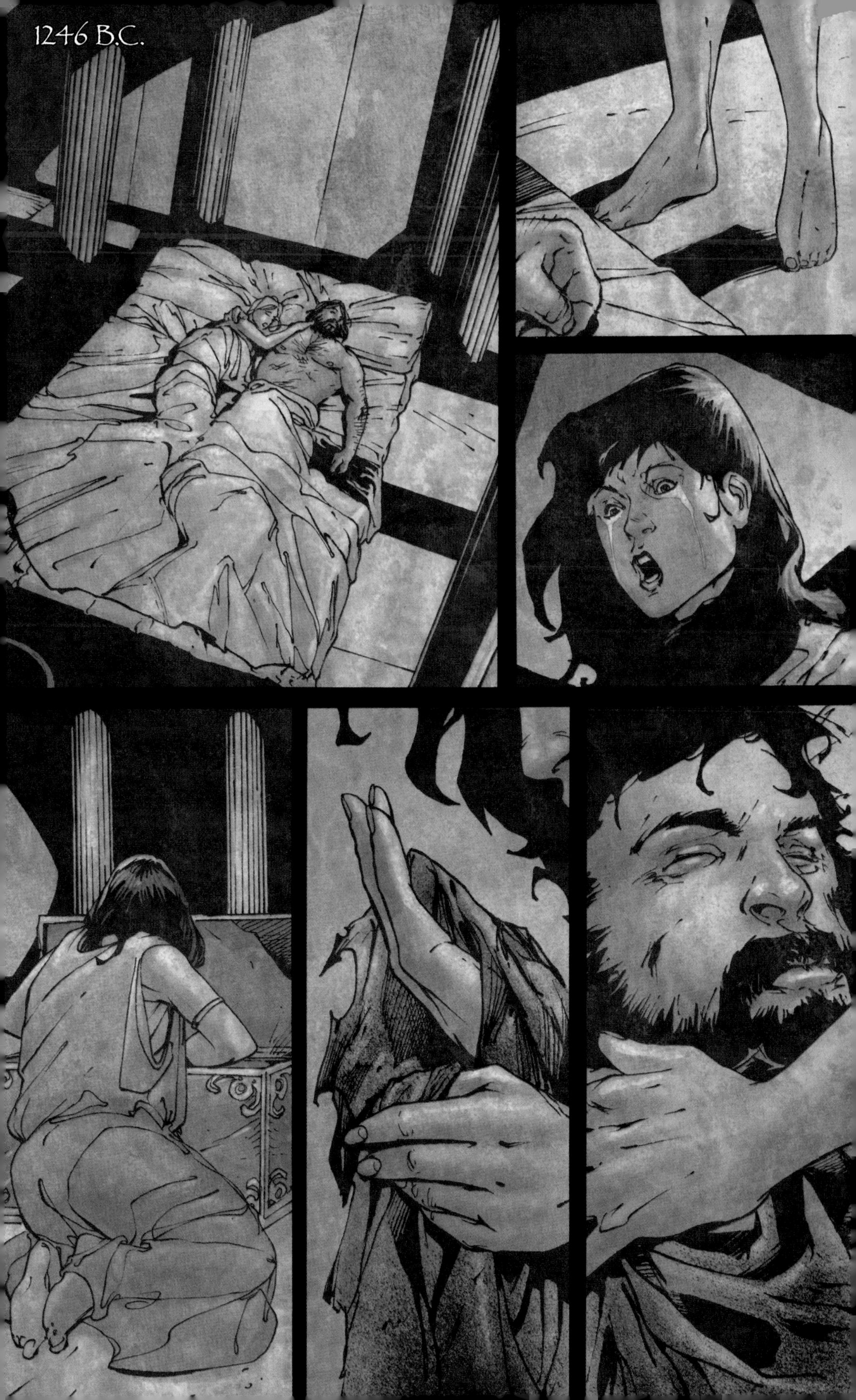
1246 B.C.

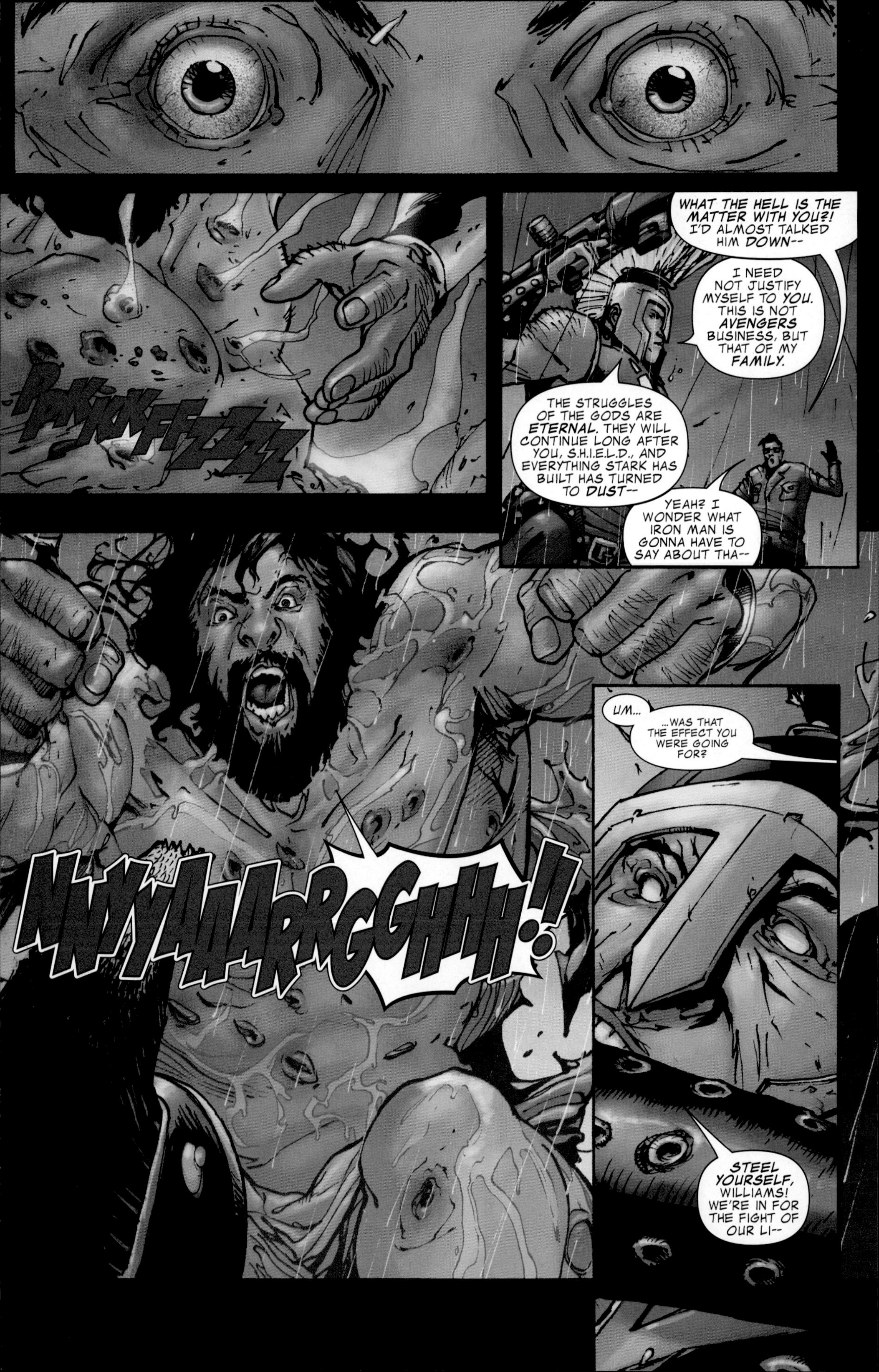
PPKKKFFZZZZZ
WHAT THE HELL IS THE MATTER WITH YOU?! I'D ALMOST TALKED HIM DOWN--
I NEED NOT JUSTIFY MYSELF TO YOU. THIS IS NOT AVENGERS BUSINESS, BUT THAT OF MY FAMILY.
THE STRUGGLES OF THE GODS ARE ETERNAL. THEY WILL CONTINUE LONG AFTER YOU, S.H.I.E.L.D., AND EVERYTHING STARK HAS BUILT HAS TURNED TO DUST--
YEAH? I WONDER WHAT IRON MAN IS GONNA HAVE TO SAY ABOUT THA--
NNYAAARRGGHHH!!
UM...
...WAS THAT THE EFFECT YOU WERE GOING FOR?
STEEL YOURSELF, WILLIAMS! WE'RE IN FOR THE FIGHT OF OUR LI--

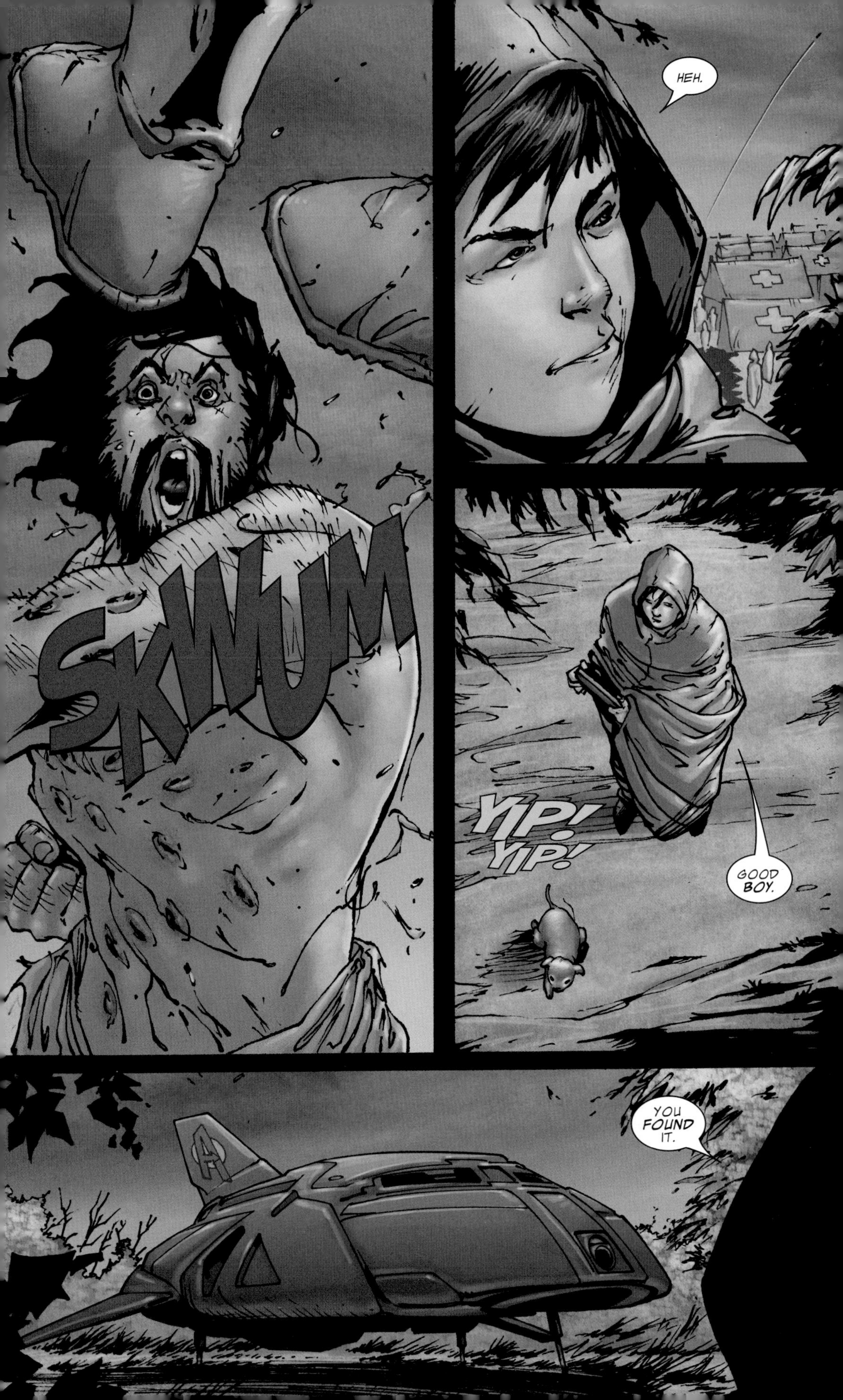
SKWUM
HEH.
YIP! YIP!
GOOD BOY.
YOU FOUND IT.

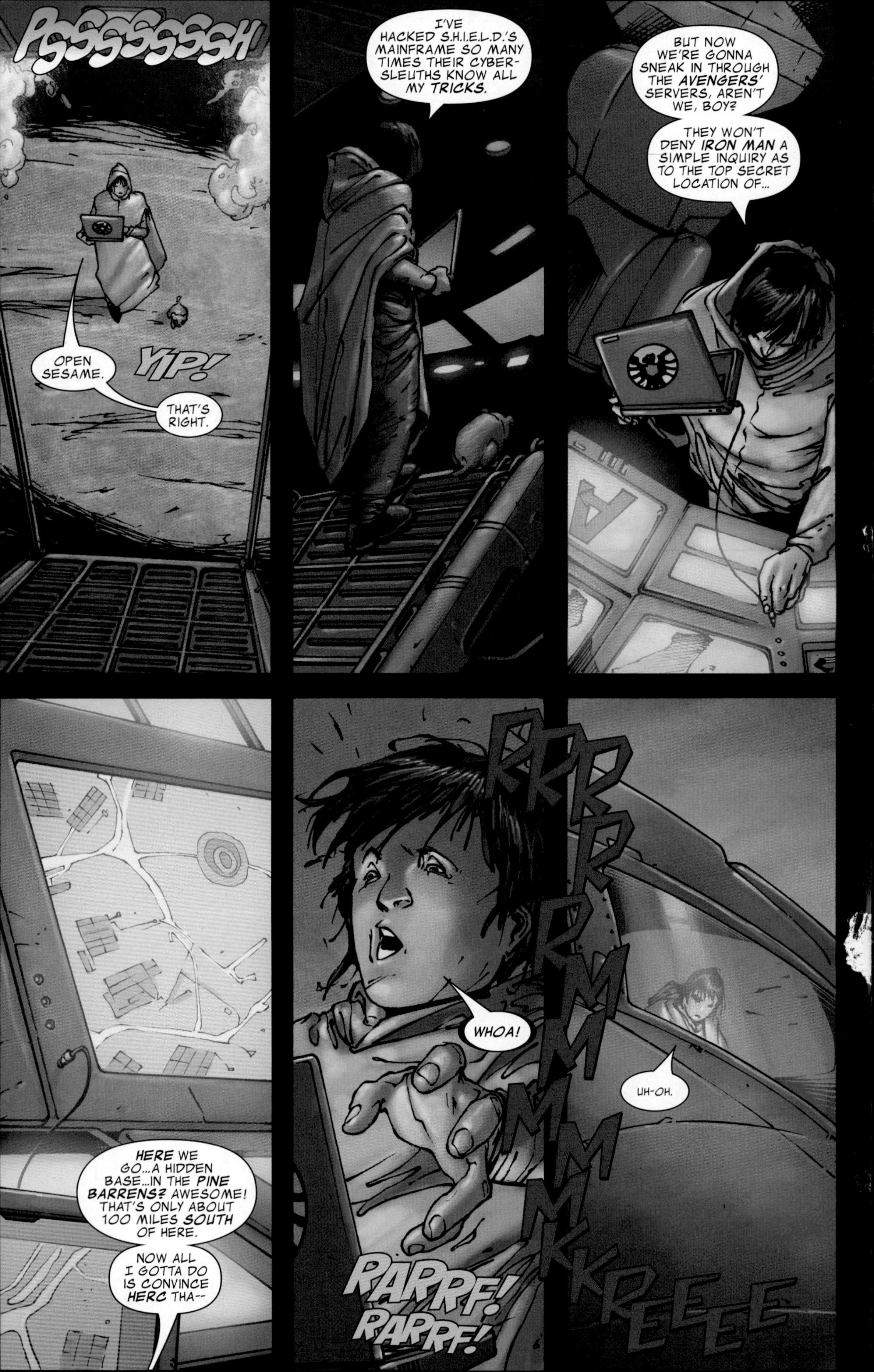
PSSSSSSSSH
OPEN SESAME.
YIP!
THAT'S RIGHT.
I'VE HACKED S.H.I.E.L.D.'S MAINFRAME SO MANY TIMES THEIR CYBER-SLEUTHS KNOW ALL MY TRICKS.
BUT NOW WE'RE GONNA SNEAK IN THROUGH THE AVENGERS' SERVERS, AREN'T WE, BOY?
THEY WON'T DENY IRON MAN A SIMPLE INQUIRY AS TO THE TOP SECRET LOCATION OF...
HERE WE GO...A HIDDEN BASE...IN THE PINE BARRENS? AWESOME! THAT'S ONLY ABOUT 100 MILES SOUTH OF HERE.
NOW ALL I GOTTA DO IS CONVINCE HERC THA--
RRRRRRRMMMMMMKKREEEEE
WHOA!
RARRF! RARRF!
UH-OH.

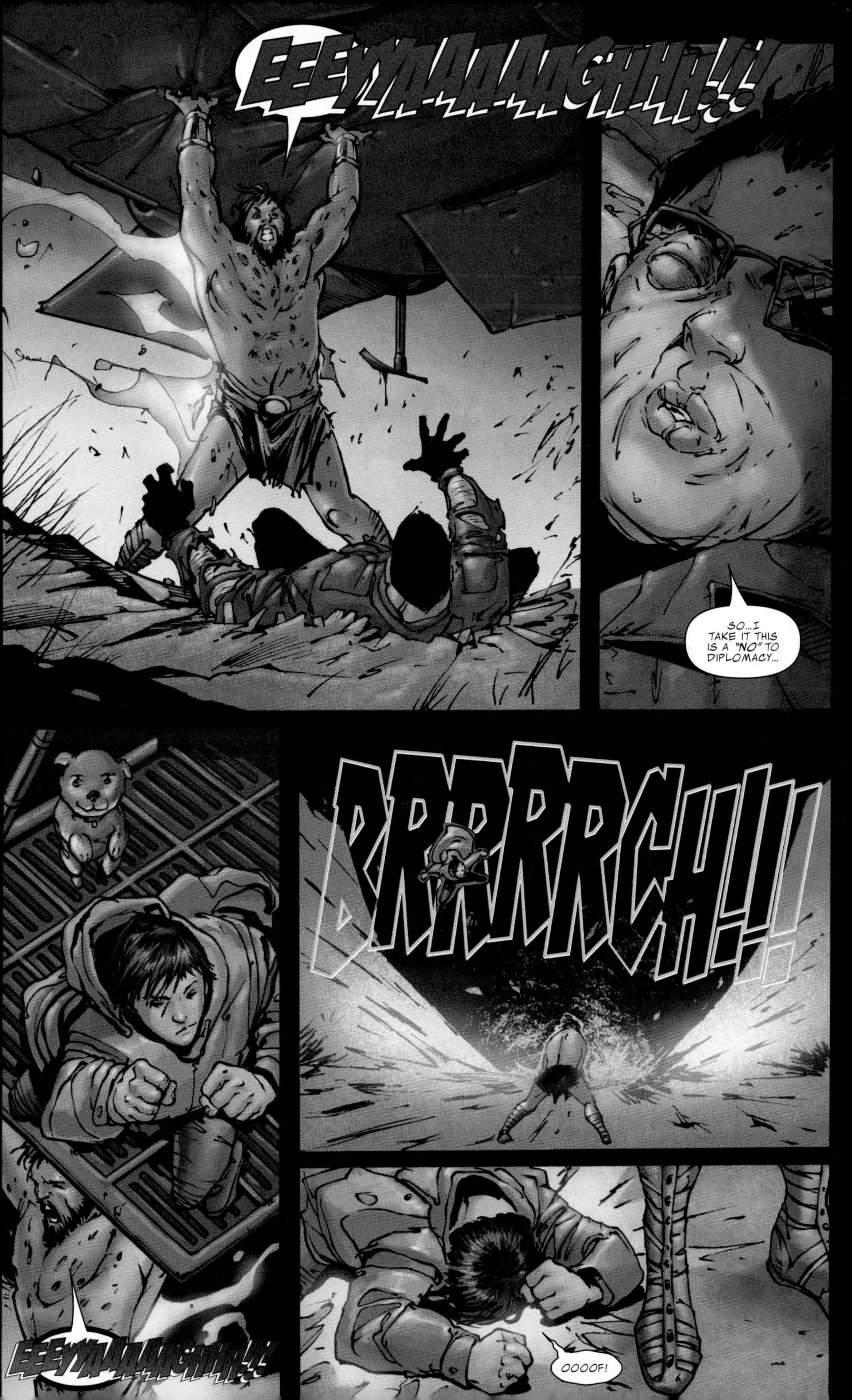
EEEYAAAAAGHHH!!
SO...I TAKE IT THIS IS A "NO" TO DIPLOMACY...
BRRRRCH!!!
EEEYAAAAAGHHH!!
OOOOF!

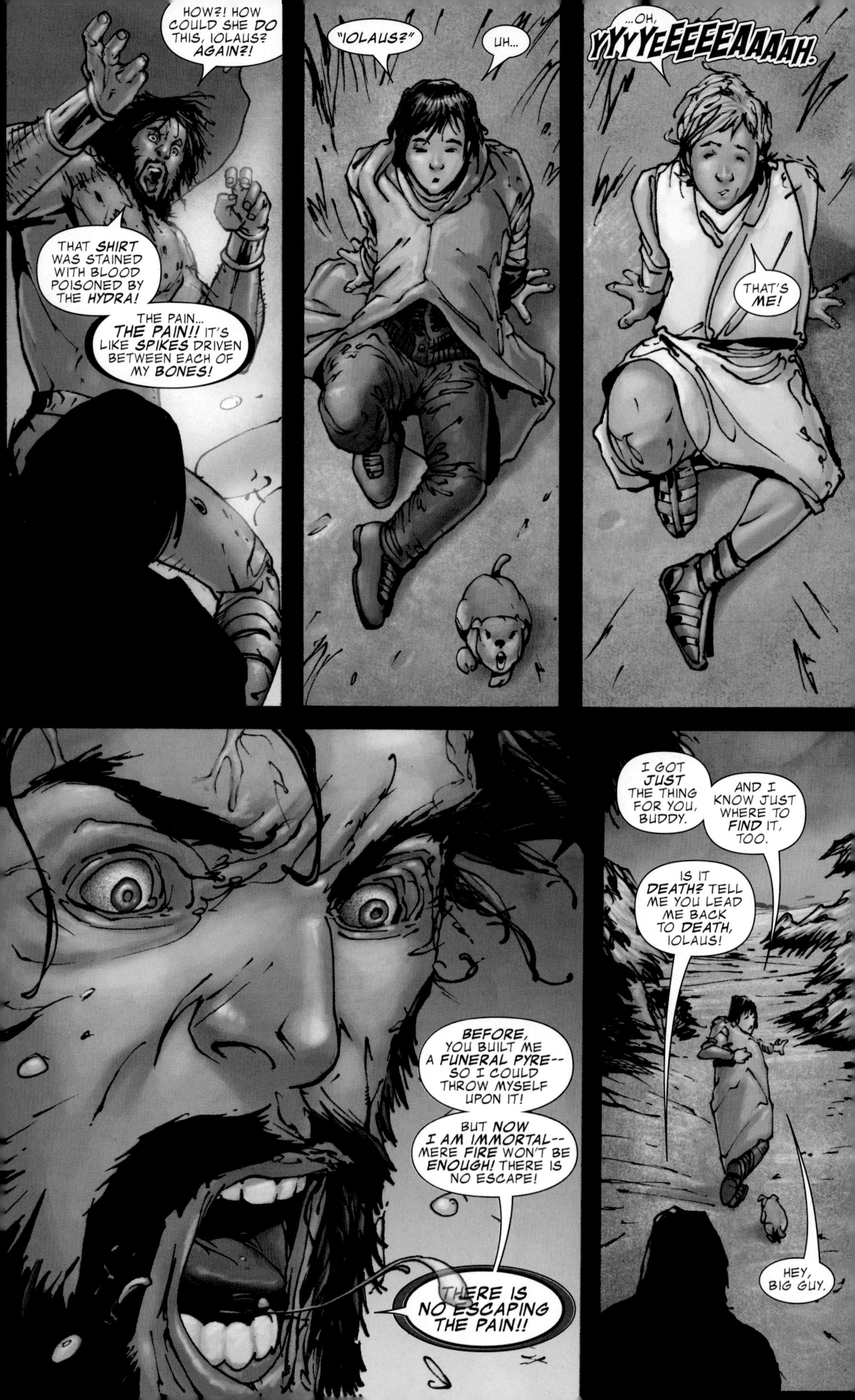
HOW?! HOW COULD SHE DO THIS, IOLAUS? AGAIN?!
THAT SHIRT WAS STAINED WITH BLOOD POISONED BY THE HYDRA!
THE PAIN... THE PAIN!! IT'S LIKE SPIKES DRIVEN BETWEEN EACH OF MY BONES!
"IOLAUS?"
UH...
...OH,
YYYYEEEEEAAAAAH.
THAT'S ME!
BEFORE, YOU BUILT ME A FUNERAL PYRE-- SO I COULD THROW MYSELF UPON IT!
BUT NOW I AM IMMORTAL-- MERE FIRE WON'T BE ENOUGH! THERE IS NO ESCAPE!
THERE IS NO ESCAPING THE PAIN!!
I GOT JUST THE THING FOR YOU, BUDDY.
AND I KNOW JUST WHERE TO FIND IT, TOO.
IS IT DEATH? TELL ME YOU LEAD ME BACK TO DEATH, IOLAUS!
HEY, BIG GUY.

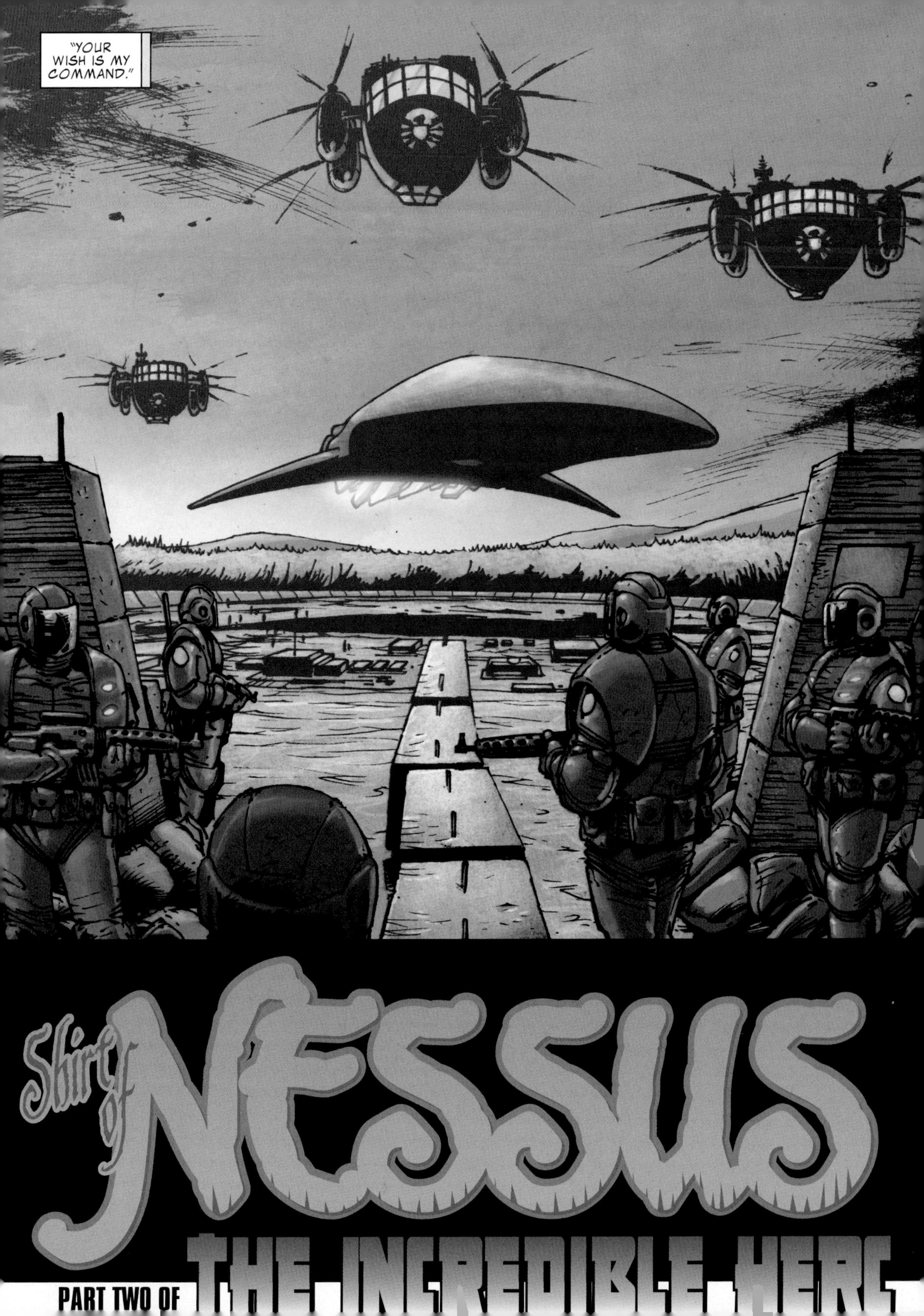
"YOUR WISH IS MY COMMAND."
Shirt of NESSUS
PART TWO OF THE INCREDIBLE HERC

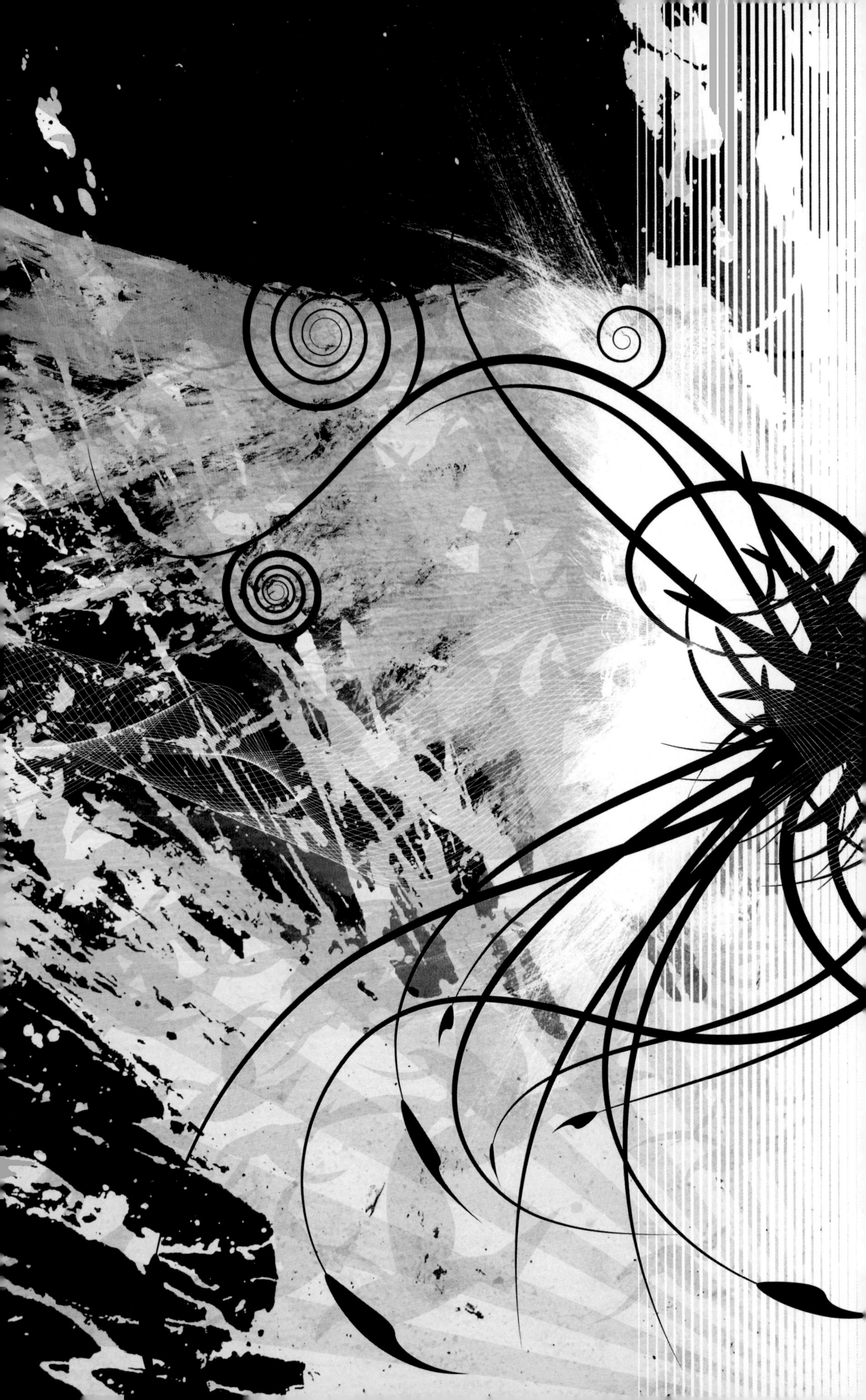

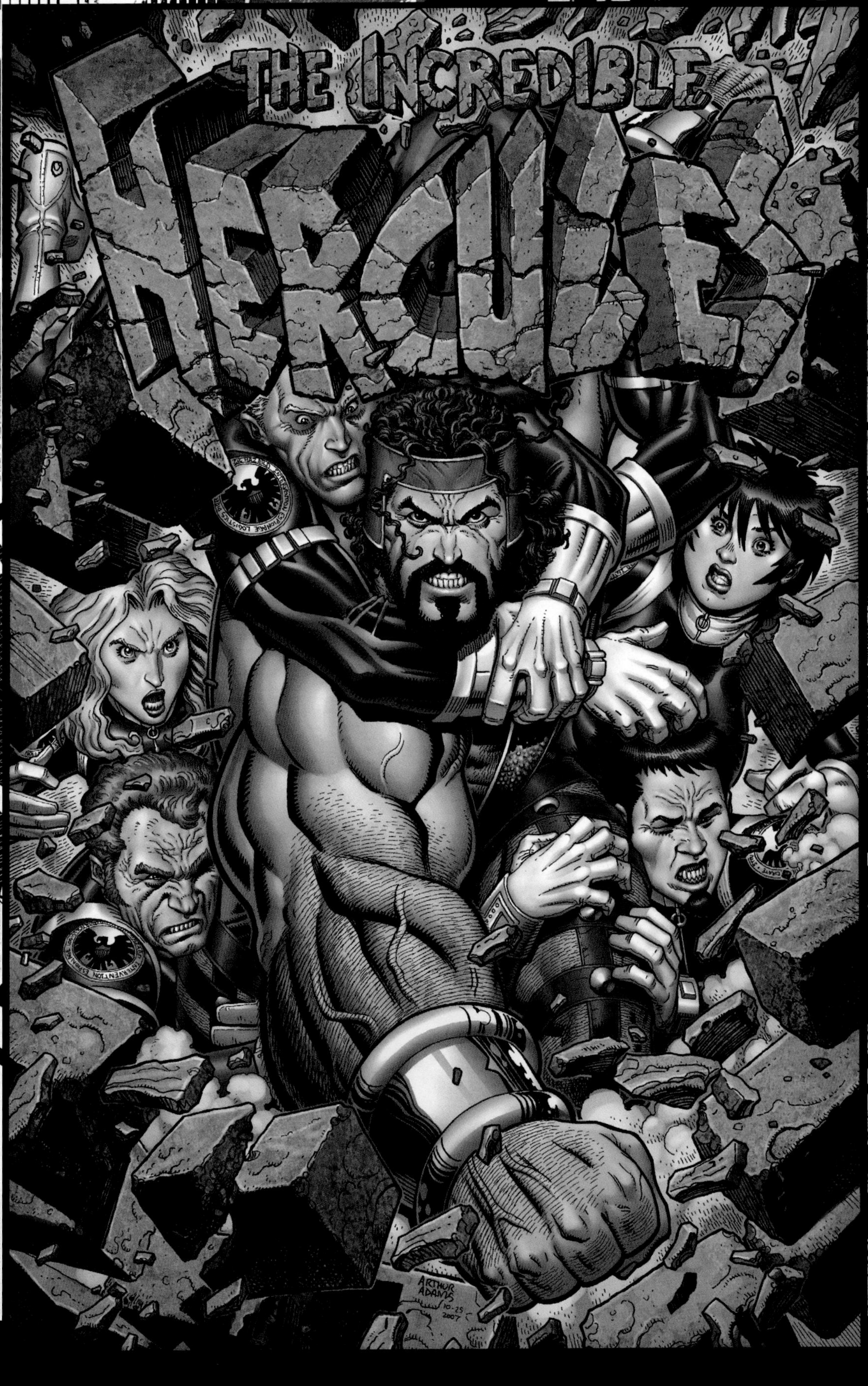
THE INCREDIBLE
HERCULES
ARTHUR ADAMS 10-25 2007

INCREDIBLE HERCULES #114

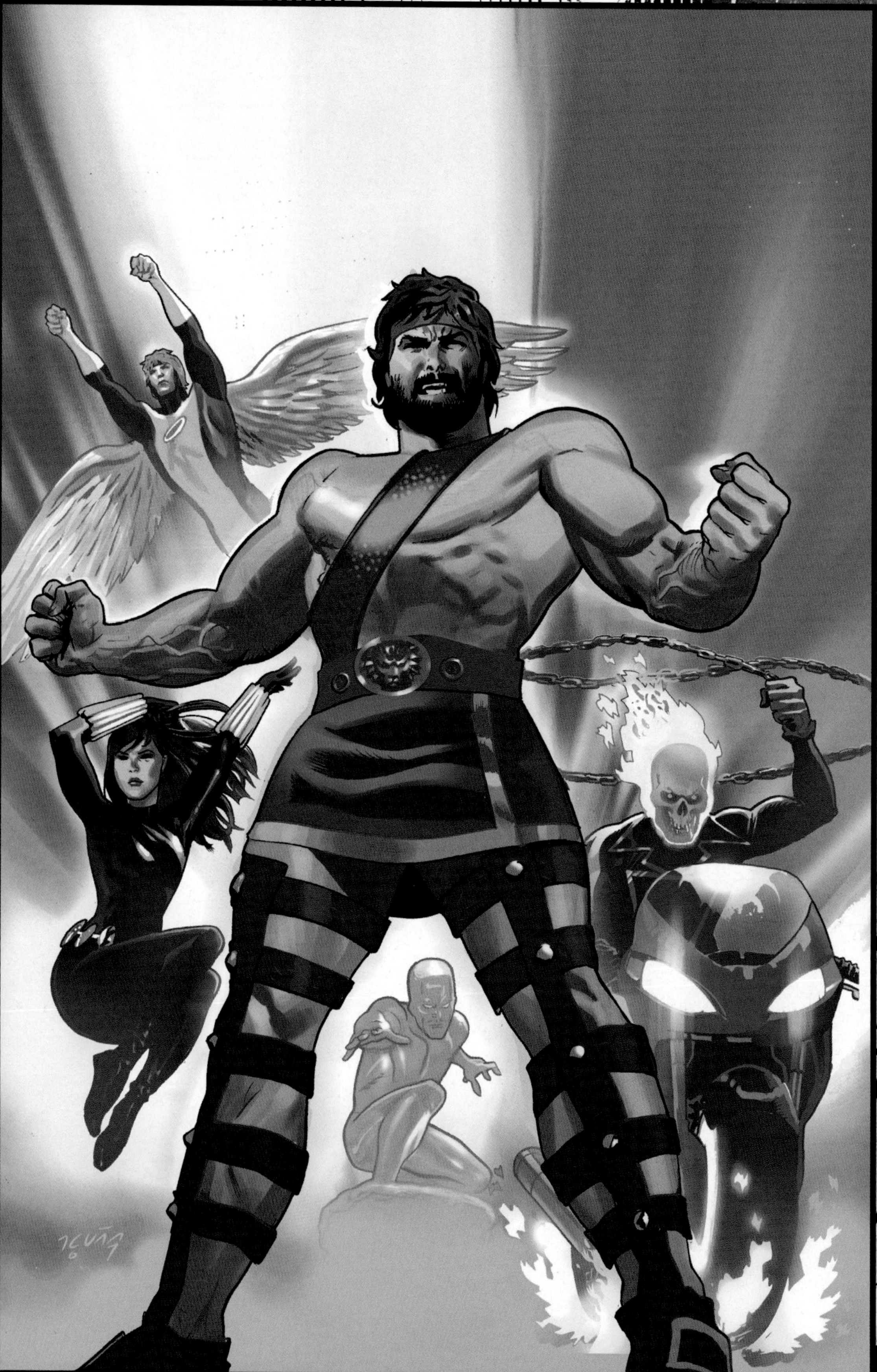

INCREDIBLE HERCULES #114 VARIANT
BY DANIEL ACUÑA

BEHOLD HERCULES.

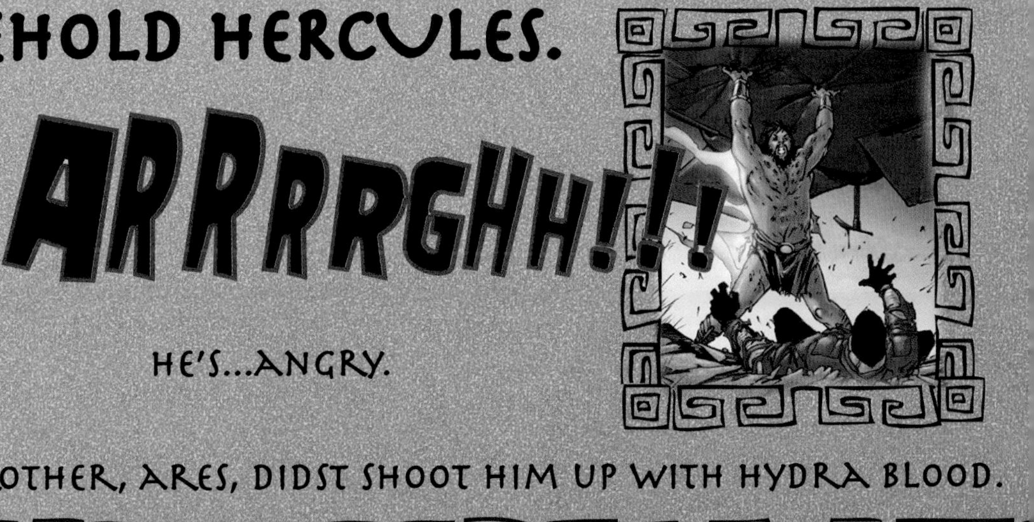

ARRRRGHH!!!

HE'S...ANGRY.

HIS BROTHER, ARES, DIDST SHOOT HIM UP WITH HYDRA BLOOD.

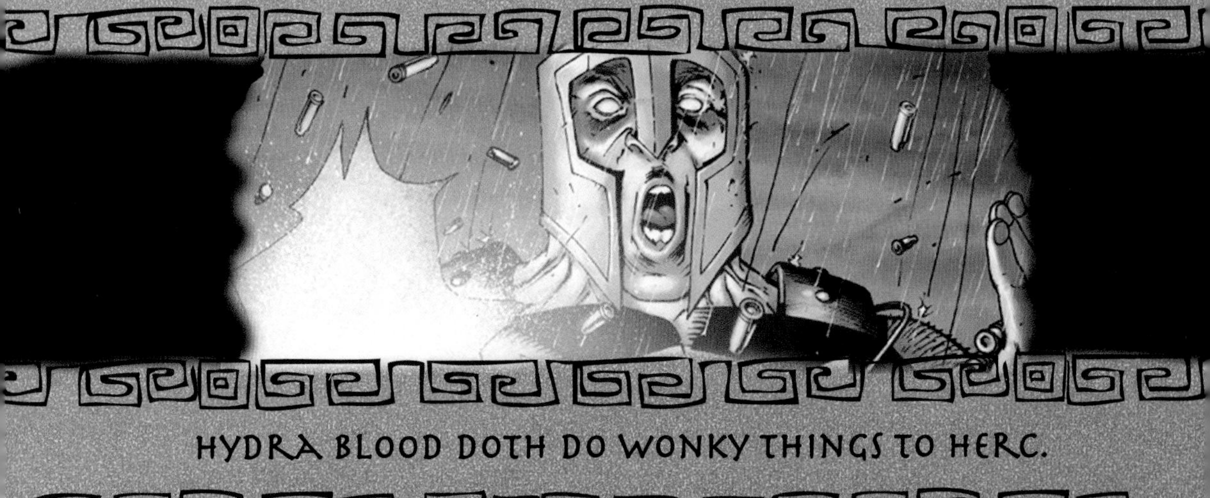

HYDRA BLOOD DOTH DO WONKY THINGS TO HERC.

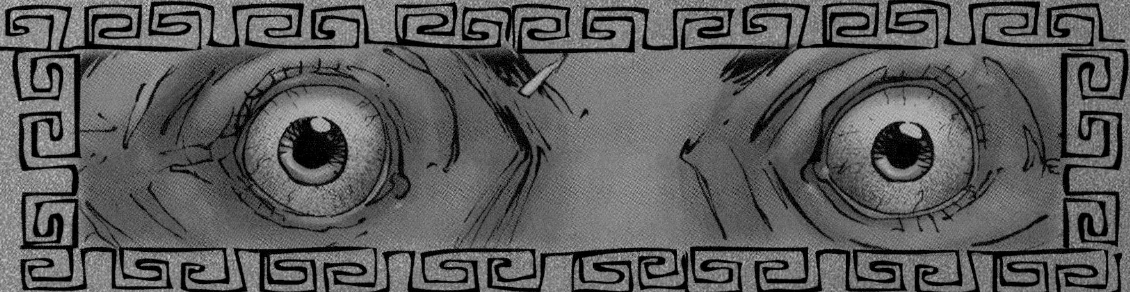

SO WHILST **AMADEUS CHO** (WITH PUP IN TOW) ATTEMPTS TO STEAL YON SHIP OF STONE... →

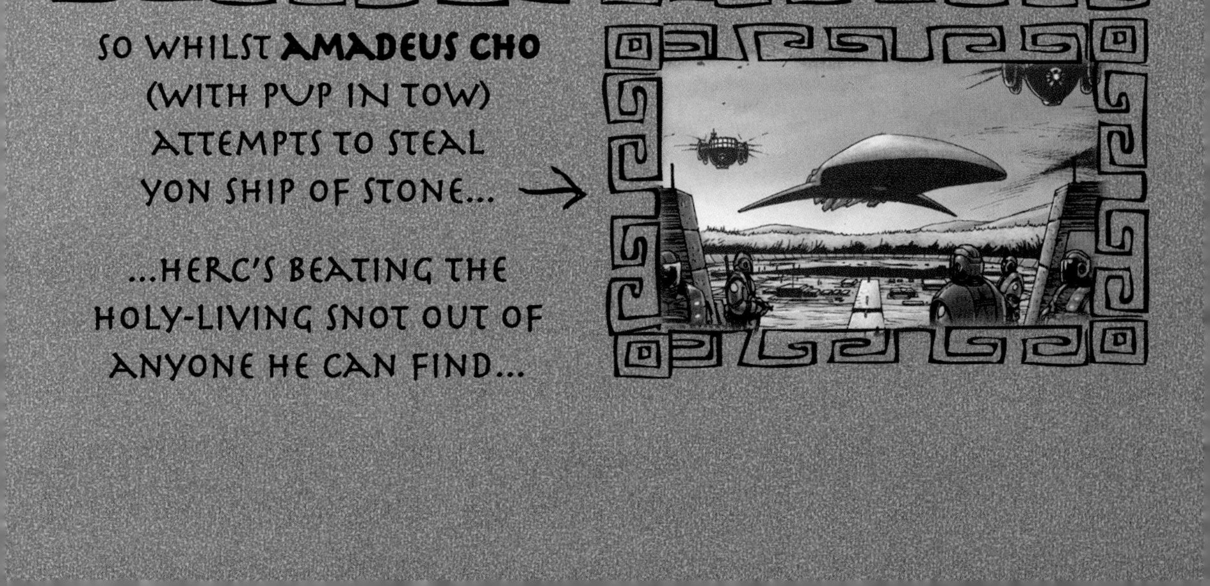

...HERC'S BEATING THE HOLY-LIVING SNOT OUT OF ANYONE HE CAN FIND...

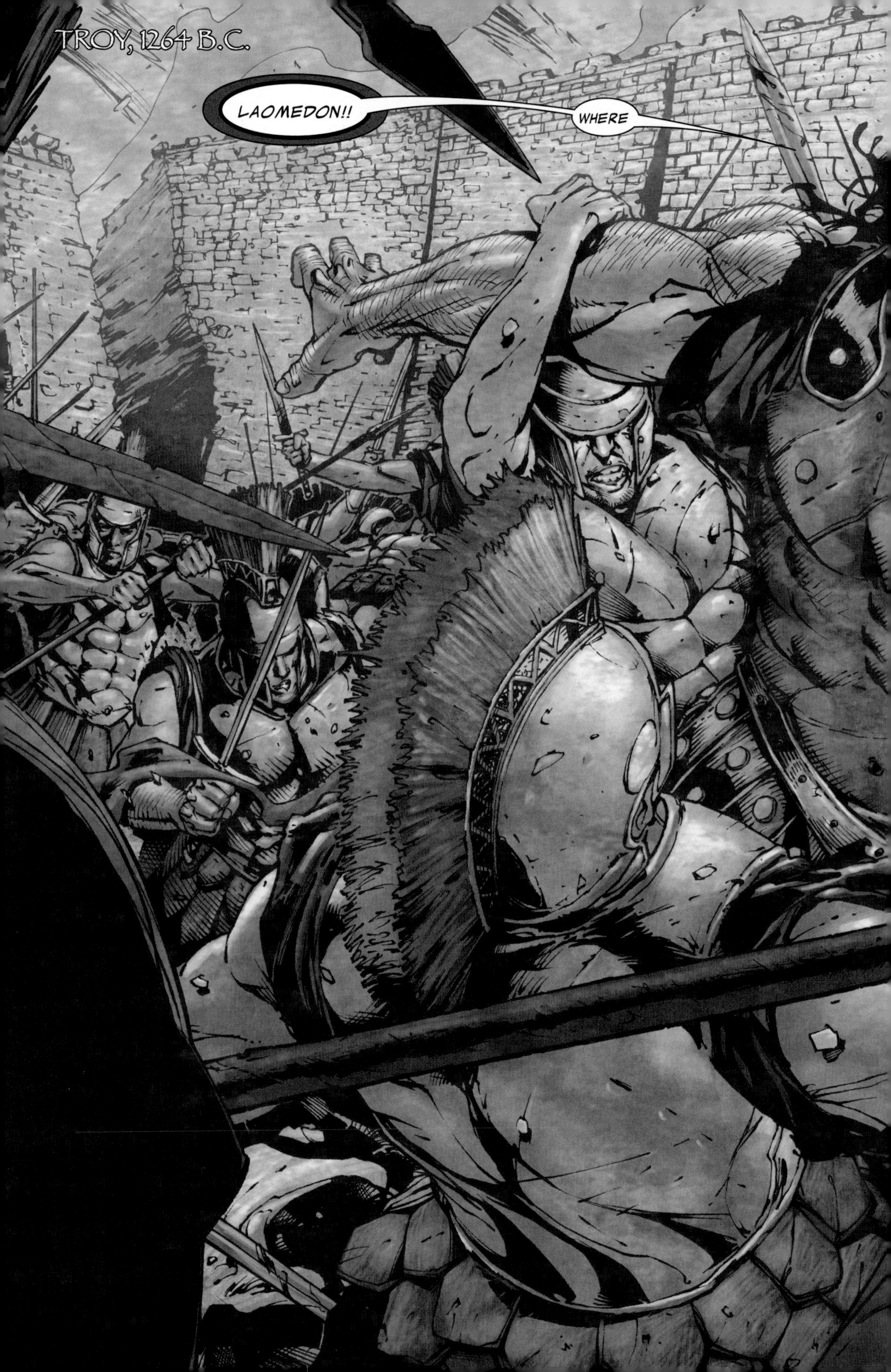
TROY, 1264 B.C.
LAOMEDON!!
WHERE

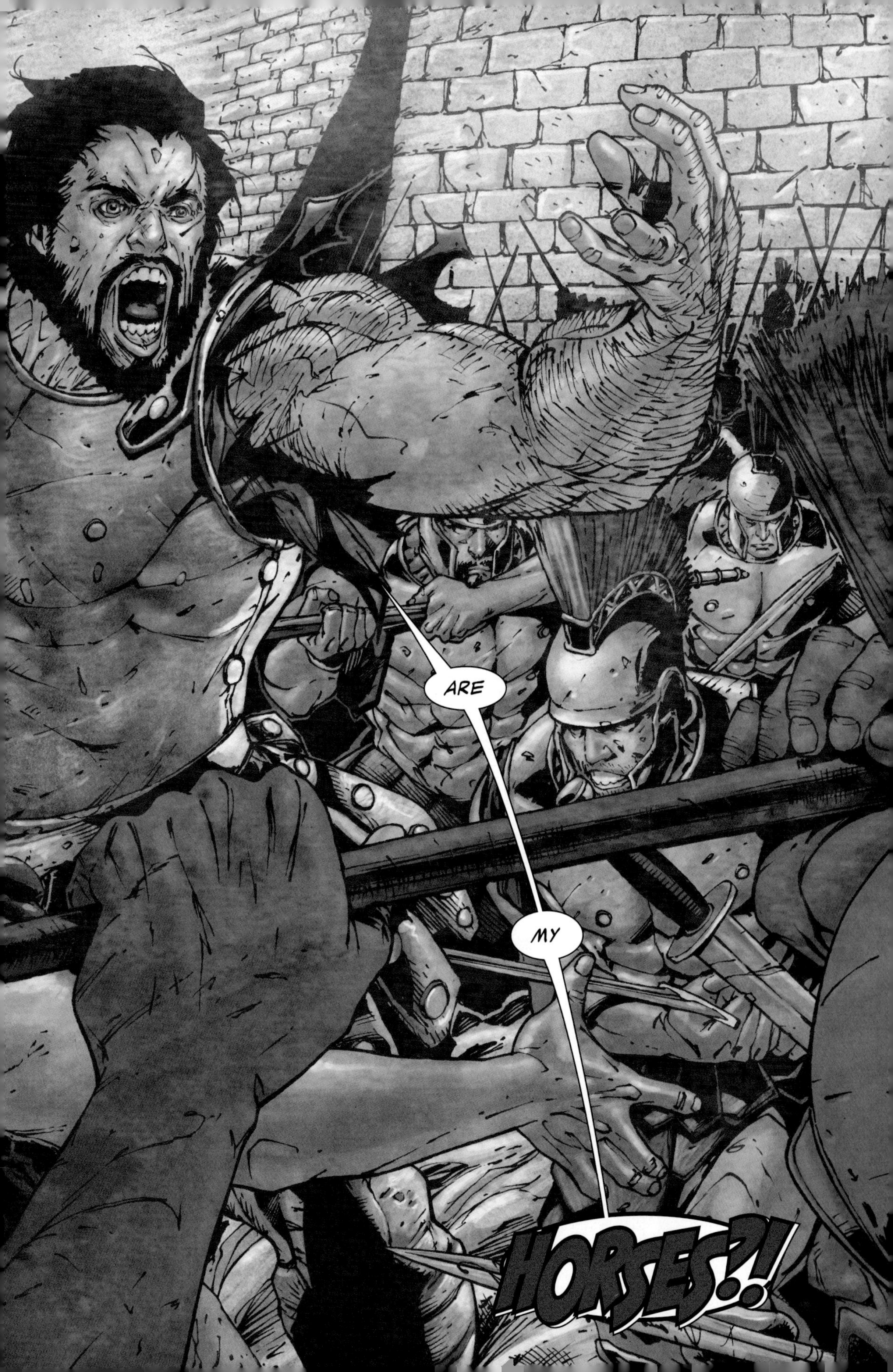
ARE
MY
HORSES?!

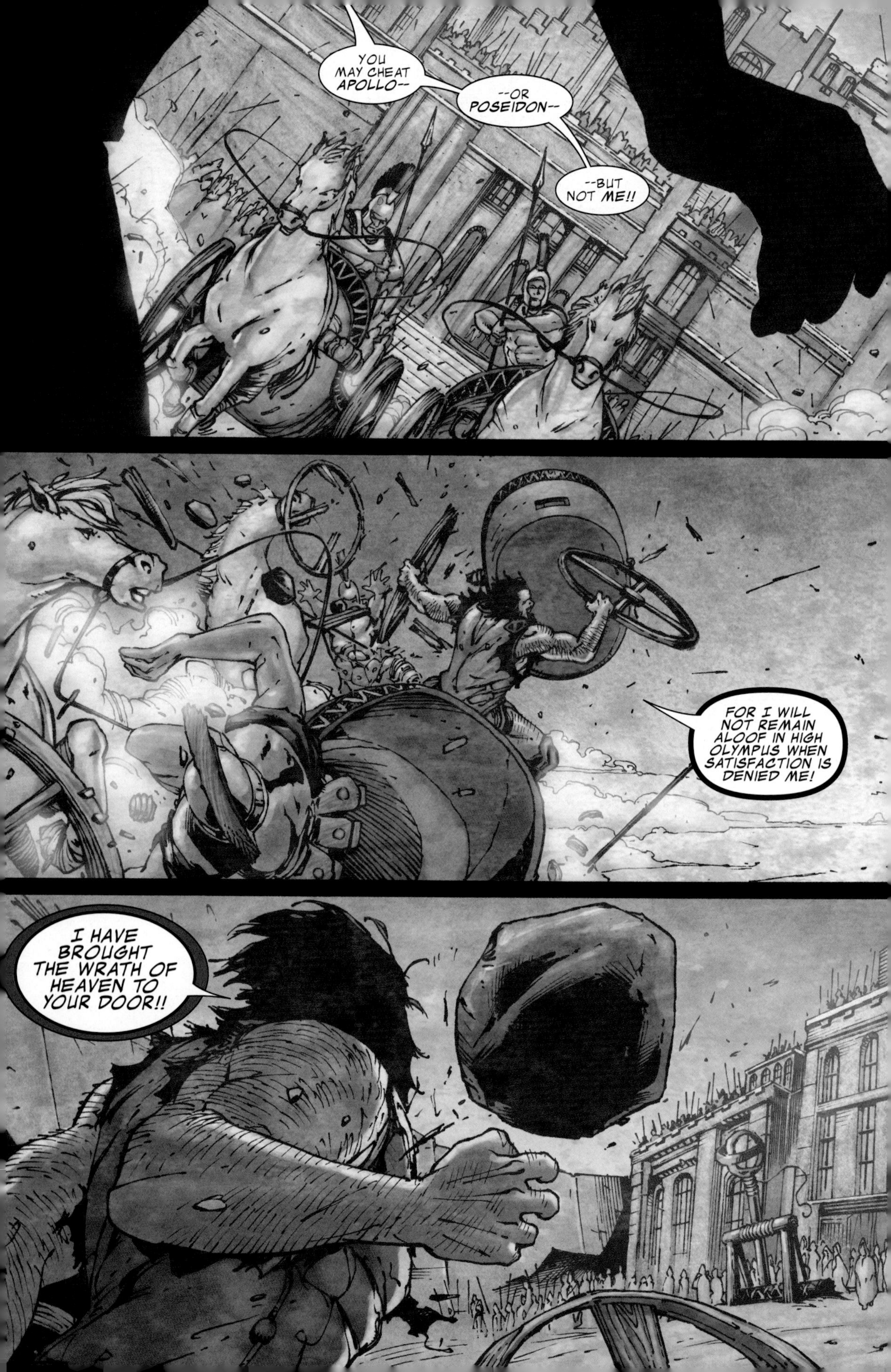
YOU MAY CHEAT APOLLO--
--OR POSEIDON--
--BUT NOT ME!!
FOR I WILL NOT REMAIN ALOOF IN HIGH OLYMPUS WHEN SATISFACTION IS DENIED ME!
I HAVE BROUGHT THE WRATH OF HEAVEN TO YOUR DOOR!!

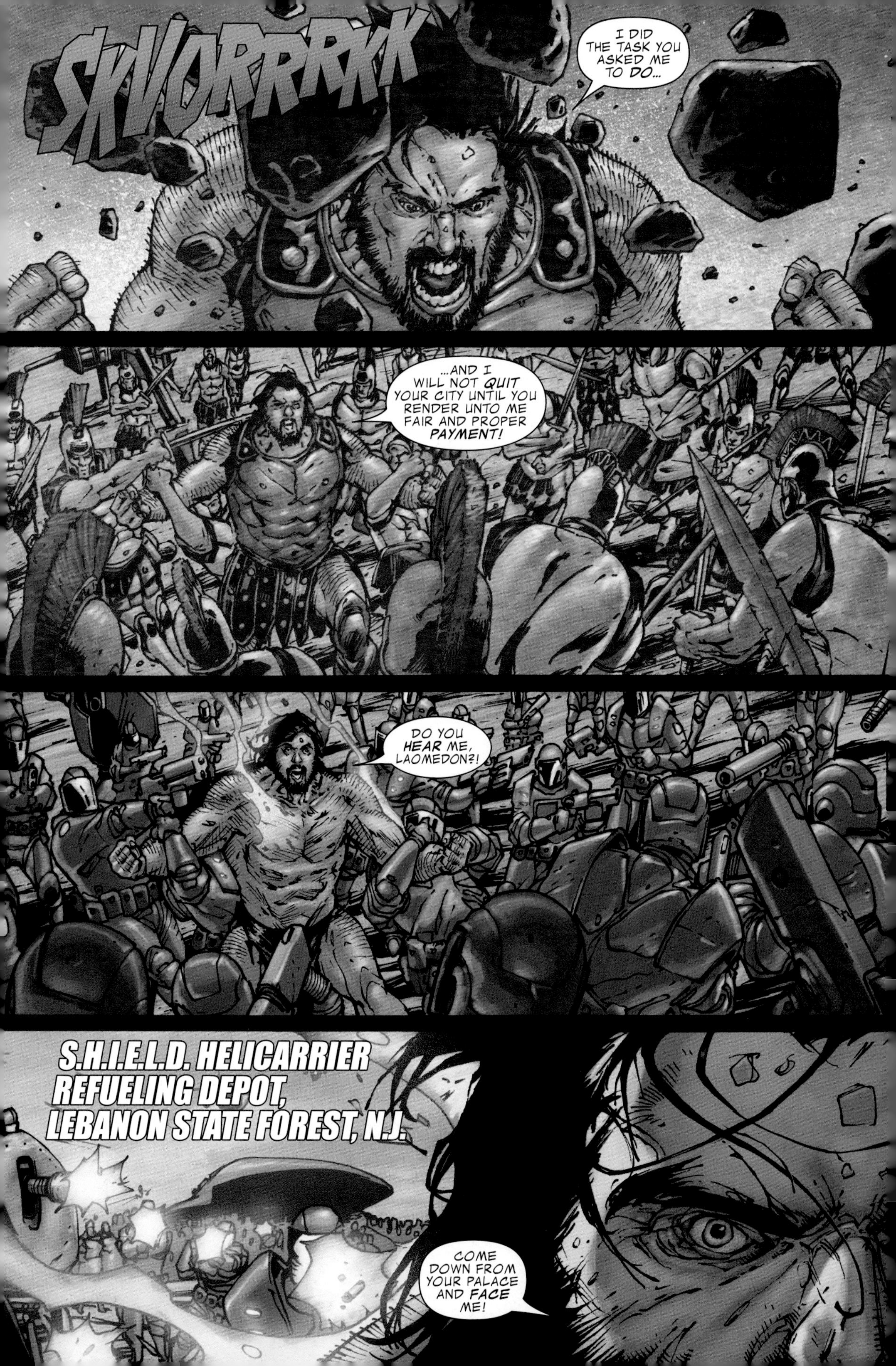
SKVORRRKK
I DID THE TASK YOU ASKED ME TO DO...
...AND I WILL NOT QUIT YOUR CITY UNTIL YOU RENDER UNTO ME FAIR AND PROPER PAYMENT!
DO YOU HEAR ME, LAOMEDON?!
S.H.I.E.L.D. HELICARRIER REFUELING DEPOT, LEBANON STATE FOREST, N.J.
COME DOWN FROM YOUR PALACE AND FACE ME!

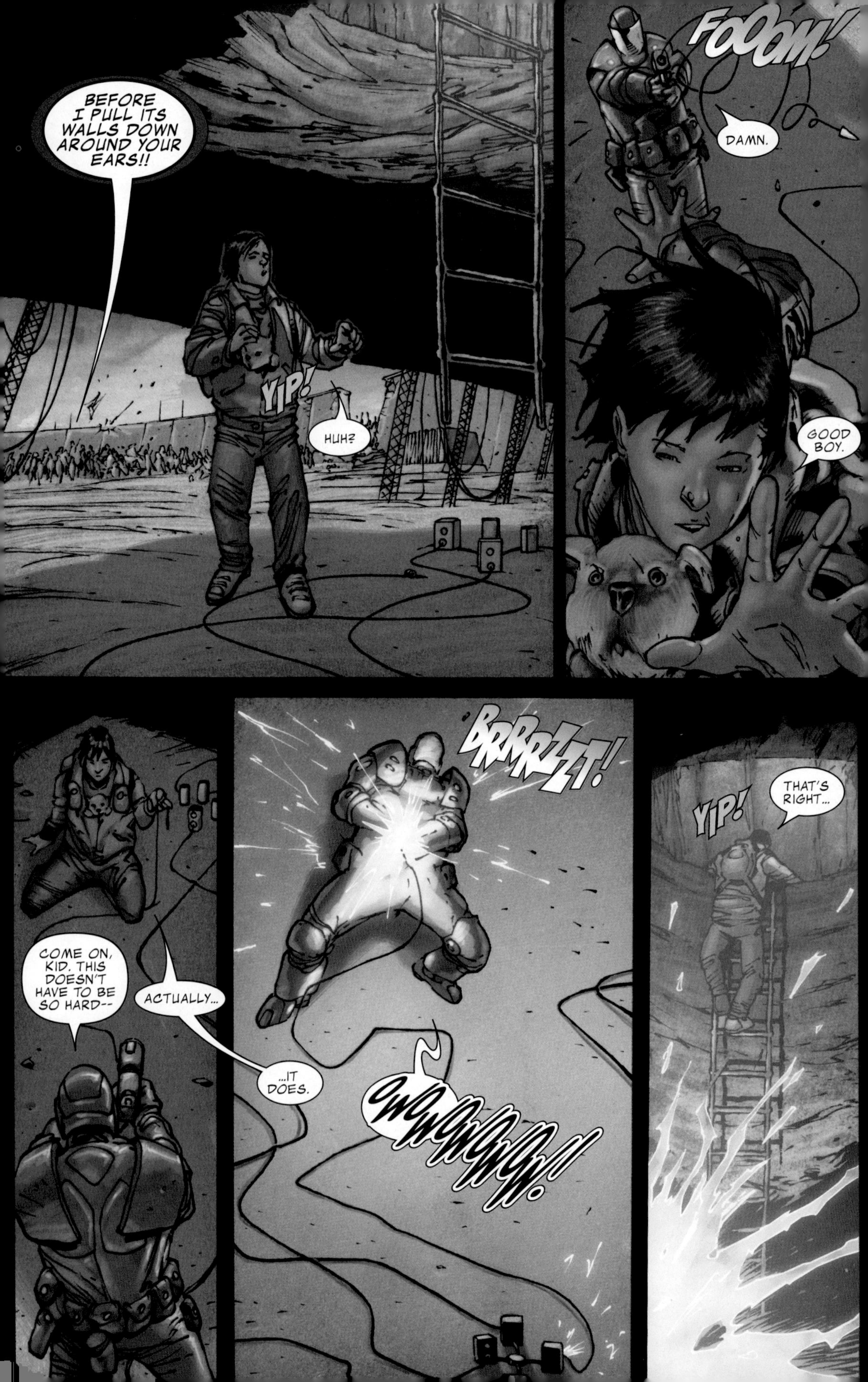
BEFORE I PULL ITS WALLS DOWN AROUND YOUR EARS!!
YIP!
HUH?
FOOOM!
DAMN.
GOOD BOY.
COME ON, KID. THIS DOESN'T HAVE TO BE SO HARD--
ACTUALLY...
...IT DOES.
BRRRZZT!
OWOWOWOWOW!
YIP!
THAT'S RIGHT...

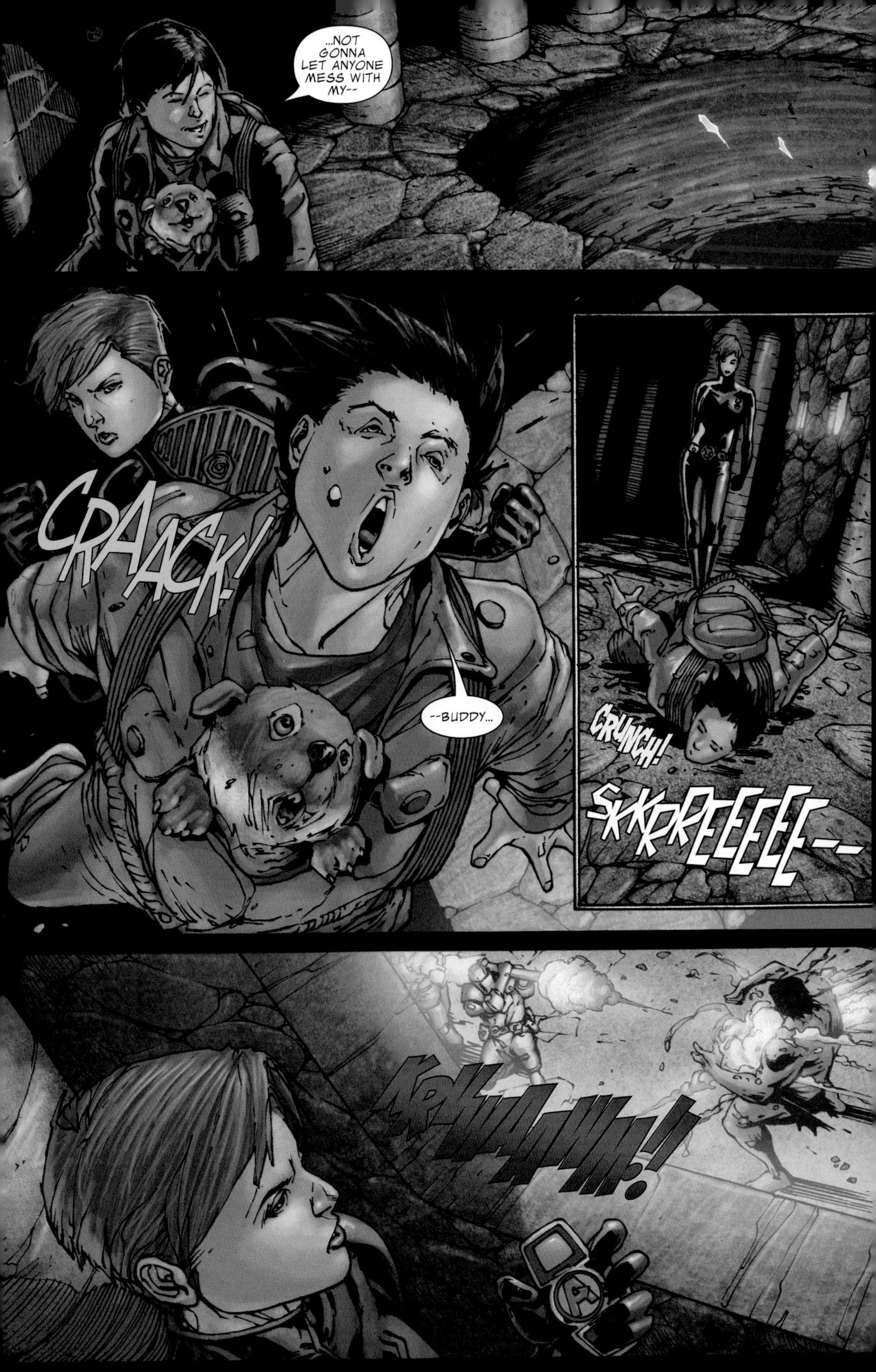
...NOT GONNA LET ANYONE MESS WITH MY--
CRAACK!
--BUDDY...
CRUNCH!
SKKRREEEEE--

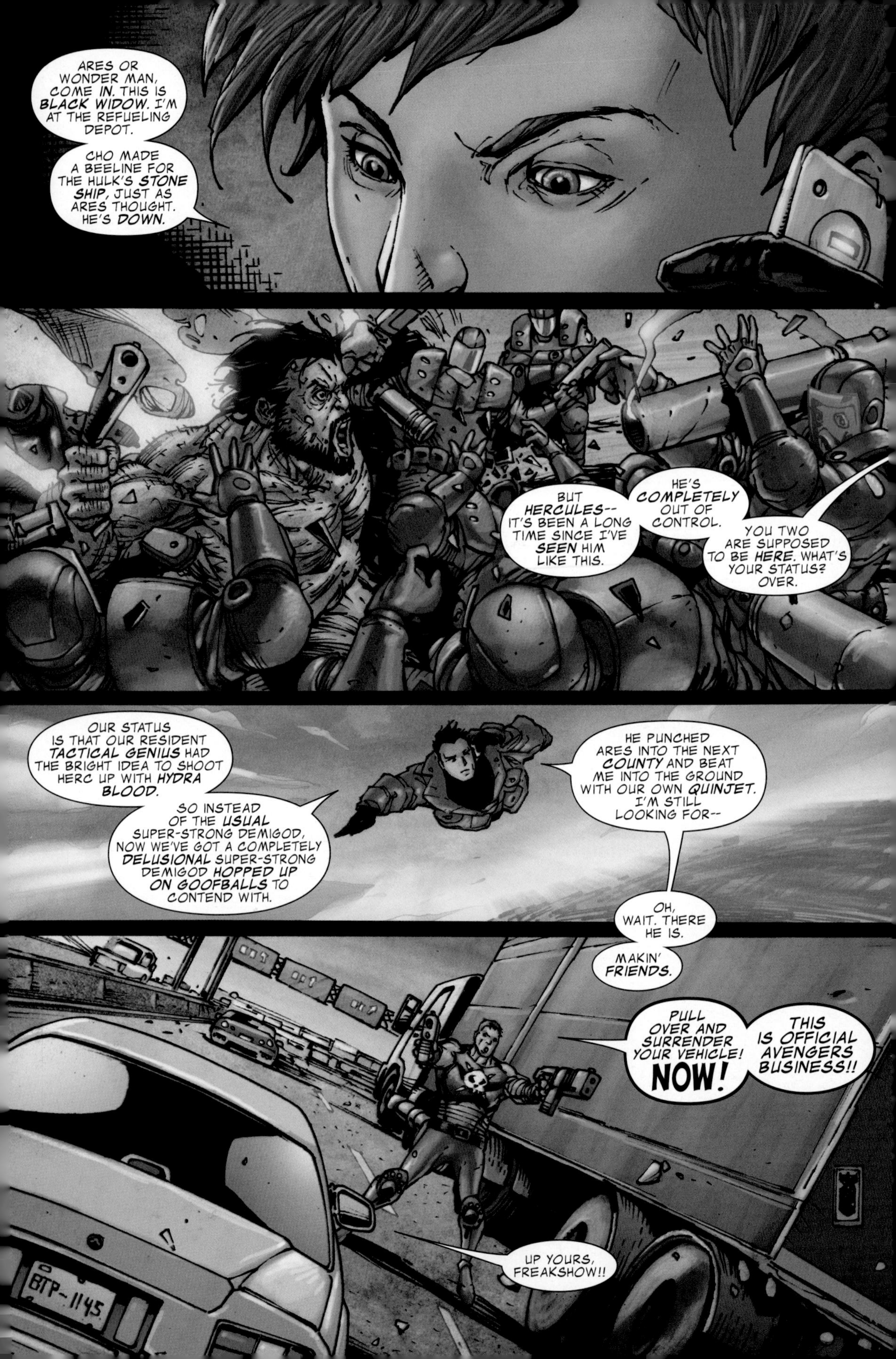

ARES OR WONDER MAN, COME IN. THIS IS BLACK WIDOW. I'M AT THE REFUELING DEPOT.
CHO MADE A BEELINE FOR THE HULK'S STONE SHIP, JUST AS ARES THOUGHT. HE'S DOWN.
BUT HERCULES-- IT'S BEEN A LONG TIME SINCE I'VE SEEN HIM LIKE THIS.
HE'S COMPLETELY OUT OF CONTROL.
YOU TWO ARE SUPPOSED TO BE HERE. WHAT'S YOUR STATUS? OVER.
OUR STATUS IS THAT OUR RESIDENT TACTICAL GENIUS HAD THE BRIGHT IDEA TO SHOOT HERC UP WITH HYDRA BLOOD.
SO INSTEAD OF THE USUAL SUPER-STRONG DEMIGOD, NOW WE'VE GOT A COMPLETELY DELUSIONAL SUPER-STRONG DEMIGOD HOPPED UP ON GOOFBALLS TO CONTEND WITH.
HE PUNCHED ARES INTO THE NEXT COUNTY AND BEAT ME INTO THE GROUND WITH OUR OWN QUINJET. I'M STILL LOOKING FOR--
OH, WAIT. THERE HE IS.
MAKIN' FRIENDS.
PULL OVER AND SURRENDER YOUR VEHICLE! NOW!
THIS IS OFFICIAL AVENGERS BUSINESS!!
UP YOURS, FREAKSHOW!!
BTP-1145

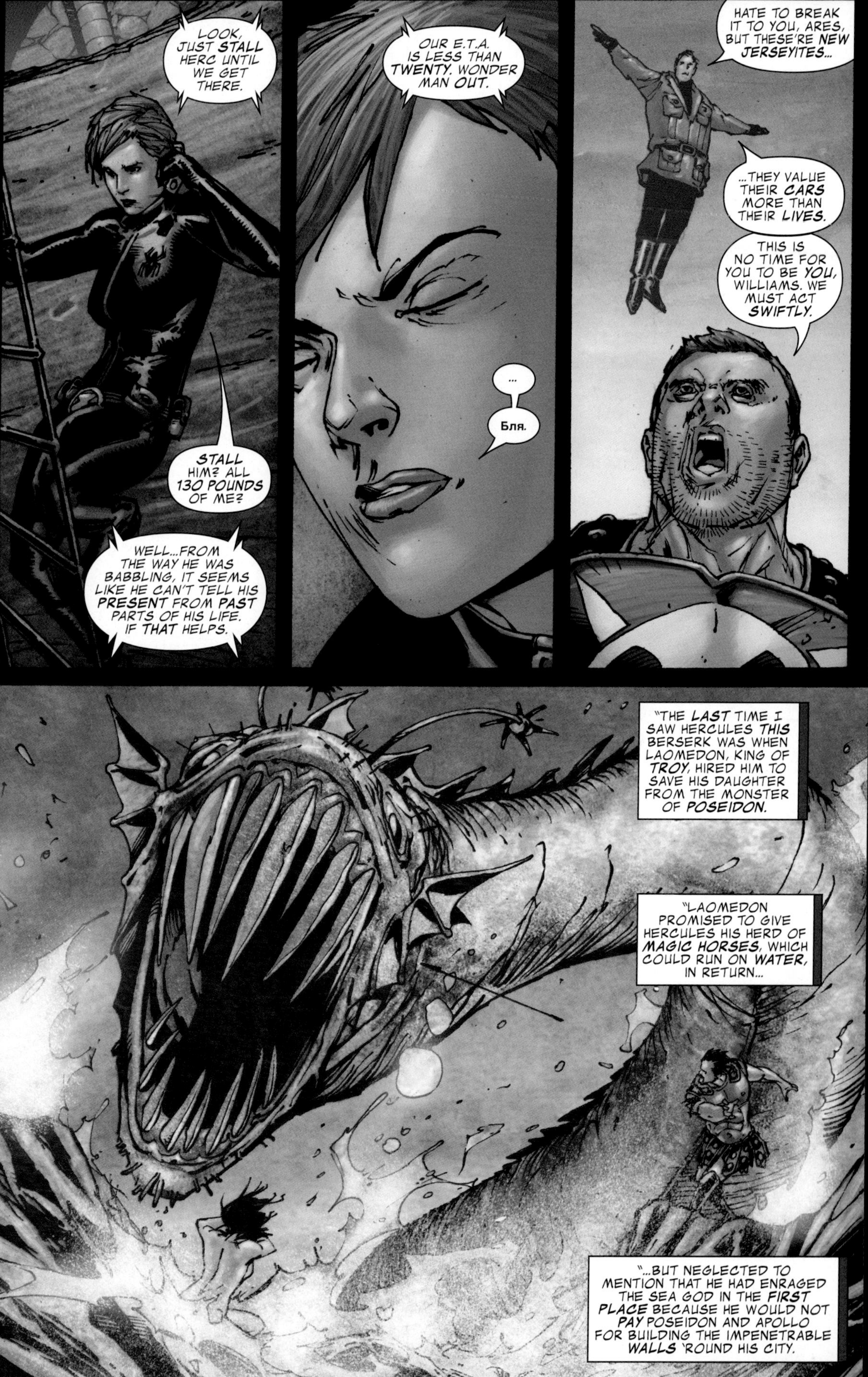
LOOK, JUST STALL HERC UNTIL WE GET THERE.
STALL HIM? ALL 130 POUNDS OF ME?
WELL...FROM THE WAY HE WAS BABBLING, IT SEEMS LIKE HE CAN'T TELL HIS PRESENT FROM PAST PARTS OF HIS LIFE. IF THAT HELPS.
OUR E.T.A. IS LESS THAN TWENTY. WONDER MAN OUT.
...
Бля.
HATE TO BREAK IT TO YOU, ARES, BUT THESE'RE NEW JERSEYITES...
...THEY VALUE THEIR CARS MORE THAN THEIR LIVES.
THIS IS NO TIME FOR YOU TO BE YOU, WILLIAMS. WE MUST ACT SWIFTLY.
"THE LAST TIME I SAW HERCULES THIS BERSERK WAS WHEN LAOMEDON, KING OF TROY, HIRED HIM TO SAVE HIS DAUGHTER FROM THE MONSTER OF POSEIDON.
"LAOMEDON PROMISED TO GIVE HERCULES HIS HERD OF MAGIC HORSES, WHICH COULD RUN ON WATER, IN RETURN...
"...BUT NEGLECTED TO MENTION THAT HE HAD ENRAGED THE SEA GOD IN THE FIRST PLACE BECAUSE HE WOULD NOT PAY POSEIDON AND APOLLO FOR BUILDING THE IMPENETRABLE WALLS 'ROUND HIS CITY.

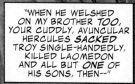

"WHEN HE WELSHED ON MY BROTHER *TOO*, YOUR CUDDLY, AVUNCULAR HERCULES *SACKED* TROY SINGLE-HANDEDLY, KILLED LAOMEDON AND ALL BUT *ONE* OF HIS SONS, THEN--"

YEAH, OKAY, WHATEVER. ENOUGH *EDITH HAMILTON* FOR ONE DAY, HUH?

FOR SOMEBODY WHO SUPPOSEDLY *HATES* HERC SO MUCH, YOU SURE AS HELL CAN'T SEEM TO *SHUT UP* ABOUT HIM...

HEY... WAIT A MINUTE...

THIS IS WHAT YOU WANTED ALL ALONG! YOU *KNEW* THE HYDRA BLOOD WOULD DRIVE HERC NUTSO--

FORCING THE AVENGERS AND WHOEVER ELSE TO USE *MAXIMUM FORCE* TO BRING HIM DOWN!

I DON'T KNOW *WHAT* YOU'RE TALKING ABOUT...

NO WONDER YOU SEEMED SO HOT TO PARTNER WITH *ME* ON THIS DEAL!

YOU THINK I'VE GOT *"CHUMP"* TATTOOED ON MY FOREHEAD, DON'T YOU--

SKREEEEEEECH!

OHMIGAWD!!

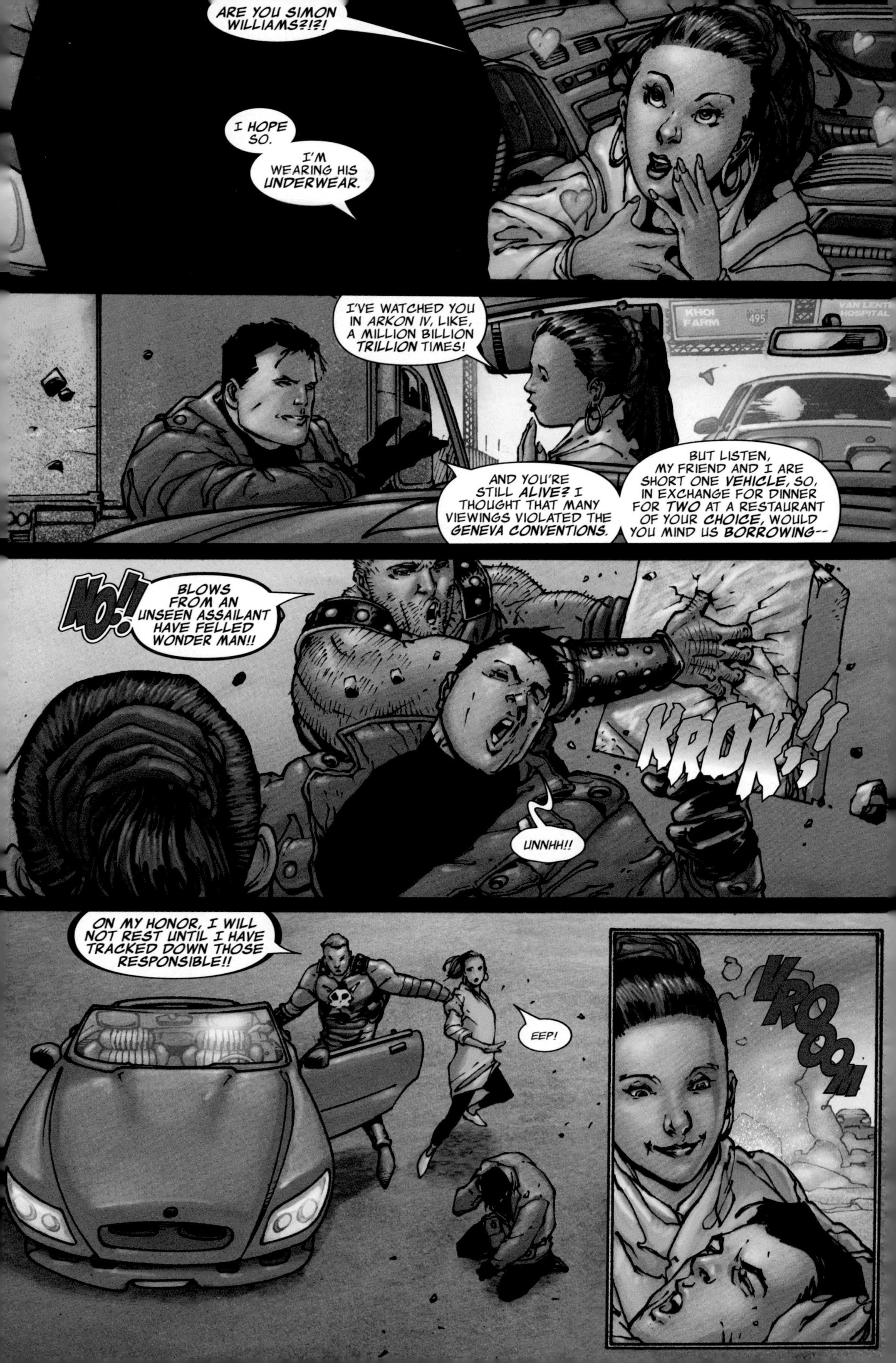
ARE YOU SIMON WILLIAMS?!?!
I HOPE SO.
I'M WEARING HIS UNDERWEAR.
I'VE WATCHED YOU IN ARKON IV, LIKE, A MILLION BILLION TRILLION TIMES!
KHOI FARM
495
VAN LENTE HOSPITAL
AND YOU'RE STILL ALIVE? I THOUGHT THAT MANY VIEWINGS VIOLATED THE GENEVA CONVENTIONS.
BUT LISTEN, MY FRIEND AND I ARE SHORT ONE VEHICLE, SO, IN EXCHANGE FOR DINNER FOR TWO AT A RESTAURANT OF YOUR CHOICE, WOULD YOU MIND US BORROWING--
NO!!
BLOWS FROM AN UNSEEN ASSAILANT HAVE FELLED WONDER MAN!!
KROK!!
UNNHH!!
ON MY HONOR, I WILL NOT REST UNTIL I HAVE TRACKED DOWN THOSE RESPONSIBLE!!
EEP!
VROOOOM

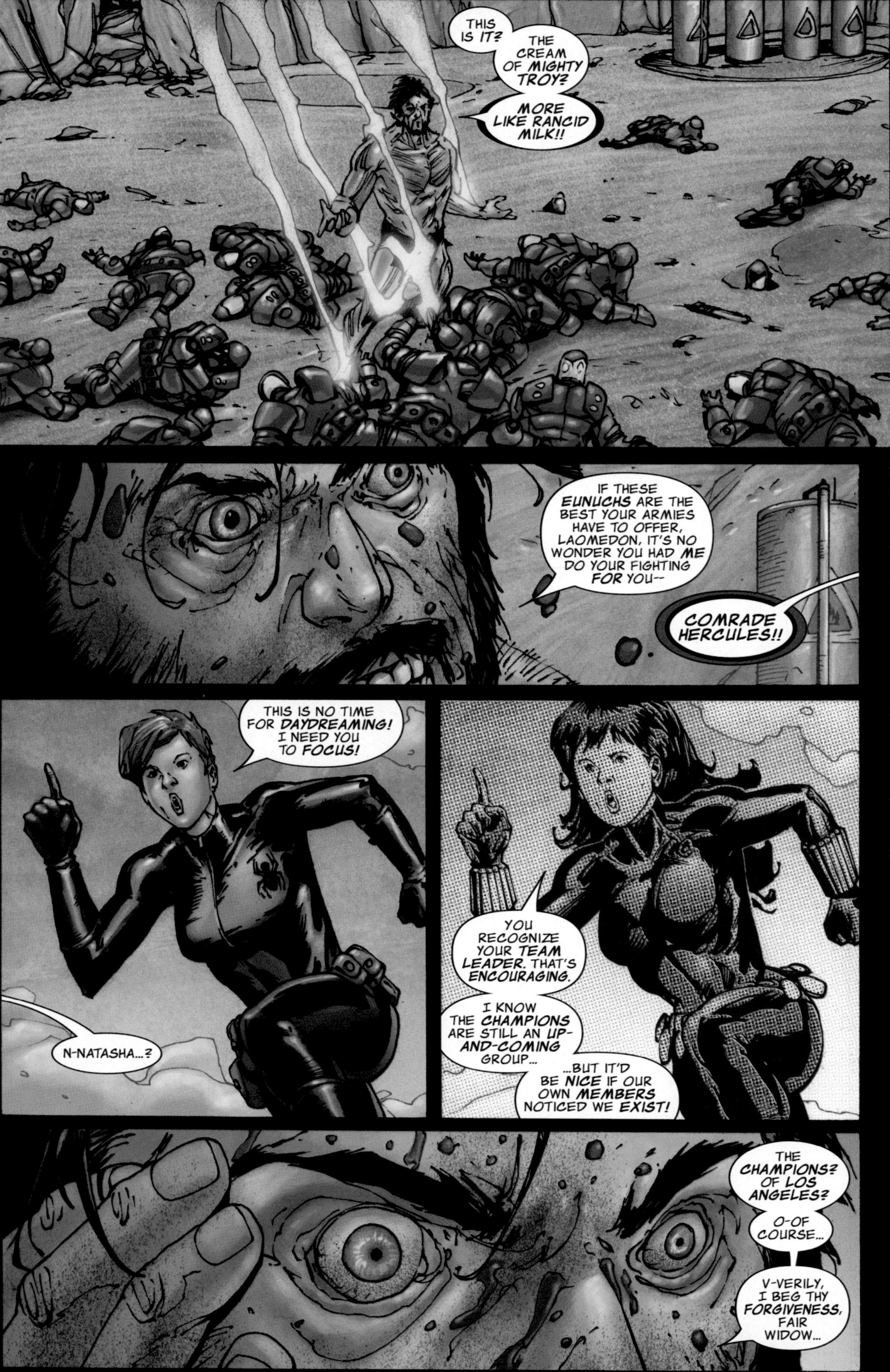

THIS IS IT? THE CREAM OF MIGHTY TROY?
MORE LIKE RANCID MILK!!
IF THESE EUNUCHS ARE THE BEST YOUR ARMIES HAVE TO OFFER, LAOMEDON, IT'S NO WONDER YOU HAD ME DO YOUR FIGHTING FOR YOU--
COMRADE HERCULES!!
THIS IS NO TIME FOR DAYDREAMING! I NEED YOU TO FOCUS!
N-NATASHA...?
YOU RECOGNIZE YOUR TEAM LEADER. THAT'S ENCOURAGING.
I KNOW THE CHAMPIONS ARE STILL AN UP-AND-COMING GROUP...
...BUT IT'D BE NICE IF OUR OWN MEMBERS NOTICED WE EXIST!
THE CHAMPIONS? OF LOS ANGELES?
O-OF COURSE...
V-VERILY, I BEG THY FORGIVENESS, FAIR WIDOW...

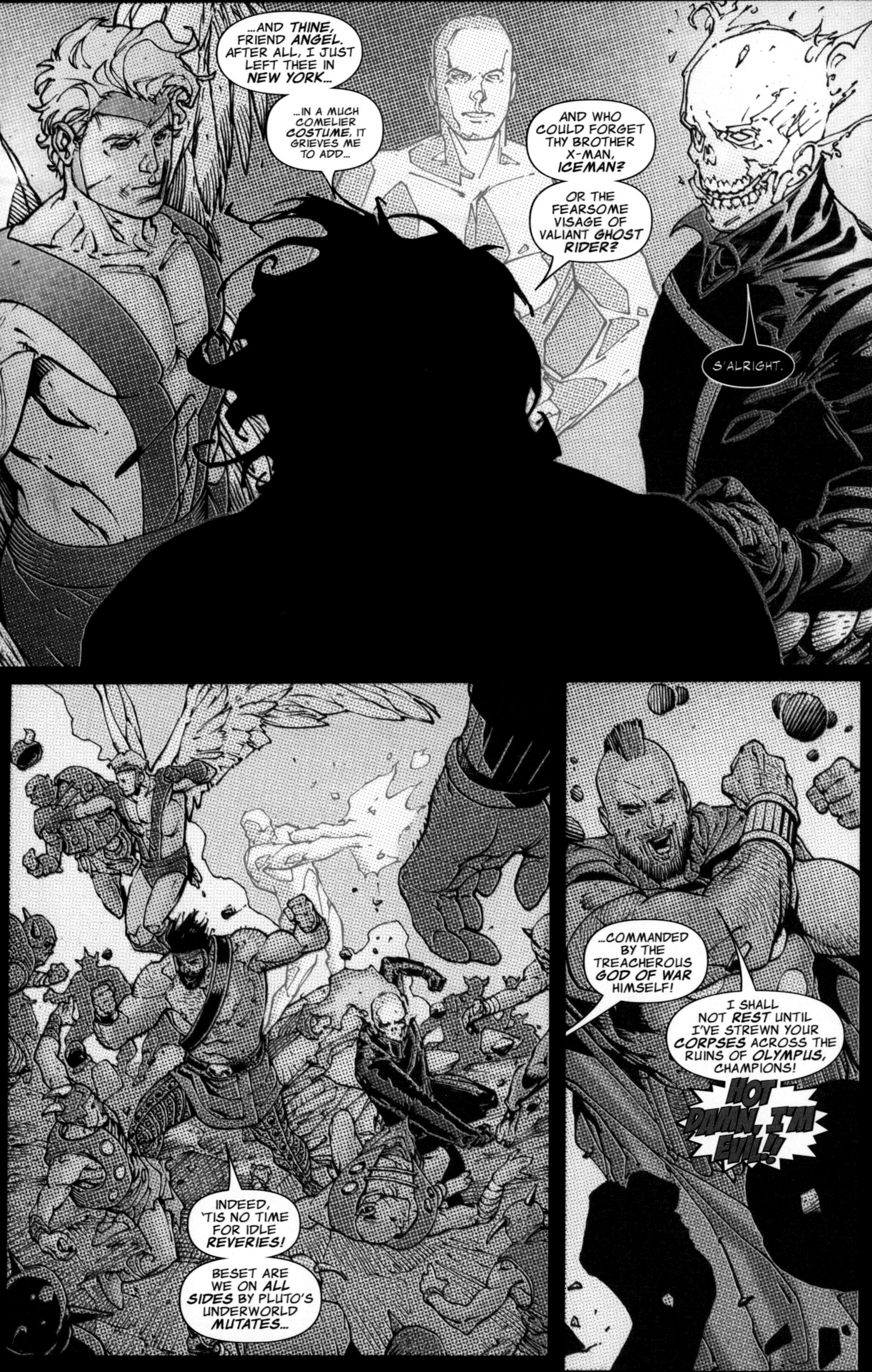
...AND THINE, FRIEND ANGEL. AFTER ALL, I JUST LEFT THEE IN NEW YORK...
...IN A MUCH COMELIER COSTUME, IT GRIEVES ME TO ADD...
AND WHO COULD FORGET THY BROTHER X-MAN, ICEMAN?
OR THE FEARSOME VISAGE OF VALIANT GHOST RIDER?
S'ALRIGHT.
INDEED, 'TIS NO TIME FOR IDLE REVERIES!
BESET ARE WE ON ALL SIDES BY PLUTO'S UNDERWORLD MUTATES...
...COMMANDED BY THE TREACHEROUS GOD OF WAR HIMSELF!
I SHALL NOT REST UNTIL I'VE STREWN YOUR CORPSES ACROSS THE RUINS OF OLYMPUS, CHAMPIONS!
HOT DAMN, I'M EVIL!!

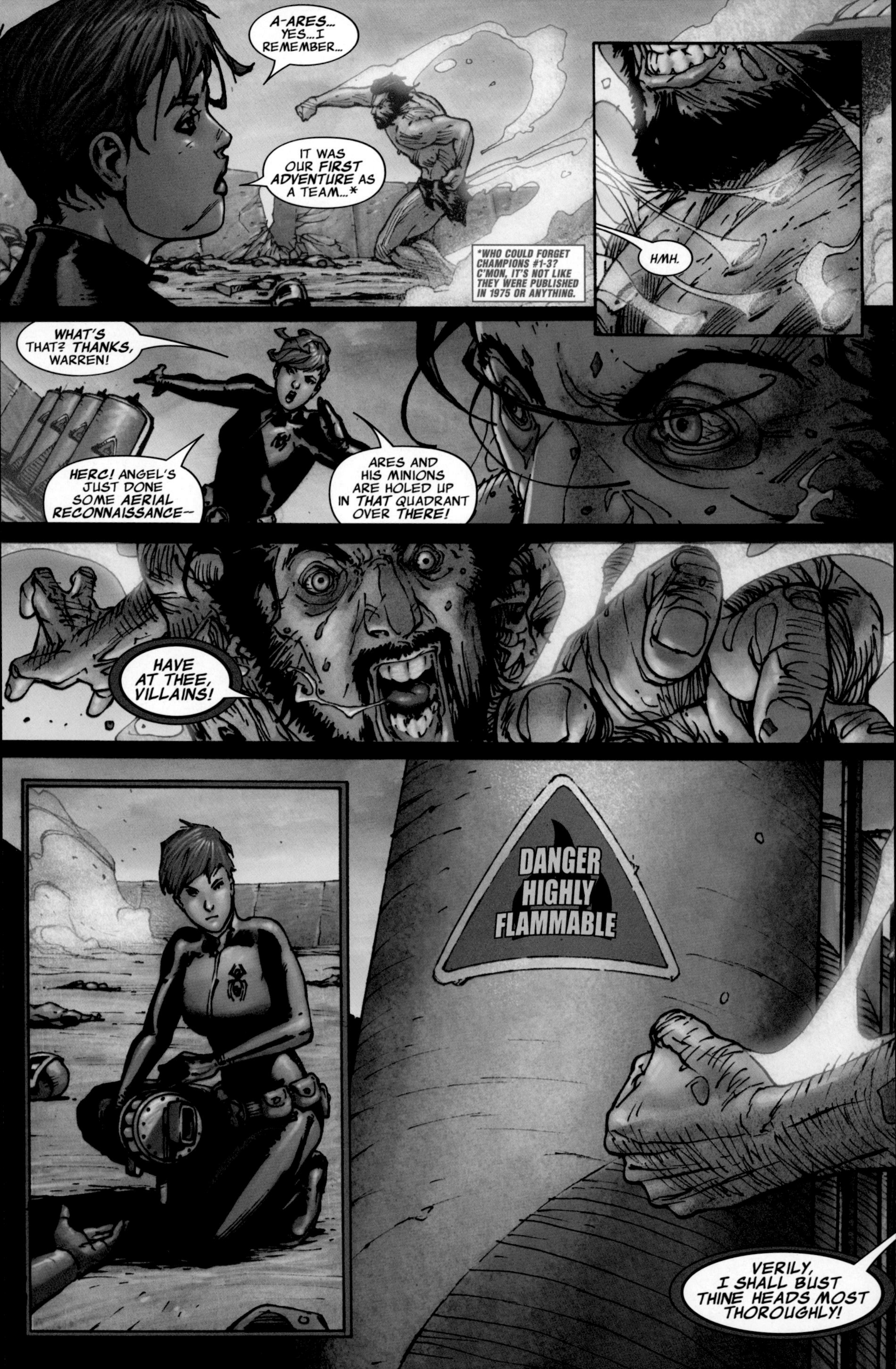
A-ARES... YES...I REMEMBER...
IT WAS OUR FIRST ADVENTURE AS A TEAM...*
*WHO COULD FORGET CHAMPIONS #1-3? C'MON, IT'S NOT LIKE THEY WERE PUBLISHED IN 1975 OR ANYTHING.
HMH.
WHAT'S THAT? THANKS, WARREN!
HERC! ANGEL'S JUST DONE SOME AERIAL RECONNAISSANCE--
ARES AND HIS MINIONS ARE HOLED UP IN THAT QUADRANT OVER THERE!
HAVE AT THEE, VILLAINS!
DANGER HIGHLY FLAMMABLE
VERILY, I SHALL BUST THINE HEADS MOST THOROUGHLY!

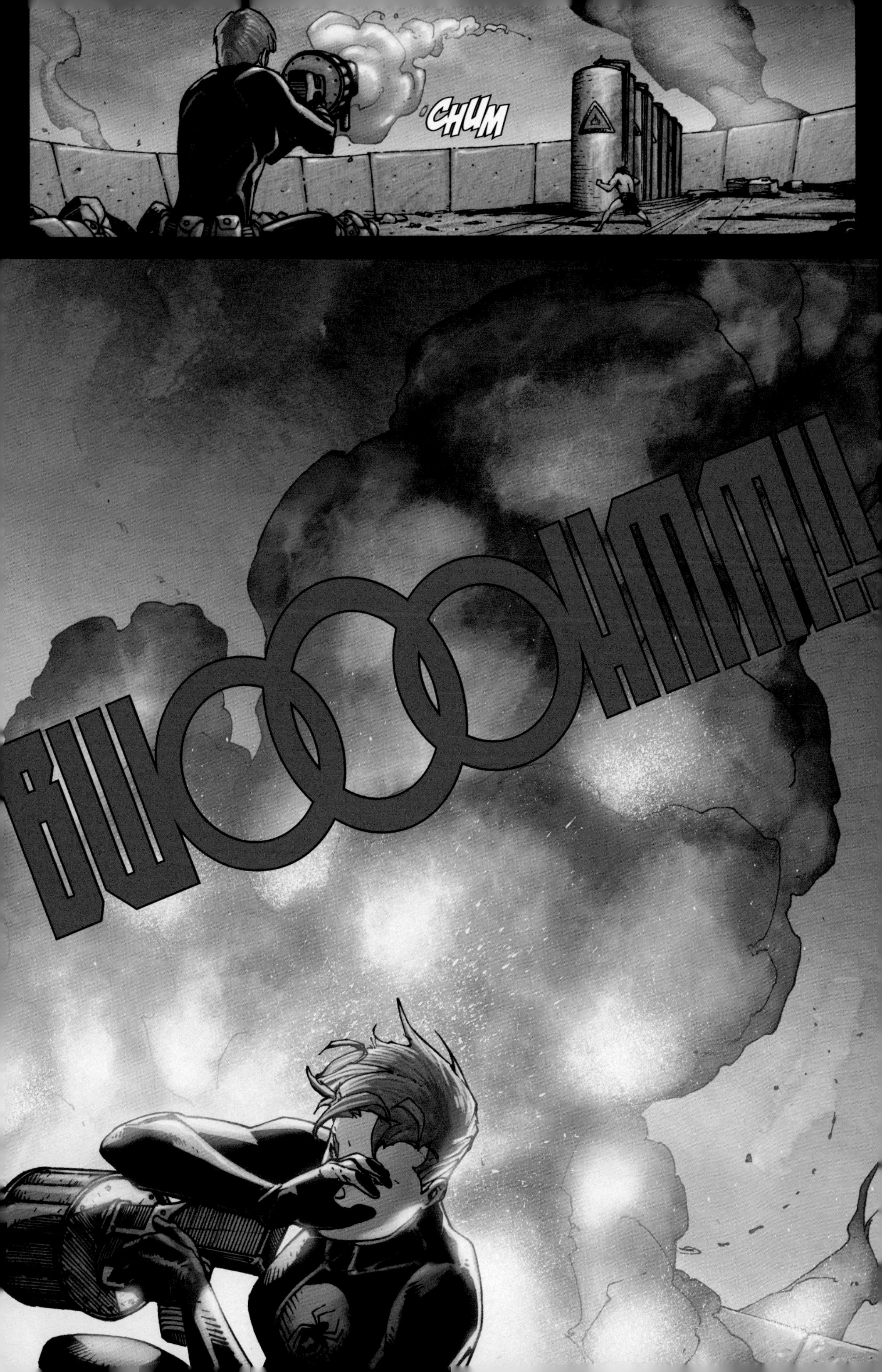
CHUM
BUOOOOHMMM!!!

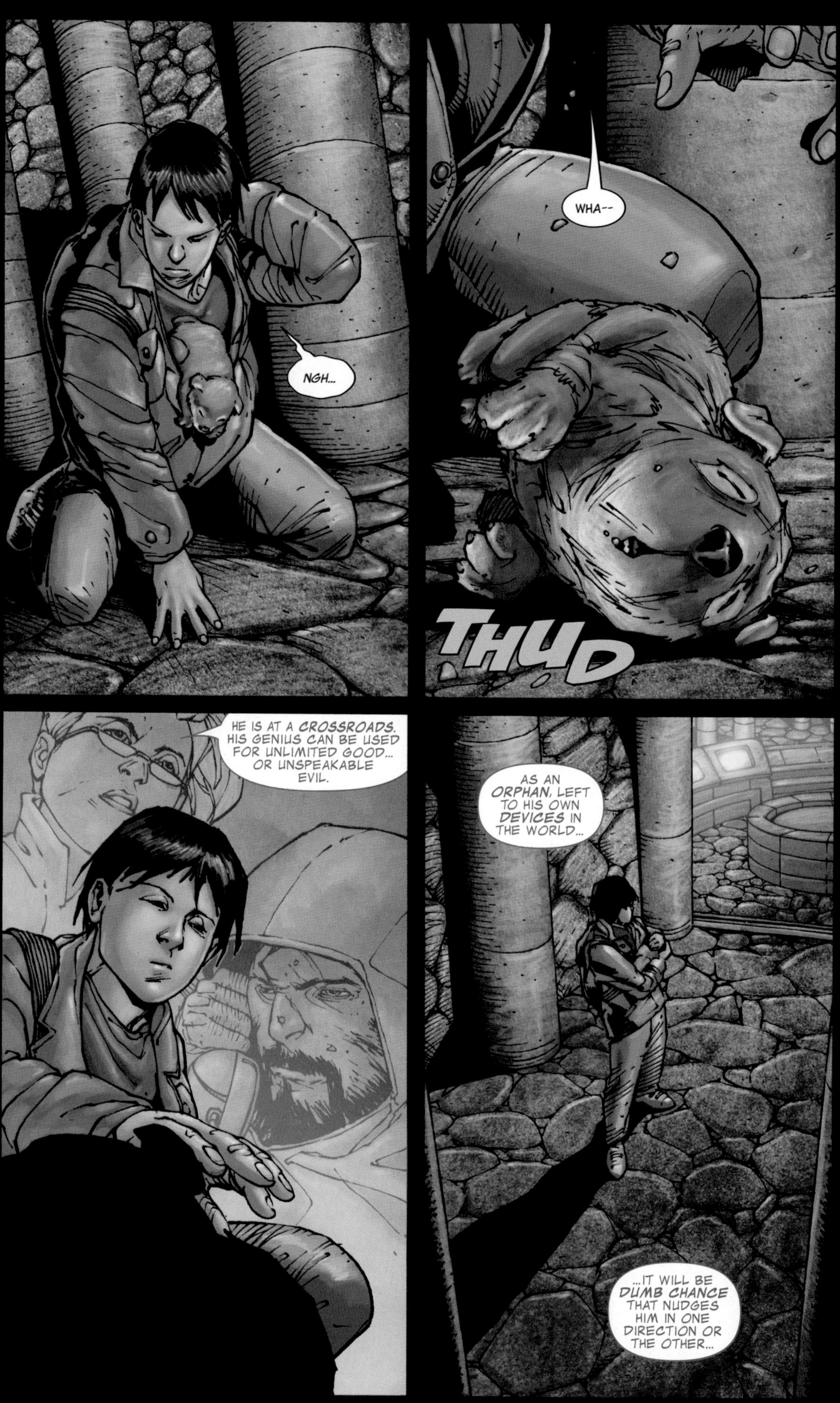
NGH...
WHA--
THUD
HE IS AT A CROSSROADS. HIS GENIUS CAN BE USED FOR UNLIMITED GOOD... OR UNSPEAKABLE EVIL.
AS AN ORPHAN, LEFT TO HIS OWN DEVICES IN THE WORLD...
...IT WILL BE DUMB CHANCE THAT NUDGES HIM IN ONE DIRECTION OR THE OTHER...

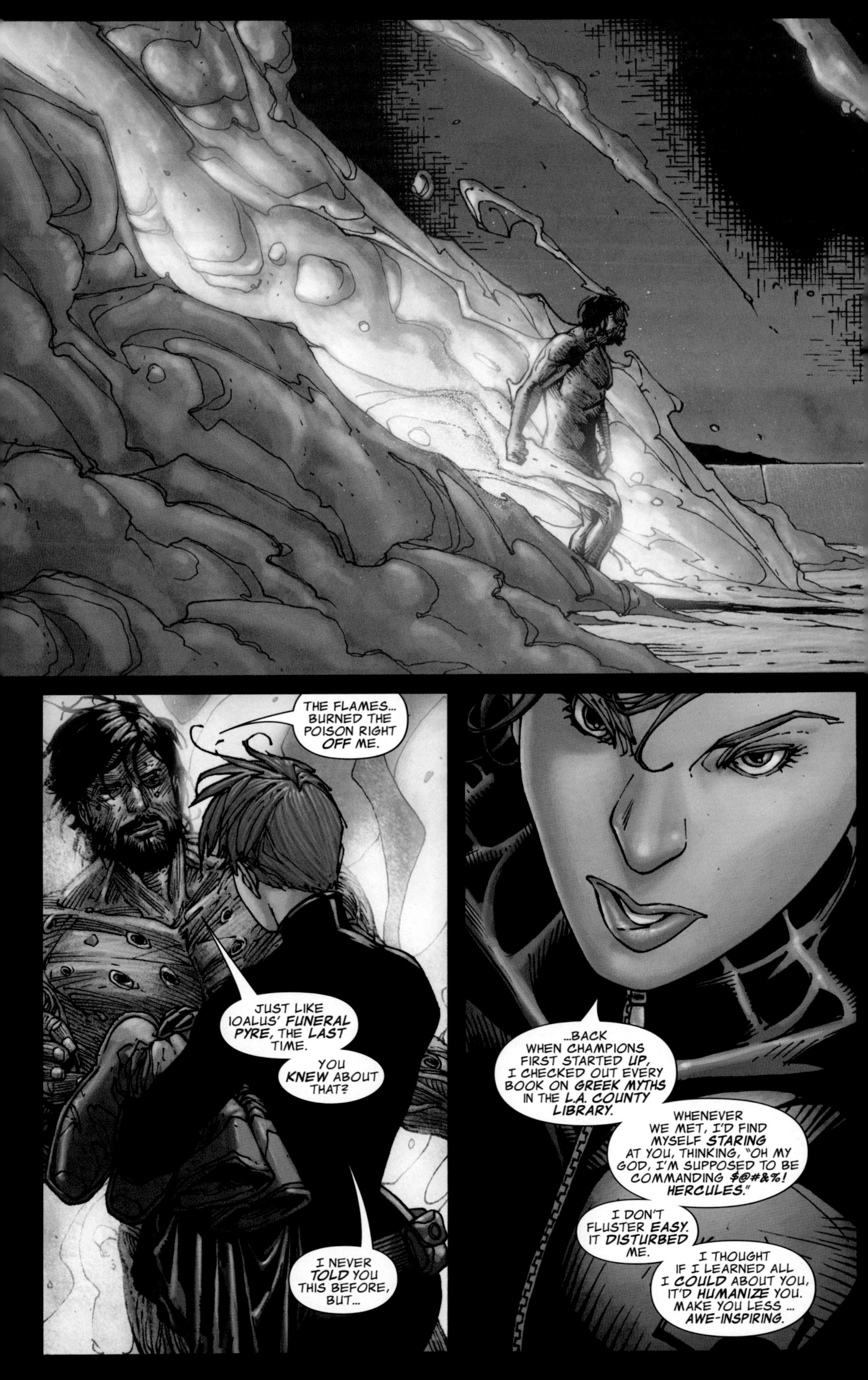
THE FLAMES... BURNED THE POISON RIGHT OFF ME.
JUST LIKE IOALUS' FUNERAL PYRE, THE LAST TIME.
YOU KNEW ABOUT THAT?
I NEVER TOLD YOU THIS BEFORE, BUT...
...BACK WHEN CHAMPIONS FIRST STARTED UP, I CHECKED OUT EVERY BOOK ON GREEK MYTHS IN THE L.A. COUNTY LIBRARY.
WHENEVER WE MET, I'D FIND MYSELF STARING AT YOU, THINKING, "OH MY GOD, I'M SUPPOSED TO BE COMMANDING $@#&%! HERCULES."
I DON'T FLUSTER EASY. IT DISTURBED ME.
I THOUGHT IF I LEARNED ALL I COULD ABOUT YOU, IT'D HUMANIZE YOU. MAKE YOU LESS ... AWE-INSPIRING.

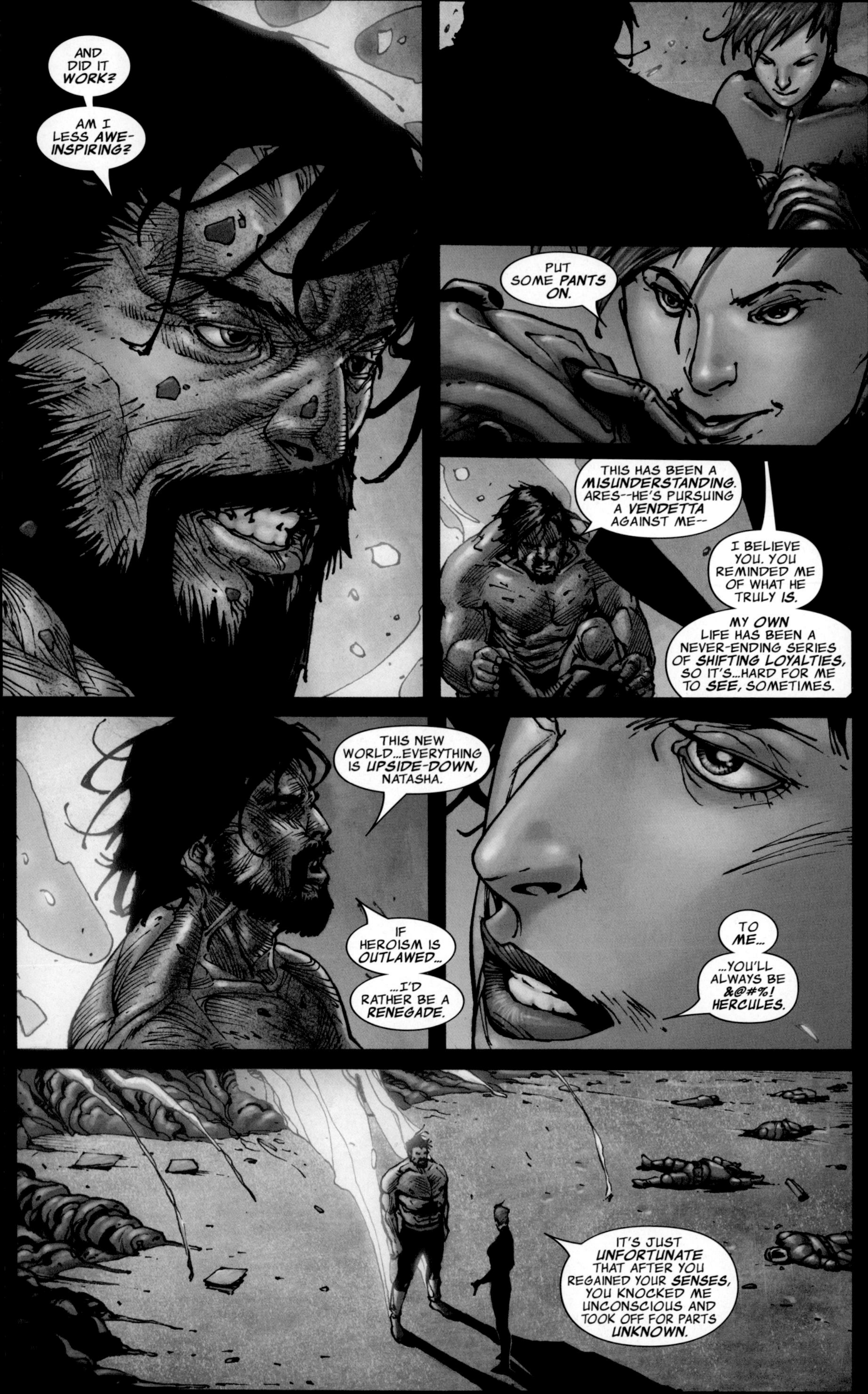
AND DID IT WORK?
AM I LESS AWE-INSPIRING?
PUT SOME PANTS ON.
THIS HAS BEEN A MISUNDERSTANDING. ARES--HE'S PURSUING A VENDETTA AGAINST ME--
I BELIEVE YOU. YOU REMINDED ME OF WHAT HE TRULY IS.
MY OWN LIFE HAS BEEN A NEVER-ENDING SERIES OF SHIFTING LOYALTIES, SO IT'S...HARD FOR ME TO SEE, SOMETIMES.
THIS NEW WORLD...EVERYTHING IS UPSIDE-DOWN, NATASHA.
IF HEROISM IS OUTLAWED...
...I'D RATHER BE A RENEGADE.
TO ME...
...YOU'LL ALWAYS BE &@#%! HERCULES.
IT'S JUST UNFORTUNATE THAT AFTER YOU REGAINED YOUR SENSES, YOU KNOCKED ME UNCONSCIOUS AND TOOK OFF FOR PARTS UNKNOWN.

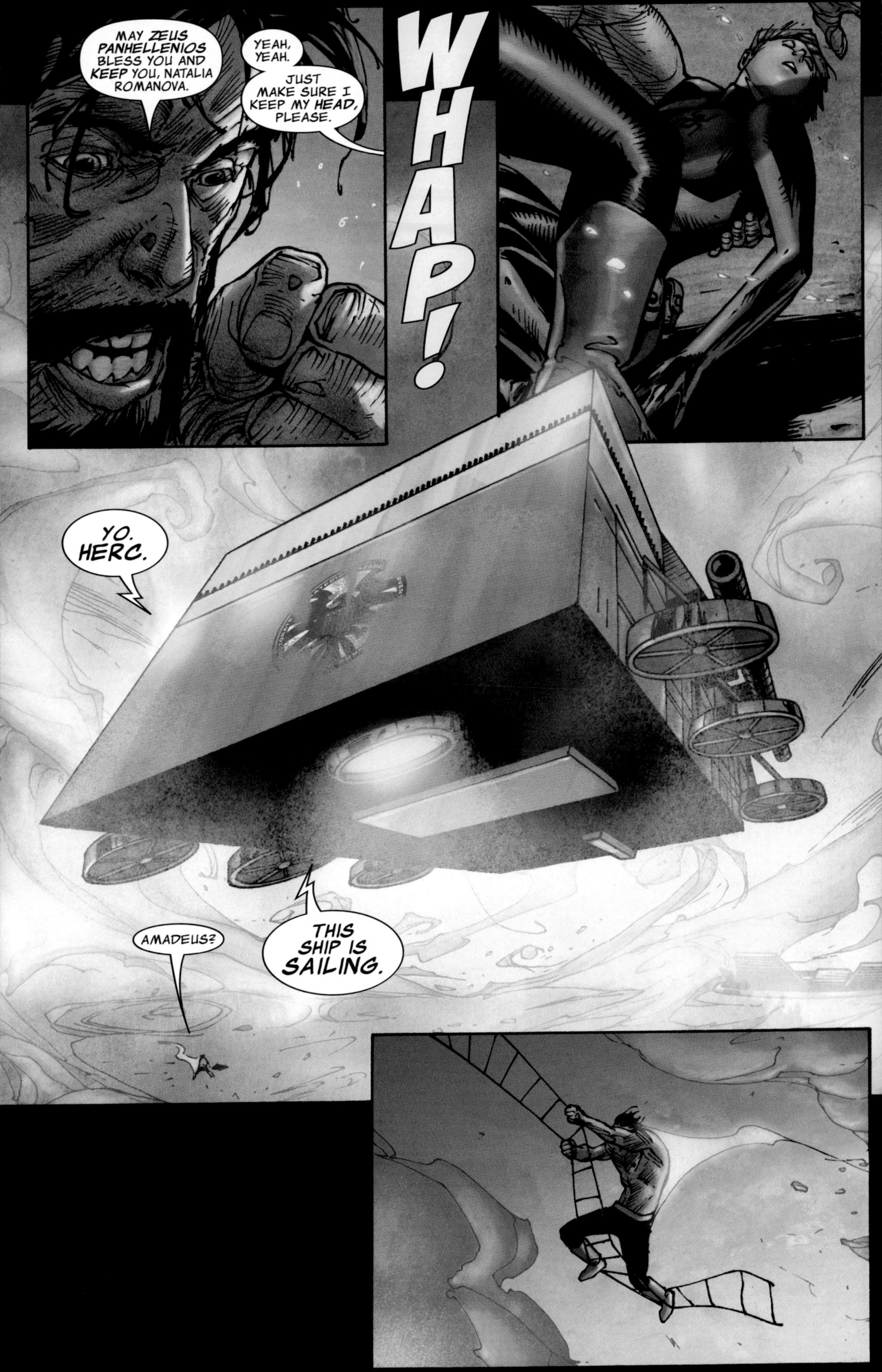
MAY ZEUS PANHELLENIOS BLESS YOU AND KEEP YOU, NATALIA ROMANOVA.
YEAH, YEAH.
JUST MAKE SURE I KEEP MY HEAD, PLEASE.
WHAP!
YO. HERC.
THIS SHIP IS SAILING.
AMADEUS?

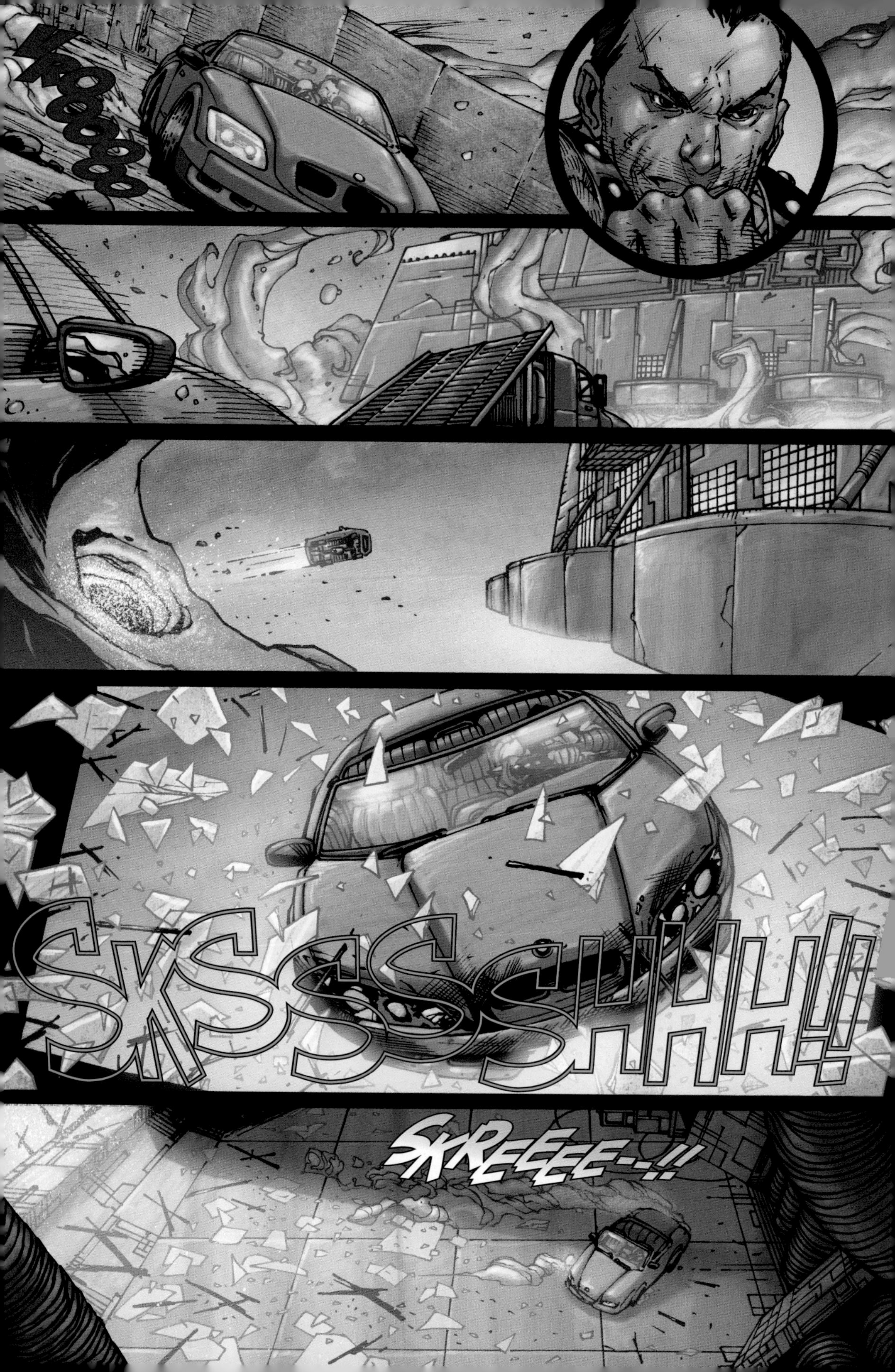
VROOOOOO
SKSSSSHHH!!
SKREEEEE--!!

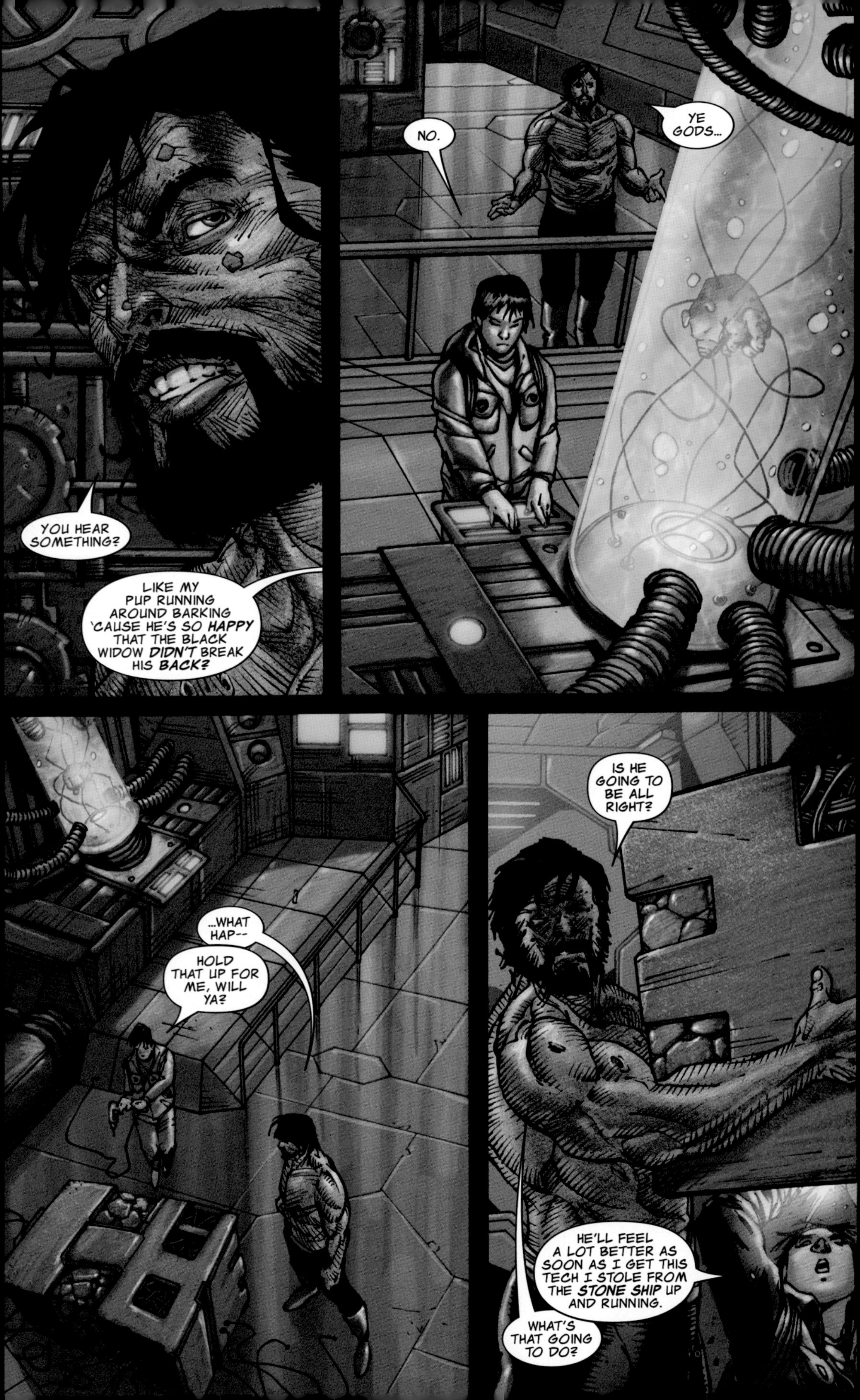
YOU HEAR SOMETHING?
LIKE MY PUP RUNNING AROUND BARKING 'CAUSE HE'S SO HAPPY THAT THE BLACK WIDOW DIDN'T BREAK HIS BACK?
NO.
YE GODS...
...WHAT HAP--
HOLD THAT UP FOR ME, WILL YA?
IS HE GOING TO BE ALL RIGHT?
HE'LL FEEL A LOT BETTER AS SOON AS I GET THIS TECH I STOLE FROM THE STONE SHIP UP AND RUNNING.
WHAT'S THAT GOING TO DO?

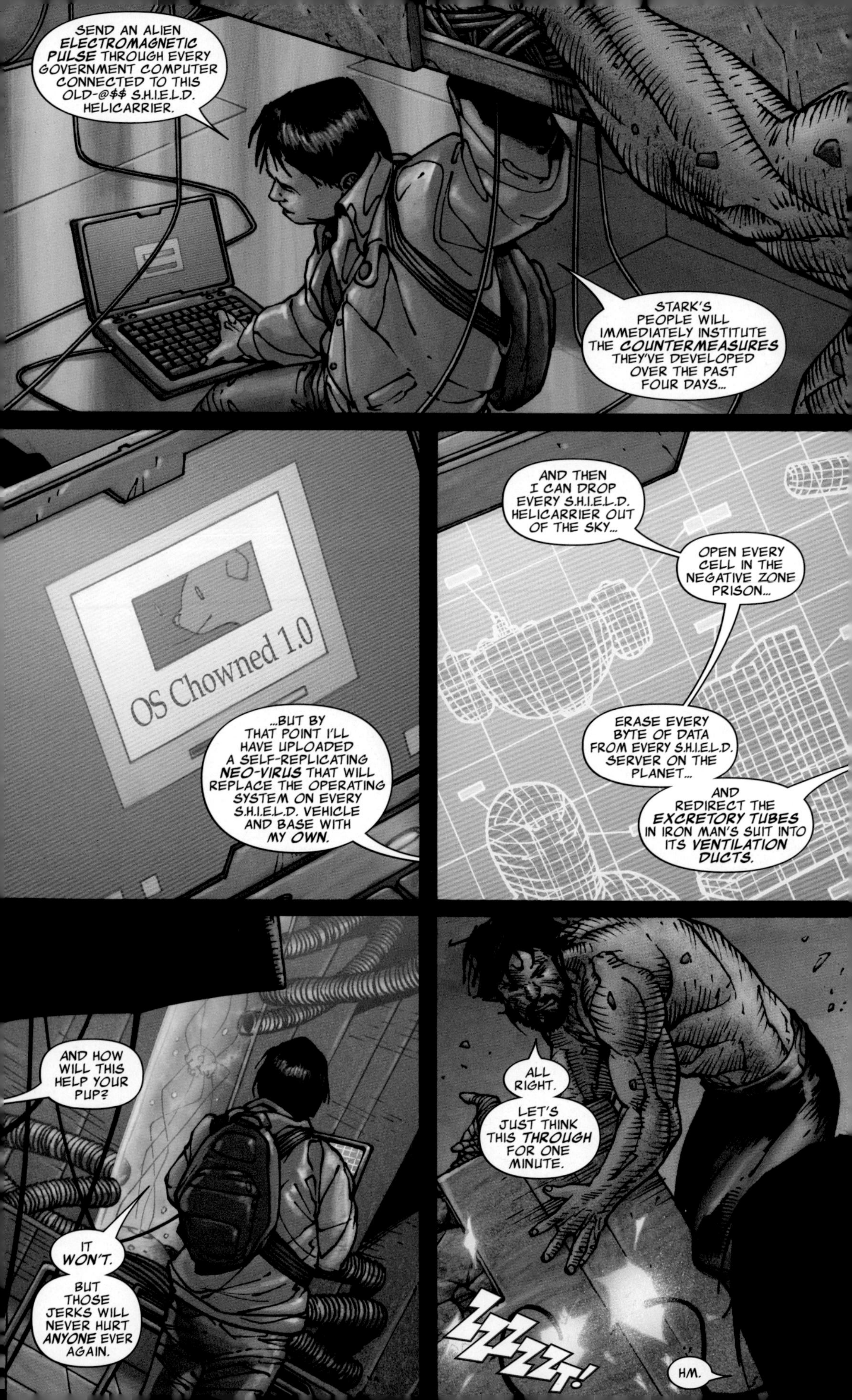
SEND AN ALIEN ELECTROMAGNETIC PULSE THROUGH EVERY GOVERNMENT COMPUTER CONNECTED TO THIS OLD-@$$ S.H.I.E.L.D. HELICARRIER.
STARK'S PEOPLE WILL IMMEDIATELY INSTITUTE THE COUNTERMEASURES THEY'VE DEVELOPED OVER THE PAST FOUR DAYS...
OS Chowned 1.0
...BUT BY THAT POINT I'LL HAVE UPLOADED A SELF-REPLICATING NEO-VIRUS THAT WILL REPLACE THE OPERATING SYSTEM ON EVERY S.H.I.E.L.D. VEHICLE AND BASE WITH MY OWN.
AND THEN I CAN DROP EVERY S.H.I.E.L.D. HELICARRIER OUT OF THE SKY...
OPEN EVERY CELL IN THE NEGATIVE ZONE PRISON...
ERASE EVERY BYTE OF DATA FROM EVERY S.H.I.E.L.D. SERVER ON THE PLANET...
AND REDIRECT THE EXCRETORY TUBES IN IRON MAN'S SUIT INTO ITS VENTILATION DUCTS.
AND HOW WILL THIS HELP YOUR PUP?
IT WON'T.
BUT THOSE JERKS WILL NEVER HURT ANYONE EVER AGAIN.
ALL RIGHT.
LET'S JUST THINK THIS THROUGH FOR ONE MINUTE.
ZZZZZT!
HM.

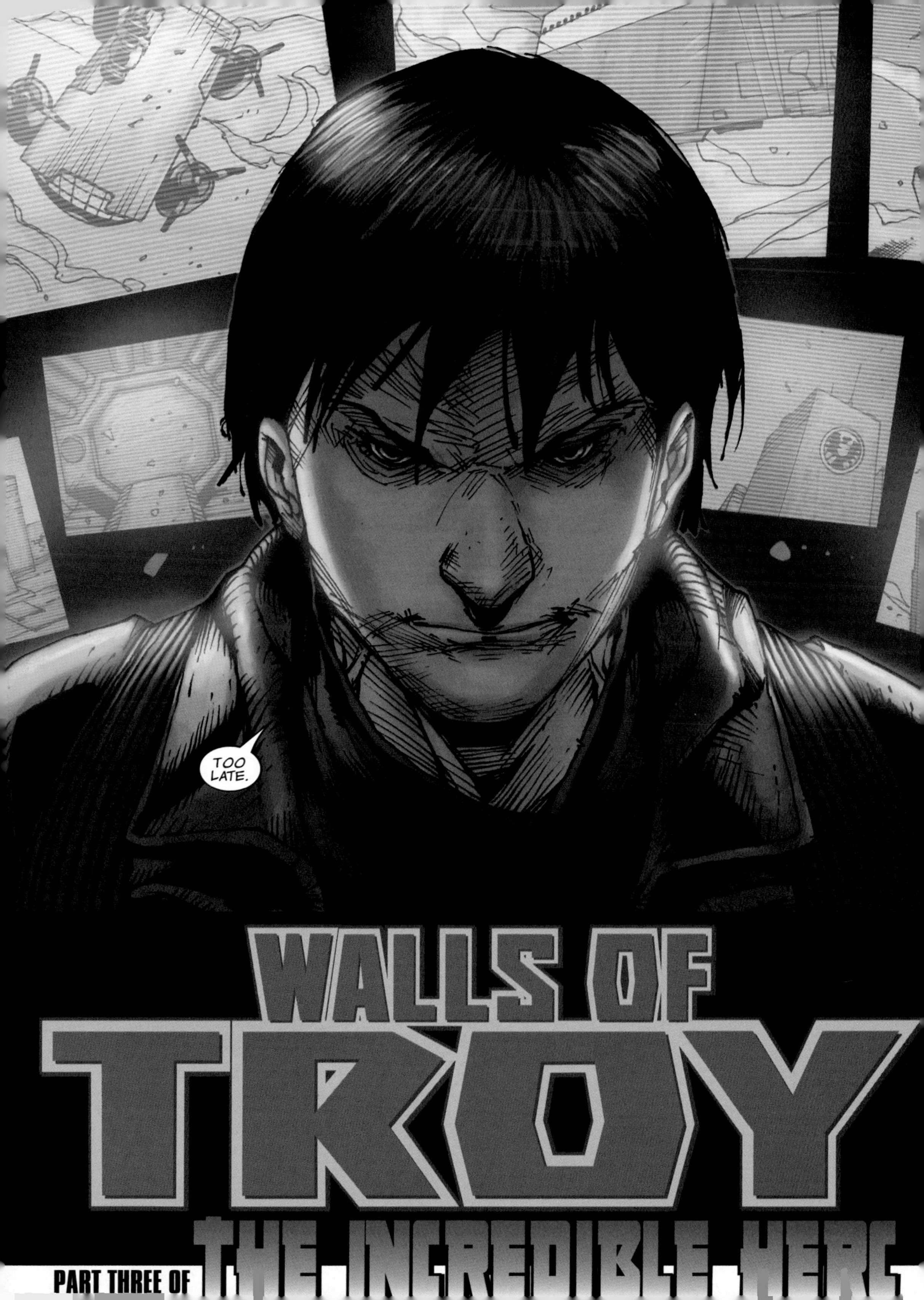
TOO LATE.
WALLS OF TROY
PART THREE OF THE INCREDIBLE HERC

e Edit View Go Message Tools Help

t Mail | Write | Address Book | Reply | Reply All | Forward | Delete | Junk | Print | Stop

Subject: PUPPY CONTEST
From: THE CHOSTER
Date: 02/13/08
To: ALL

HTTP://WWW.PUPPYCHO.COM

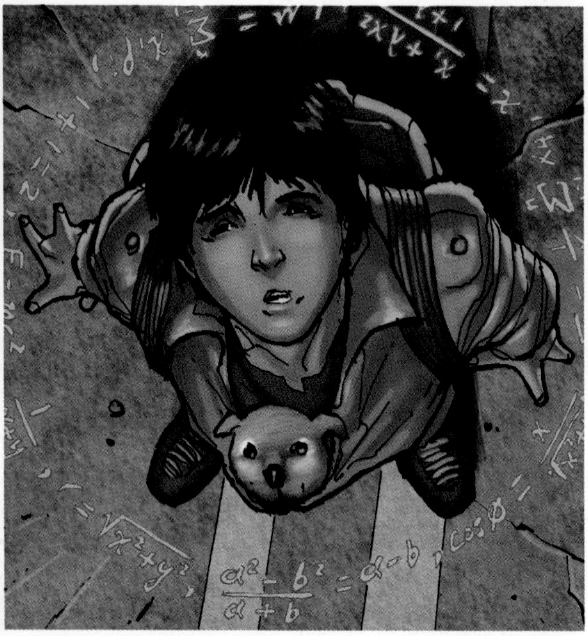

DREAMGRLZ97: he's so cute

HELFRALL0223: name him po! so he can be cho's po!

PANICMP112: CHODESTER!!!!!!!!!

BEEJAIZ1984: cats rule!

POPPYPALS: what about HOWLER!

MANGOGIRL0081: HEY CHO! i think precious would be a puuurfect name! or brighteyes, or snookems, or lady, yeah lady is the best...

KATSEYES113: MY DOG IS BETTER THAN URS!

RICHGHALO7: PLUTOOO!

MUFASSA7272: YAY DAWG! MINES WOULD BEZ SPARKS YO!

MRCOSBIE: YO CHO! NAME HIM KILLA B!

Yo.
This is Cho.

Got a lot on my plate right now. (as you may have just read)

So while I attempt to take over the world and stuff, I need you name my puppy.

He's a coyote (NOT Wile. E.). His mom's dead (NOT Bambi). He lives inside my jacket (NOT Jake...which is the name of the bird that Brooks keeps in his jacket in Shawshank Redemption. Shut up, I like that movie)

Send your name ideas to:

mondomarvel@marvel.com

You can call this a "contest" if ya want, but it's in no way, shape, or form fair. I'm naming him whatever I want. Might be one of your names, might be something Herc comes up with.

--No mo' Cho

THIS IS THE NAME THE PUPPY CONTEST PAGE WE PUT INTO HERC #114. WE GOT OVER 150 RESPONSES FOR THIS SUCKER (NOTE: THE CONTEST IS OVER, BUT FEEL FREE TO KEEP SENDING IN IDEAS).

--ASSISTANT EDITOR NATHAN COSBY

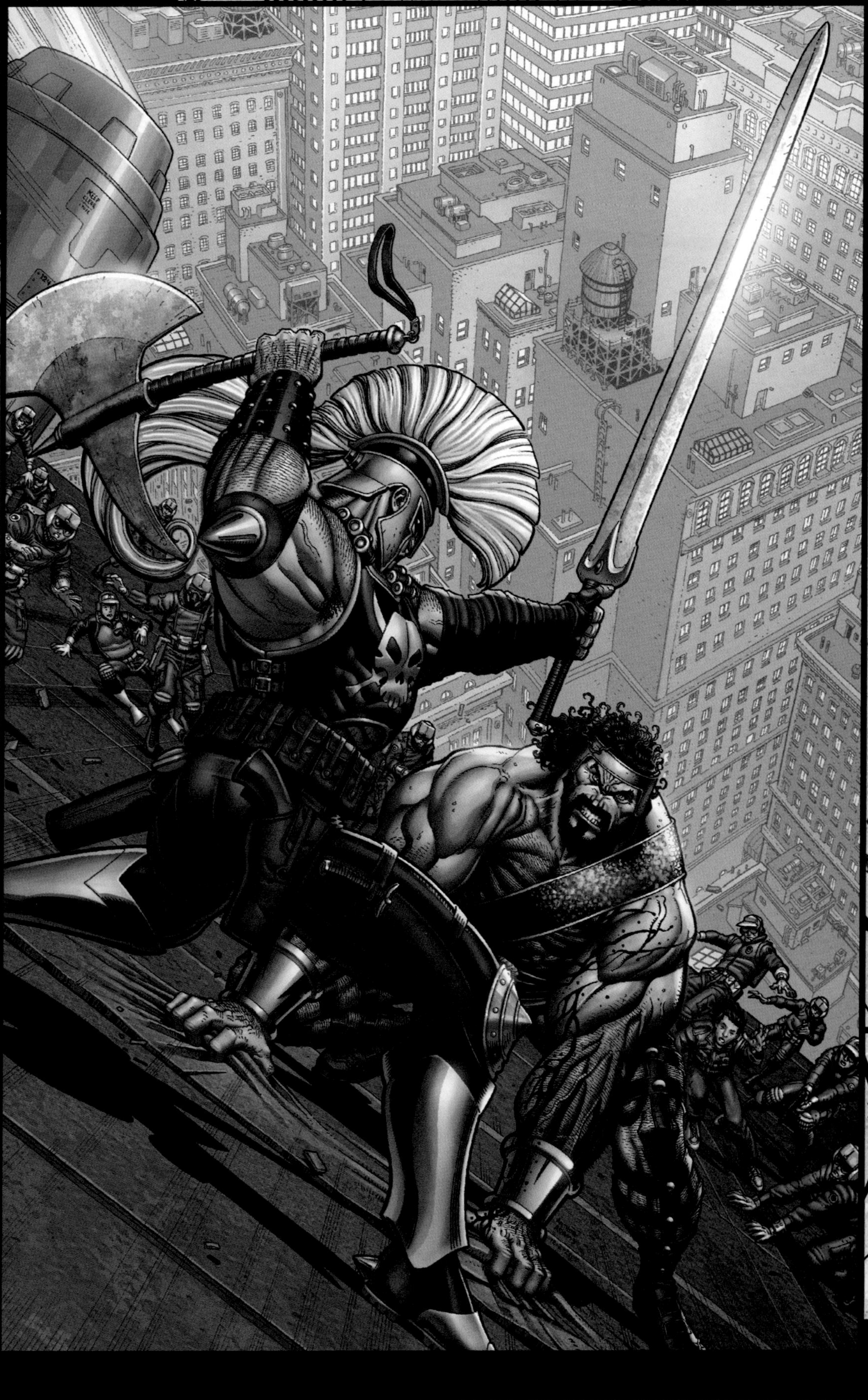

INCREDIBLE HERCULES #115

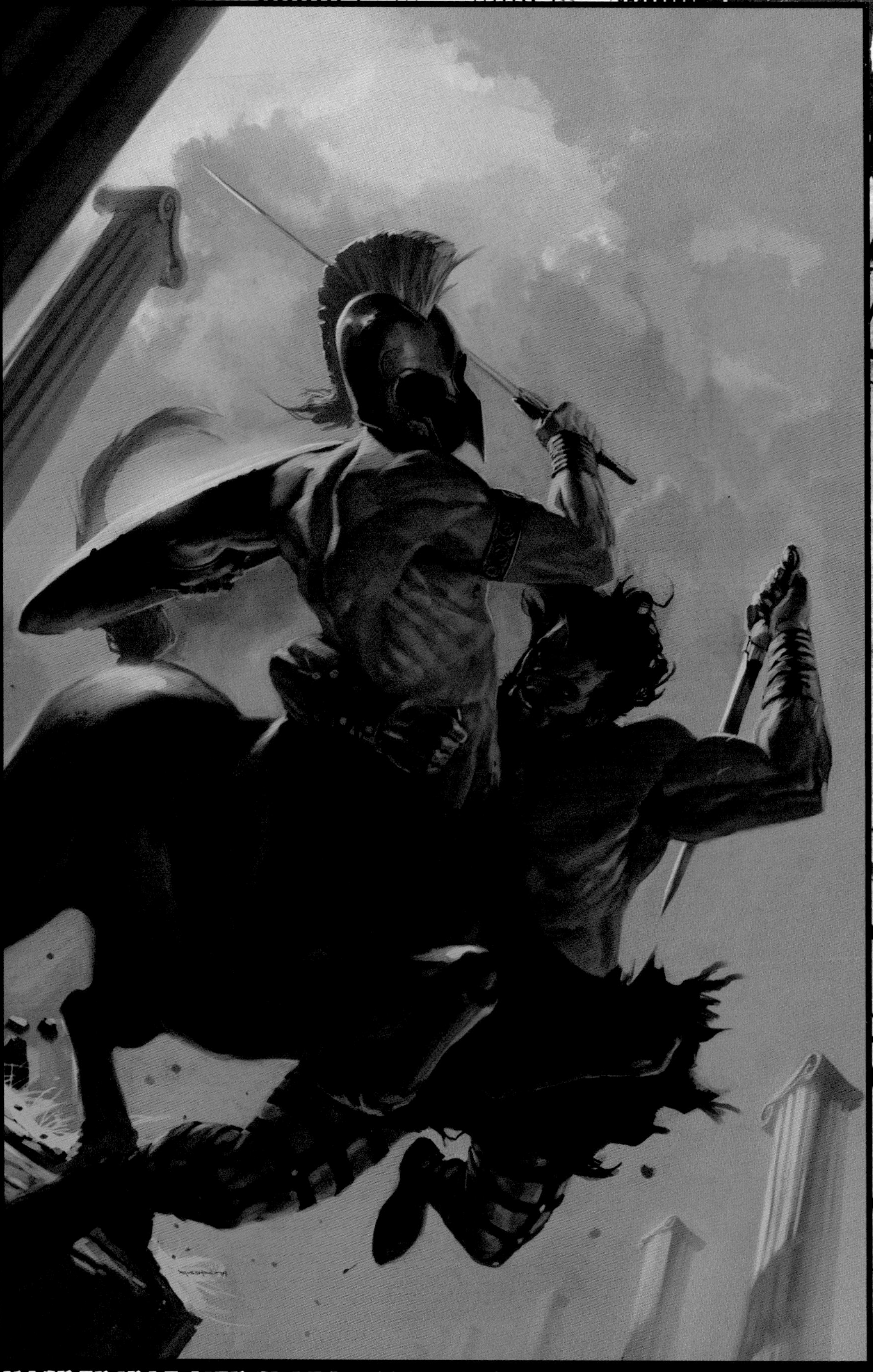

INCREDIBLE HERCULES #115 VARIANT

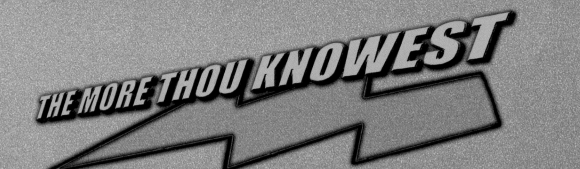

THE MORE THOU KNOWEST

THINKEST THOU LIFE IS ALL MUTTON AND MAIDENS?

NAY.

CONSIDER POWERFUL **HERCULES.** GREATEST OF HEROES. PARAGON OF MASCULINITY. HIS SHOULD BE A LIFE OF GRANDEUR.

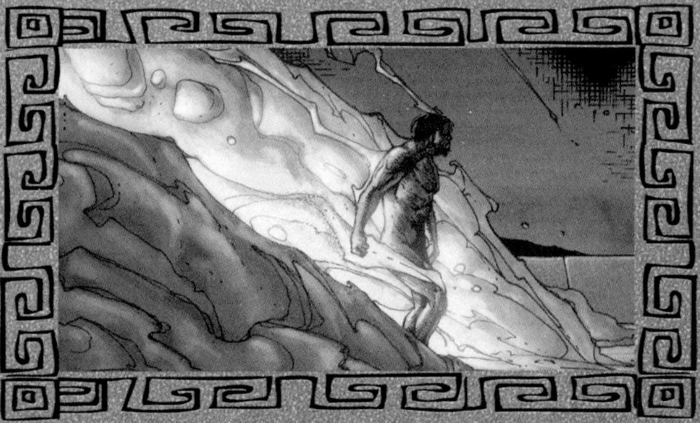

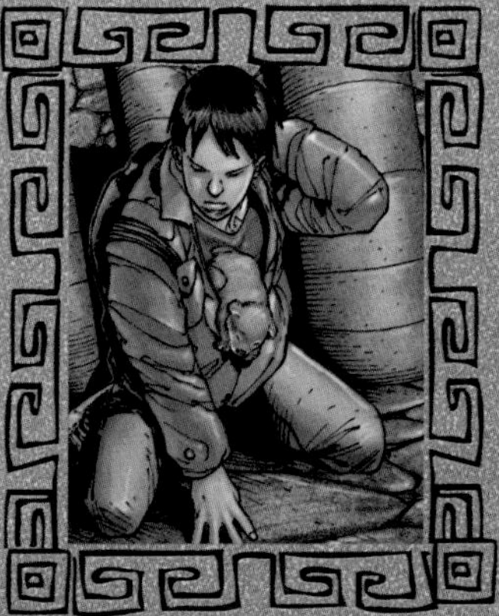

AND YET THE PATHWAY HERCULES TREADS IS FRAUGHT WITH PERIL, THROUGH FAULT PRINCIPALLY OF **AMADEUS CHO** (WITH PUP IN TOW).

CHO DEEMS S.H.I.E.L.D. RESPONSIBLE FOR WOUNDING HIS PUP, AND SO A FURIOUS CAN OF GANGSTA-STYLE WHUP-@$$ DESCENDS UPON THE MORTAL ENFORCEMENT AGENCY...

...IN THE SHAPE OF A SELF-REPLICATING **NEO-VIRUS** THAT SHALL WREAK BEDLAM UPON YON JUMPSUITED SPY-GUYS' OPERATIONS THE WORLD OVER.

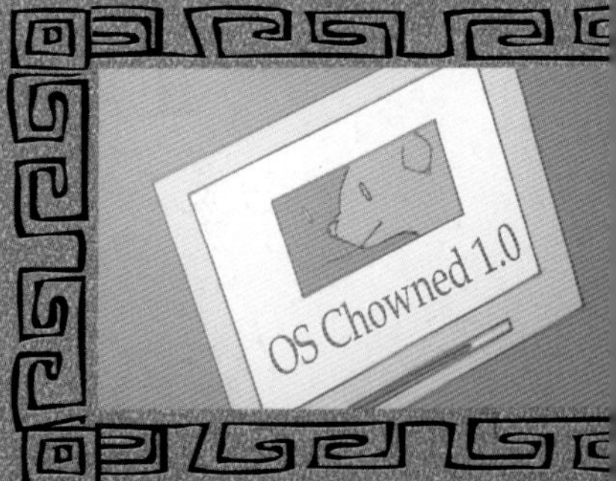
OS Chowned 1.0

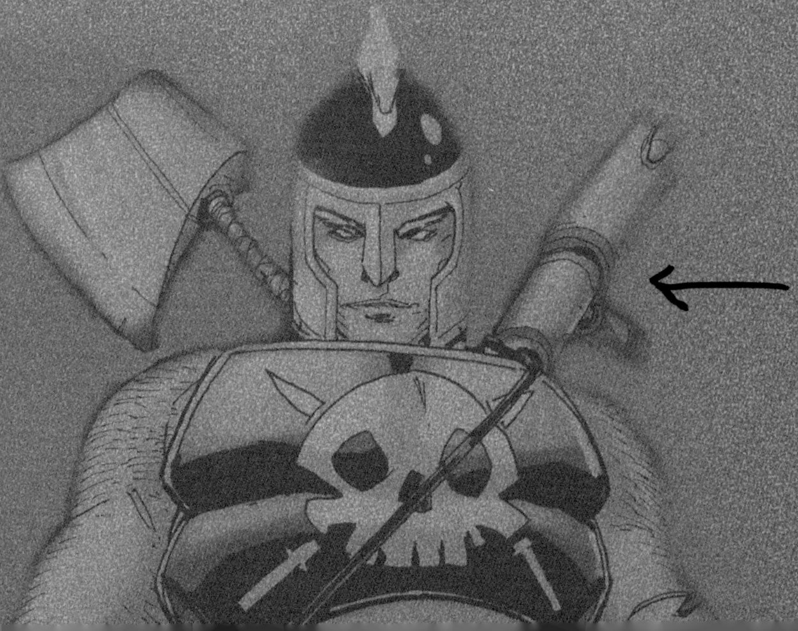

BUT WHILST HERCULES ENDEAVORS TO CONVINCE CHO TO LET HIS IRE GO, LET US NOT FORGET THAT **ARES**, BROTHER OF HERCULES AND **GOD OF #%*&IN' WAR**, WAITS TO STRIKE...

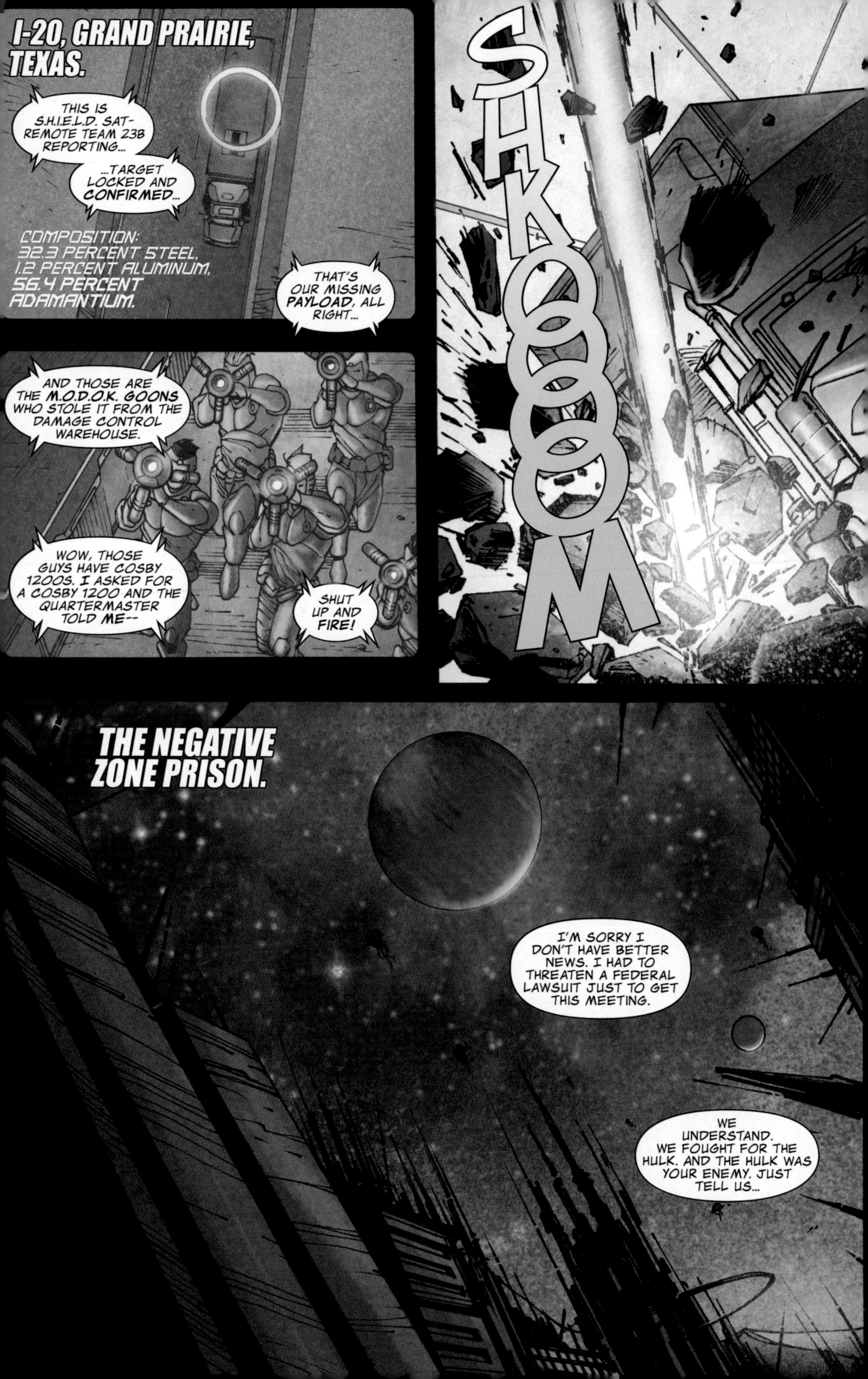
I-20, GRAND PRAIRIE, TEXAS.
THIS IS S.H.I.E.L.D. SAT-REMOTE TEAM 23B REPORTING...
...TARGET LOCKED AND CONFIRMED...
COMPOSITION: 32.3 PERCENT STEEL, 1.2 PERCENT ALUMINUM, 56.4 PERCENT ADAMANTIUM.
THAT'S OUR MISSING PAYLOAD, ALL RIGHT...
AND THOSE ARE THE M.O.D.O.K. GOONS WHO STOLE IT FROM THE DAMAGE CONTROL WAREHOUSE.
WOW, THOSE GUYS HAVE COSBY 1200S. I ASKED FOR A COSBY 1200 AND THE QUARTERMASTER TOLD ME--
SHUT UP AND FIRE!
SHKOOOOOM
THE NEGATIVE ZONE PRISON.
I'M SORRY I DON'T HAVE BETTER NEWS. I HAD TO THREATEN A FEDERAL LAWSUIT JUST TO GET THIS MEETING.
WE UNDERSTAND. WE FOUGHT FOR THE HULK. AND THE HULK WAS YOUR ENEMY. JUST TELL US...

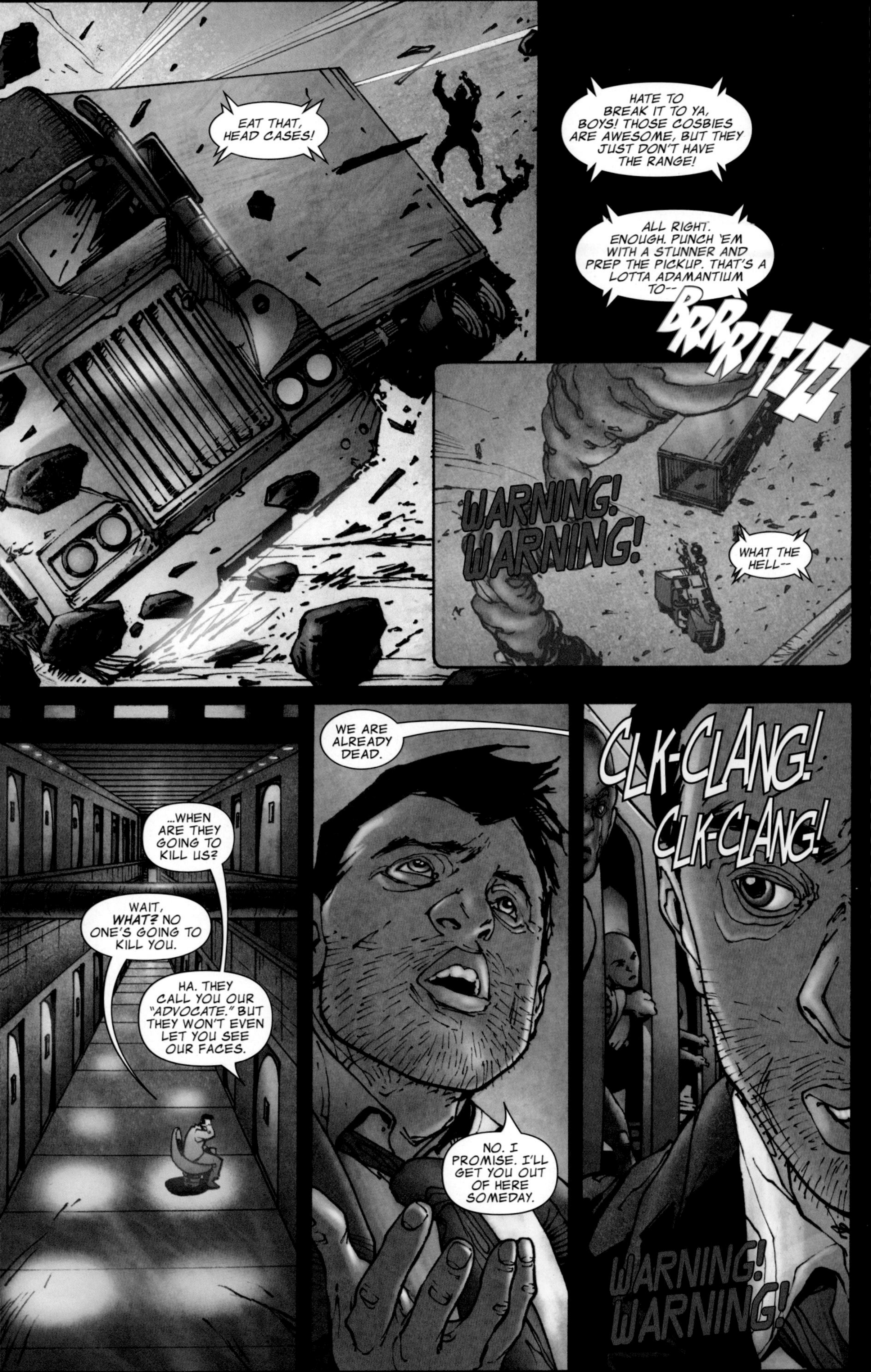
EAT THAT, HEAD CASES!
HATE TO BREAK IT TO YA, BOYS! THOSE COSBIES ARE AWESOME, BUT THEY JUST DON'T HAVE THE RANGE!
ALL RIGHT. ENOUGH. PUNCH 'EM WITH A STUNNER AND PREP THE PICKUP. THAT'S A LOTTA ADAMANTIUM TO--
BRRRRTZZZ
WARNING! WARNING!
WHAT THE HELL--
...WHEN ARE THEY GOING TO KILL US?
WAIT, WHAT? NO ONE'S GOING TO KILL YOU.
HA. THEY CALL YOU OUR "ADVOCATE." BUT THEY WON'T EVEN LET YOU SEE OUR FACES.
WE ARE ALREADY DEAD.
NO. I PROMISE. I'LL GET YOU OUT OF HERE SOMEDAY.
CLK-CLANG! CLK-CLANG!
WARNING! WARNING!

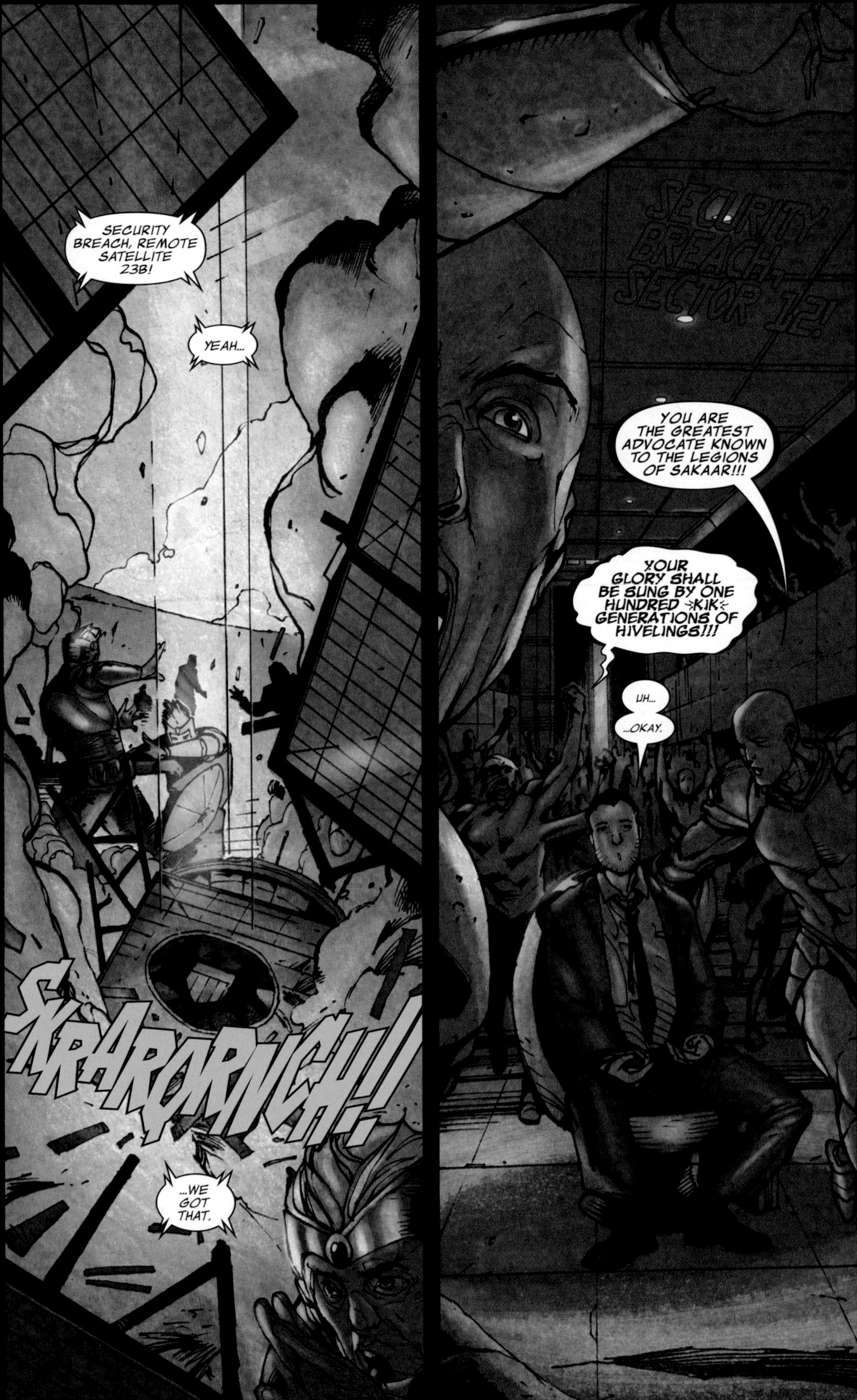
SECURITY BREACH, REMOTE SATELLITE 23B!
YEAH...
SKRARQRNCH!!
...WE GOT THAT.
SECURITY BREACH, SECTOR 12!
YOU ARE THE GREATEST ADVOCATE KNOWN TO THE LEGIONS OF SAKAAR!!!
YOUR GLORY SHALL BE SUNG BY ONE HUNDRED ⋺KIK⋲ GENERATIONS OF HIVELINGS!!!
UH...
...OKAY.

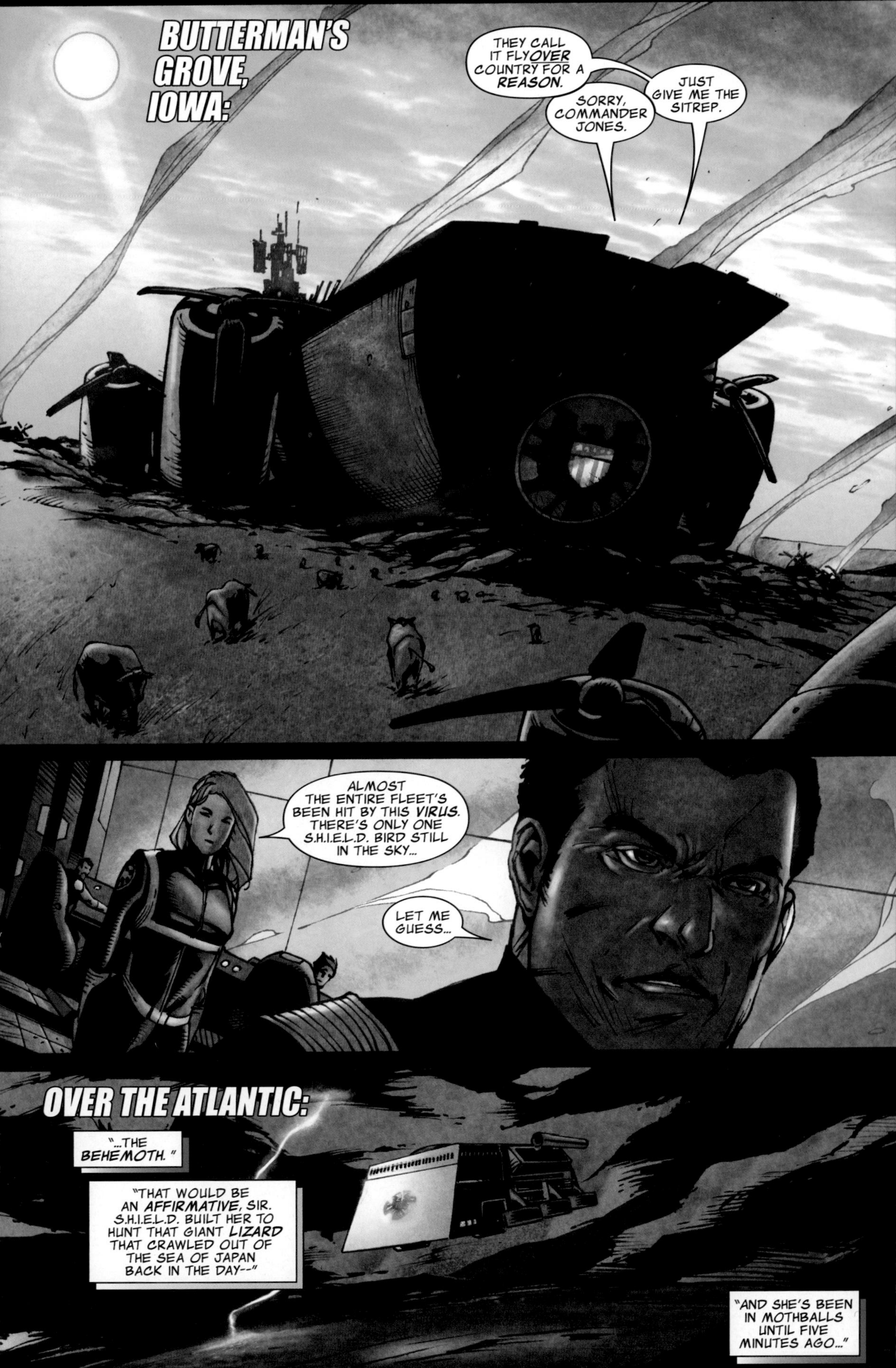
BUTTERMAN'S GROVE, IOWA:
THEY CALL IT FLYOVER COUNTRY FOR A REASON.
SORRY, COMMANDER JONES.
JUST GIVE ME THE SITREP.
ALMOST THE ENTIRE FLEET'S BEEN HIT BY THIS VIRUS. THERE'S ONLY ONE S.H.I.E.L.D. BIRD STILL IN THE SKY...
LET ME GUESS...
OVER THE ATLANTIC:
"...THE BEHEMOTH."
"THAT WOULD BE AN AFFIRMATIVE, SIR. S.H.I.E.L.D. BUILT HER TO HUNT THAT GIANT LIZARD THAT CRAWLED OUT OF THE SEA OF JAPAN BACK IN THE DAY--"
"AND SHE'S BEEN IN MOTHBALLS UNTIL FIVE MINUTES AGO..."

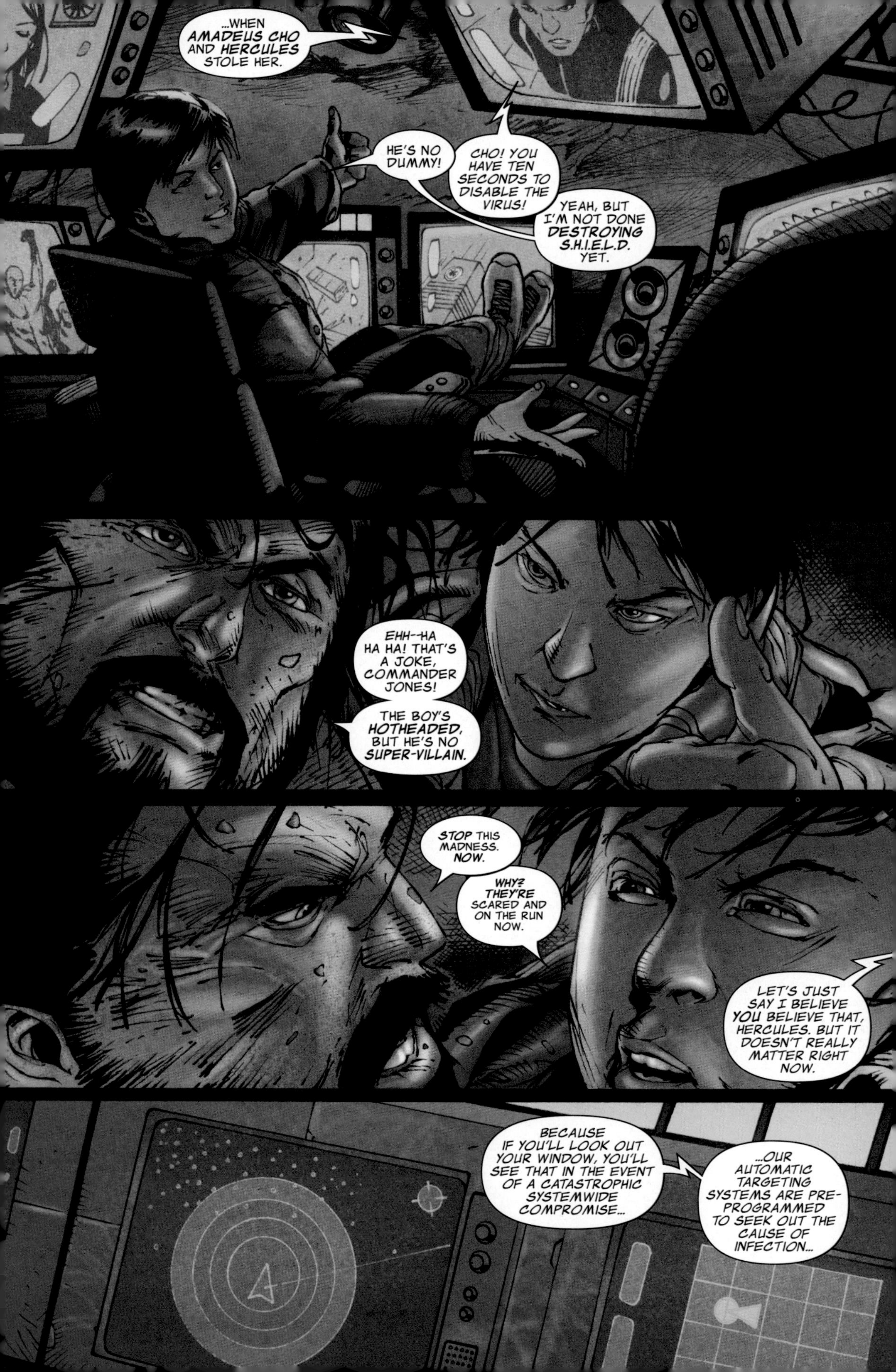
...WHEN AMADEUS CHO AND HERCULES STOLE HER.
HE'S NO DUMMY!
CHO! YOU HAVE TEN SECONDS TO DISABLE THE VIRUS!
YEAH, BUT I'M NOT DONE DESTROYING S.H.I.E.L.D. YET.
EHH--HA HA HA! THAT'S A JOKE, COMMANDER JONES!
THE BOY'S HOTHEADED, BUT HE'S NO SUPER-VILLAIN.
STOP THIS MADNESS. NOW.
WHY? THEY'RE SCARED AND ON THE RUN NOW.
LET'S JUST SAY I BELIEVE YOU BELIEVE THAT, HERCULES. BUT IT DOESN'T REALLY MATTER RIGHT NOW.
BECAUSE IF YOU'LL LOOK OUT YOUR WINDOW, YOU'LL SEE THAT IN THE EVENT OF A CATASTROPHIC SYSTEMWIDE COMPROMISE...
...OUR AUTOMATIC TARGETING SYSTEMS ARE PRE-PROGRAMMED TO SEEK OUT THE CAUSE OF INFECTION...

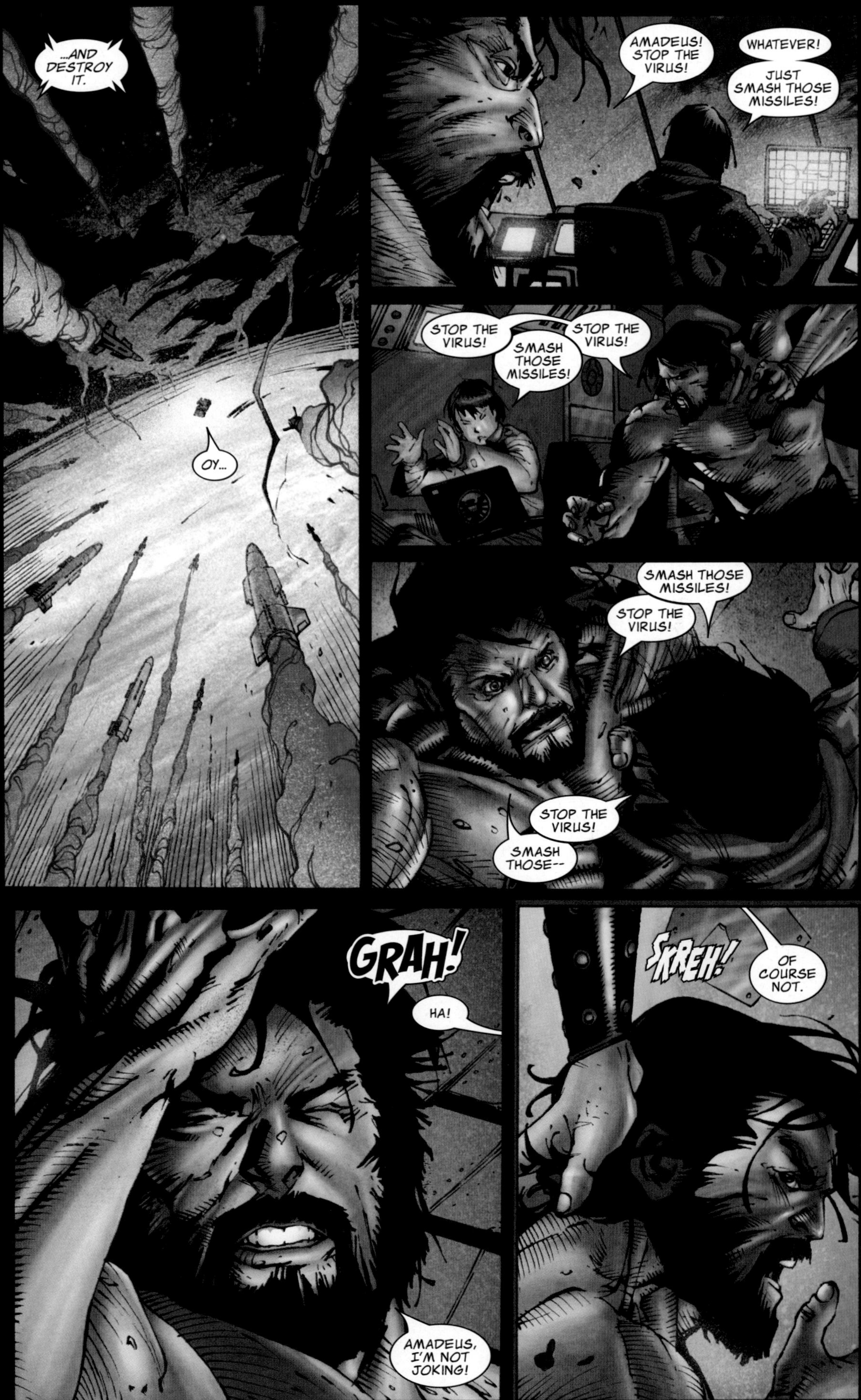
...AND DESTROY IT.
OY...
AMADEUS! STOP THE VIRUS!
WHATEVER!
JUST SMASH THOSE MISSILES!
STOP THE VIRUS!
STOP THE VIRUS!
SMASH THOSE MISSILES!
SMASH THOSE MISSILES!
STOP THE VIRUS!
STOP THE VIRUS!
SMASH THOSE--
GRAH!
HA!
AMADEUS, I'M NOT JOKING!
SKREH!
OF COURSE NOT.

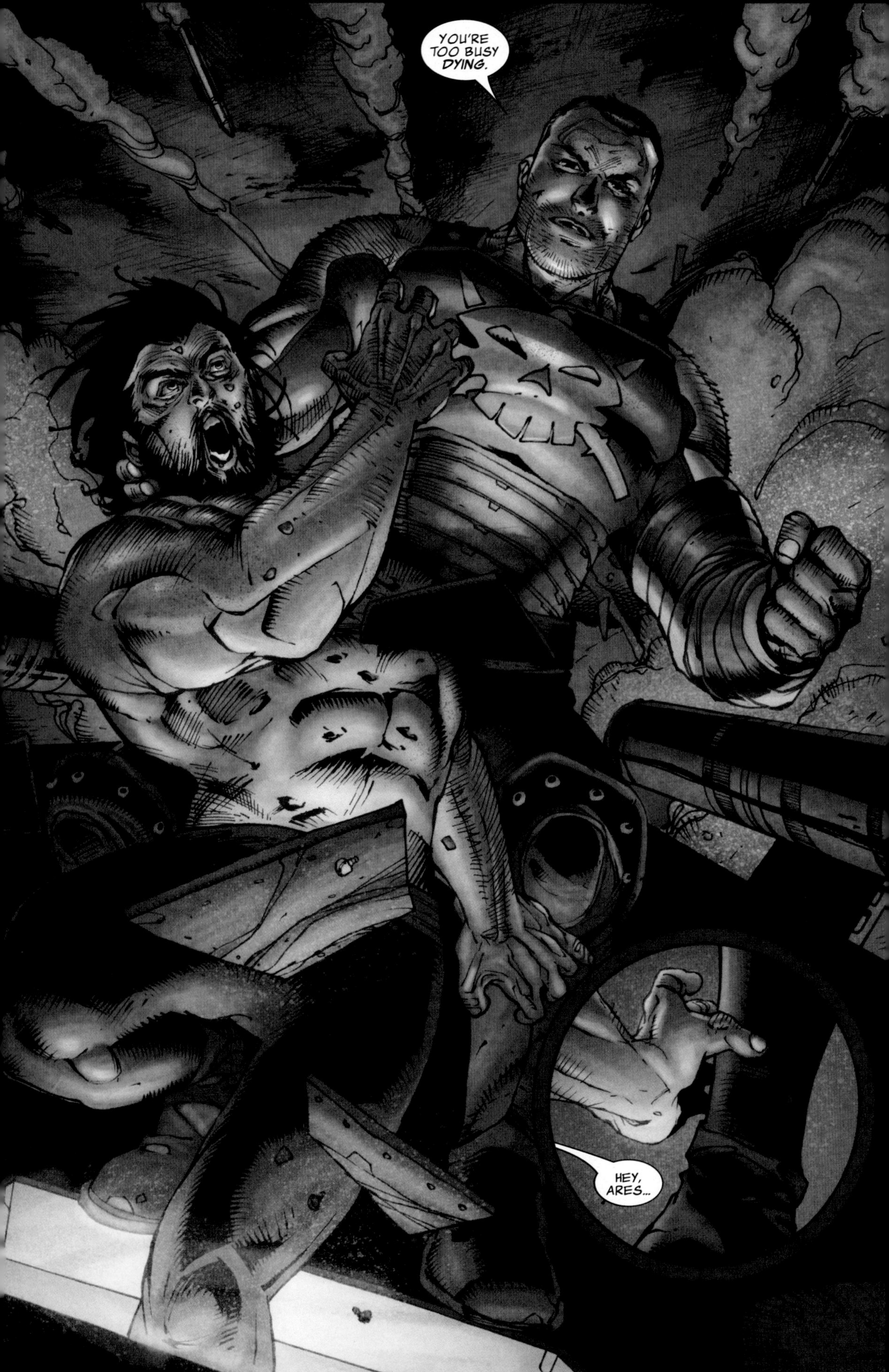
YOU'RE TOO BUSY DYING.
HEY, ARES...

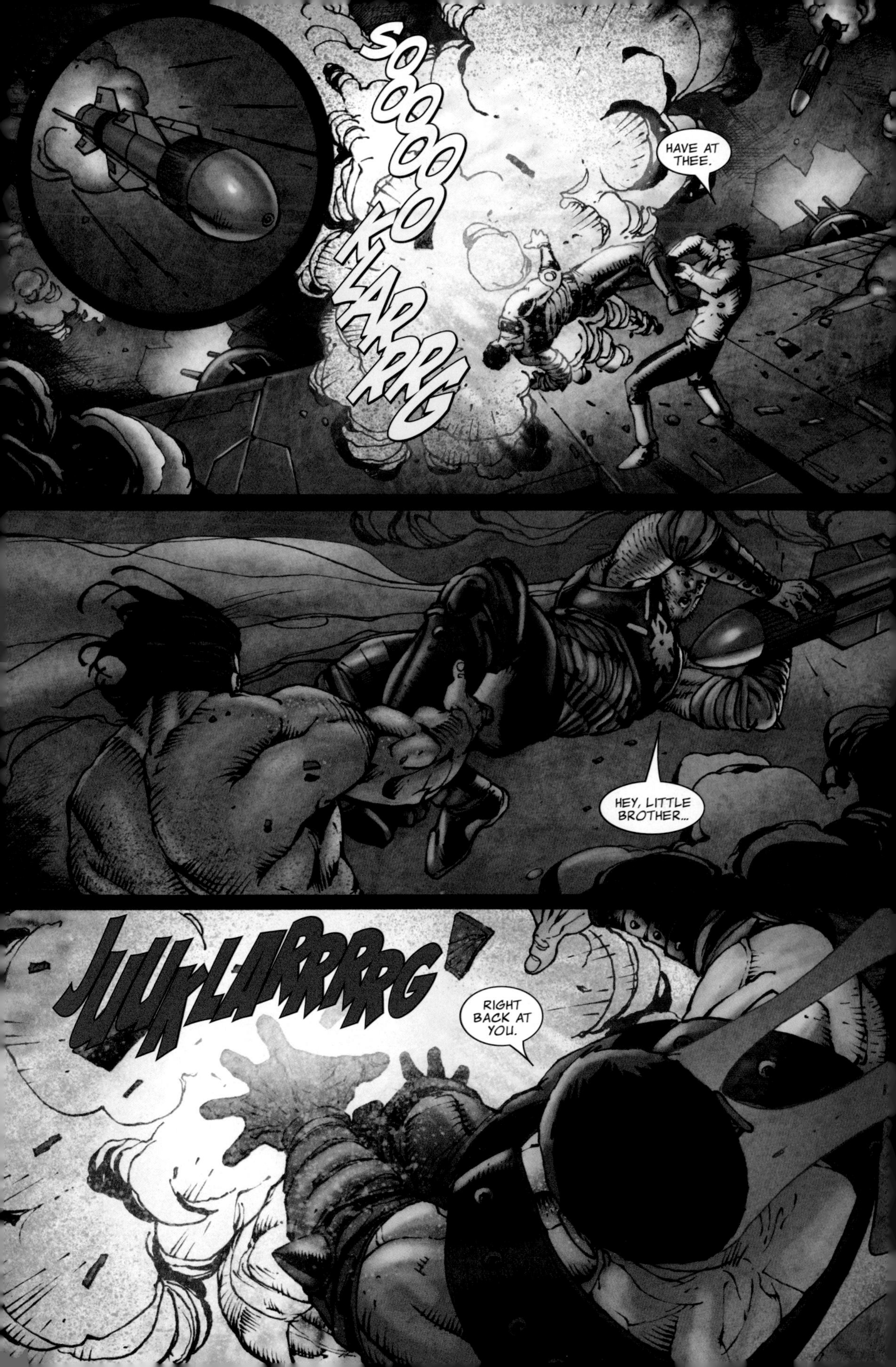
SOOOOOOKLARRG
HAVE AT THEE.
HEY, LITTLE BROTHER...
JUUKLARRRRG
RIGHT BACK AT YOU.

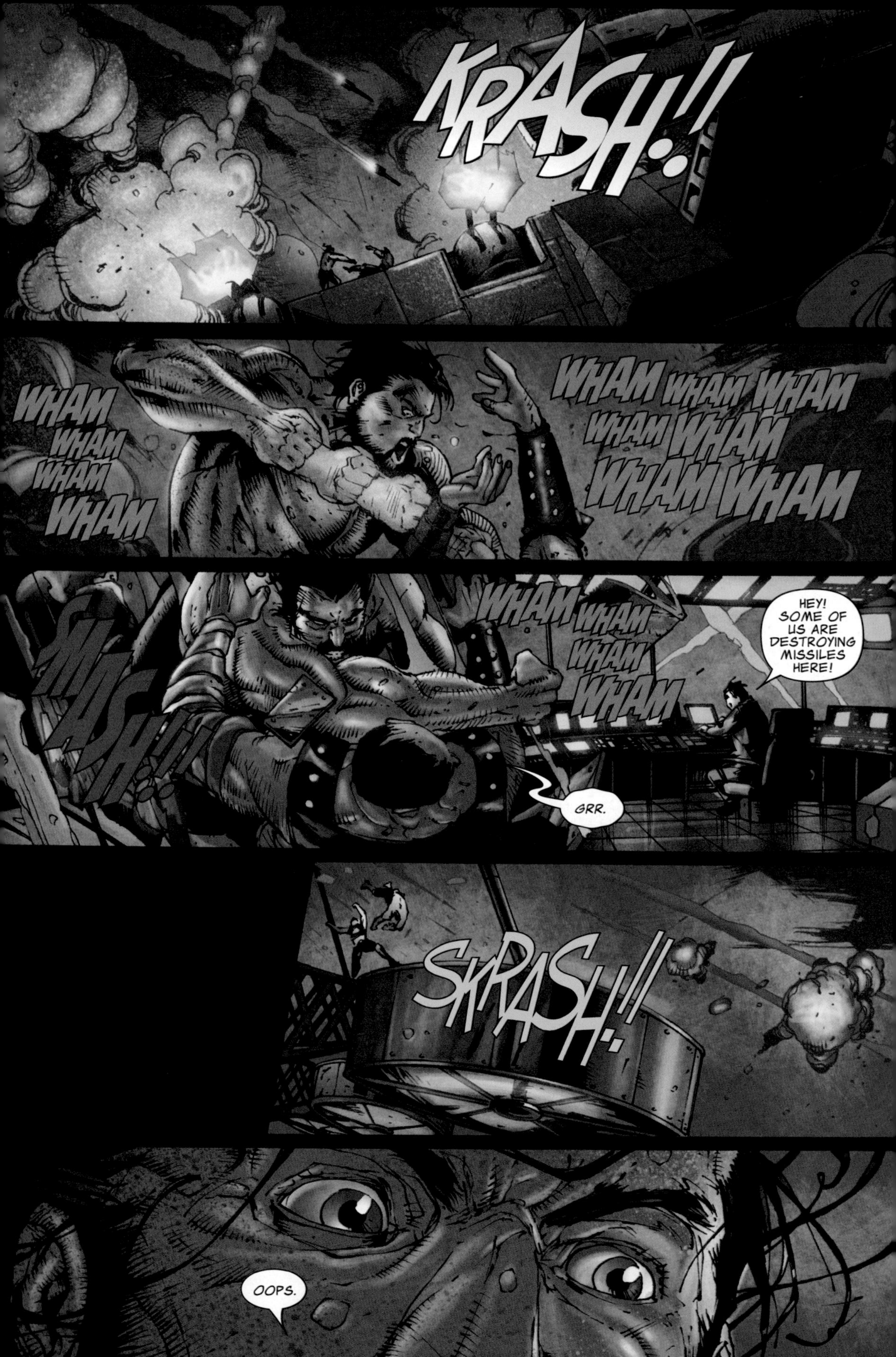
KRASH!!
WHAM WHAM WHAM WHAM
WHAM WHAM WHAM WHAM WHAM WHAM WHAM
KRASH!!
WHAM WHAM WHAM WHAM
HEY! SOME OF US ARE DESTROYING MISSILES HERE!
GRR.
SKRASH!!
OOPS.

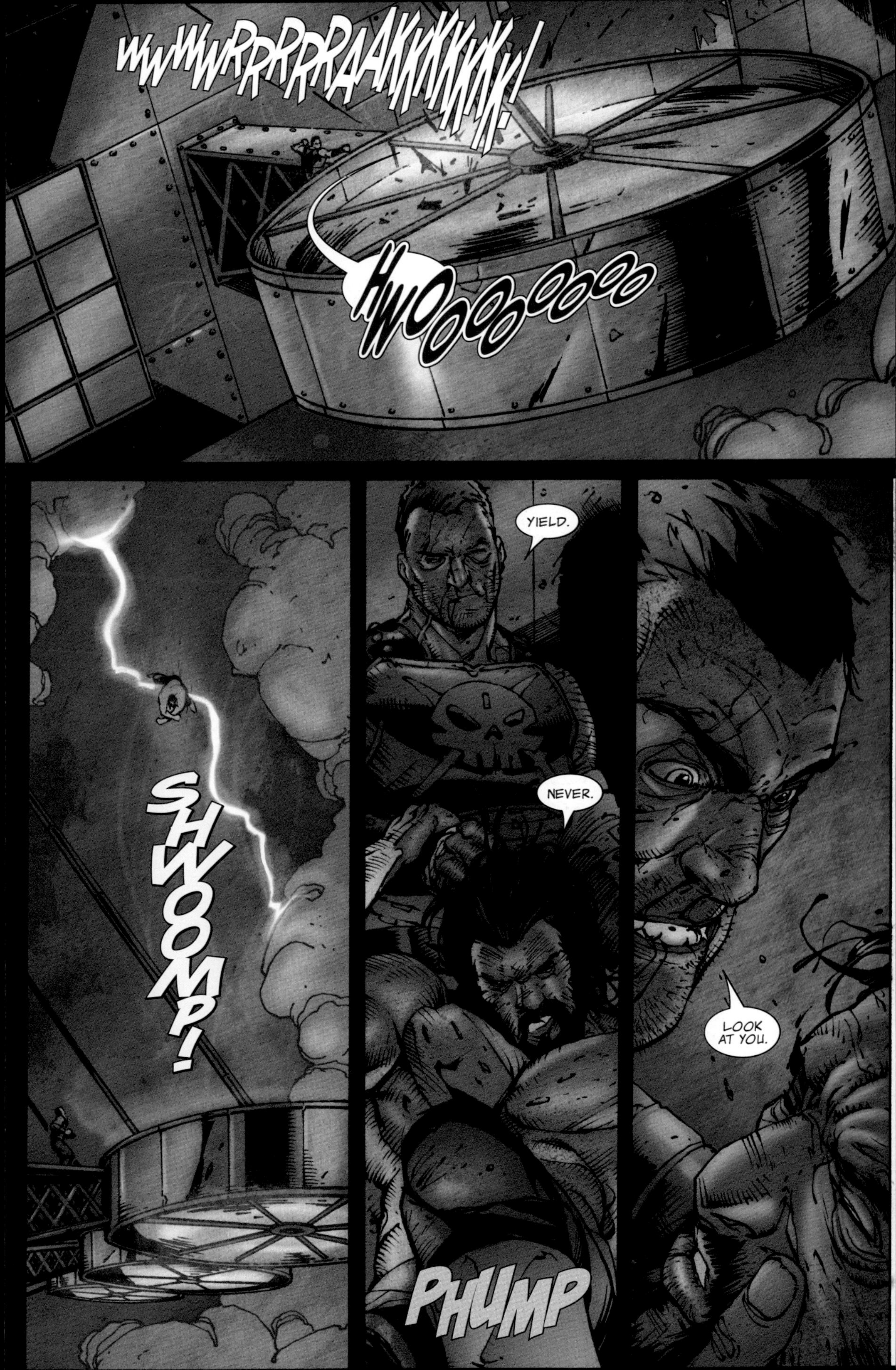
WWWWRRRRRRAAKKKKKKK!
HWOOOOOOOO
SHWOOOMP!
YIELD.
NEVER.
PHUMP
LOOK AT YOU.

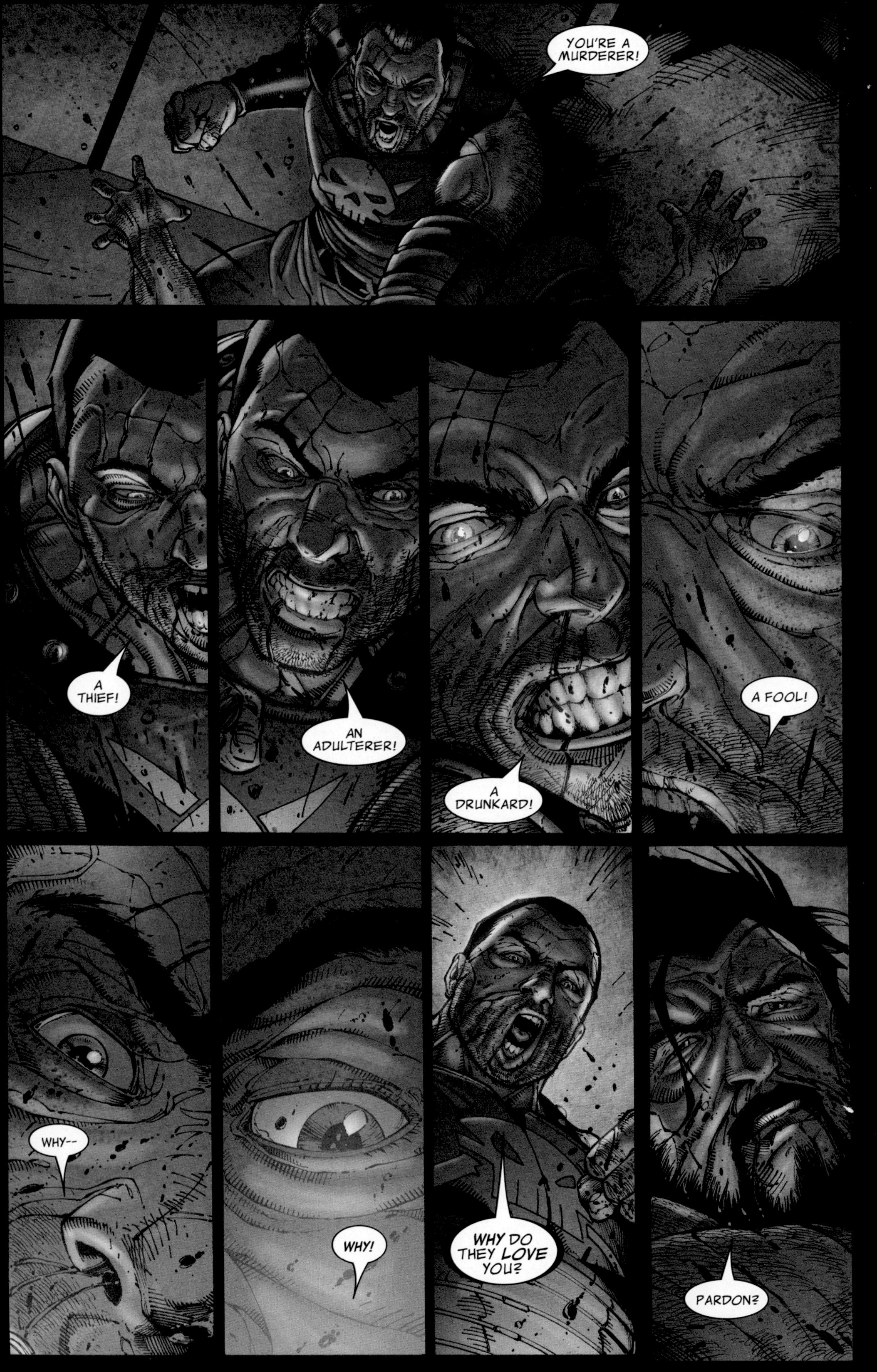
YOU'RE A MURDERER!
A THIEF!
AN ADULTERER!
A DRUNKARD!
A FOOL!
WHY--
WHY!
WHY DO THEY LOVE YOU?
PARDON?

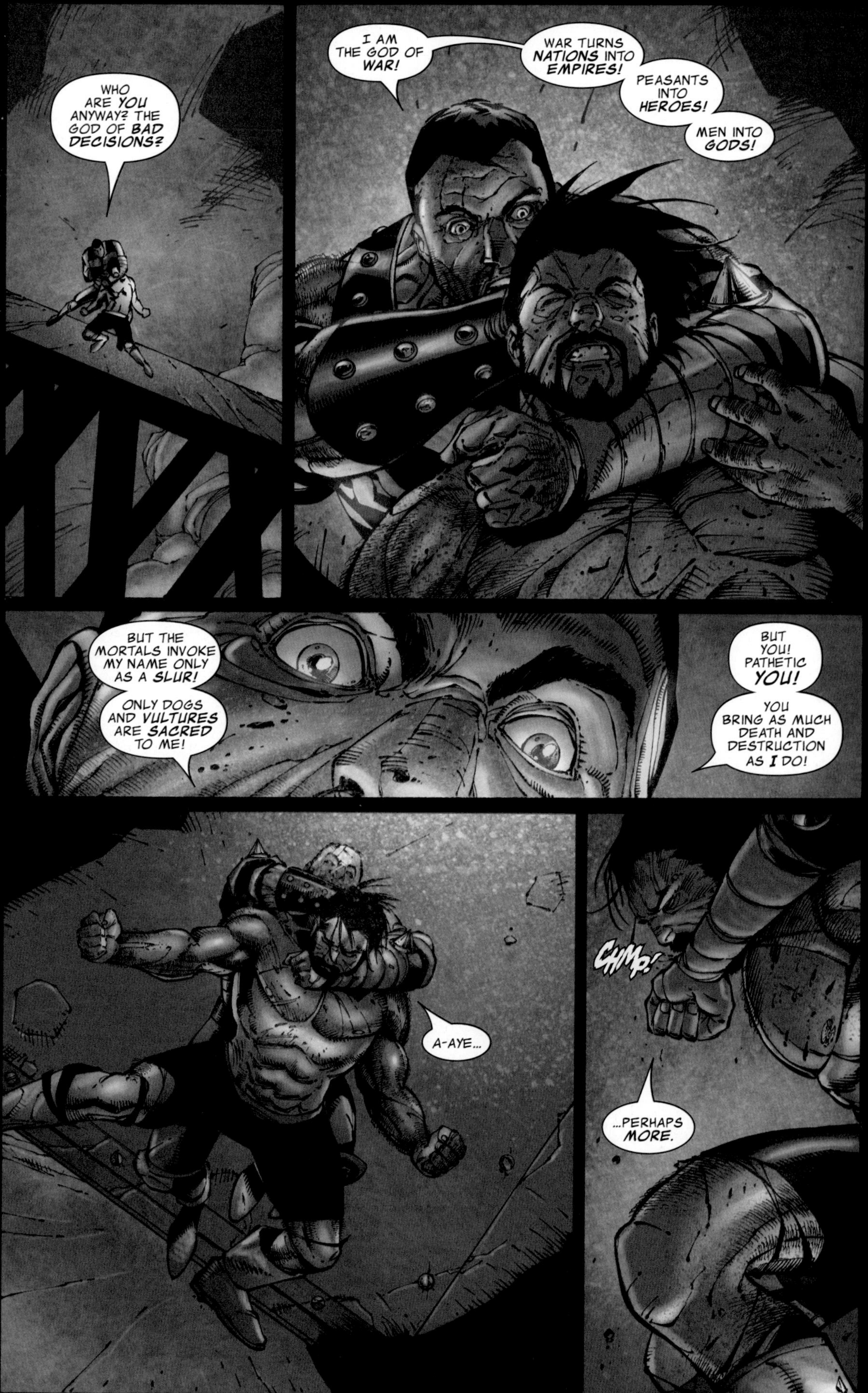
WHO ARE YOU ANYWAY? THE GOD OF BAD DECISIONS?
I AM THE GOD OF WAR!
WAR TURNS NATIONS INTO EMPIRES!
PEASANTS INTO HEROES!
MEN INTO GODS!
BUT THE MORTALS INVOKE MY NAME ONLY AS A SLUR!
ONLY DOGS AND VULTURES ARE SACRED TO ME!
BUT YOU! PATHETIC YOU!
YOU BRING AS MUCH DEATH AND DESTRUCTION AS I DO!
A-AYE...
CHMP!
...PERHAPS MORE.

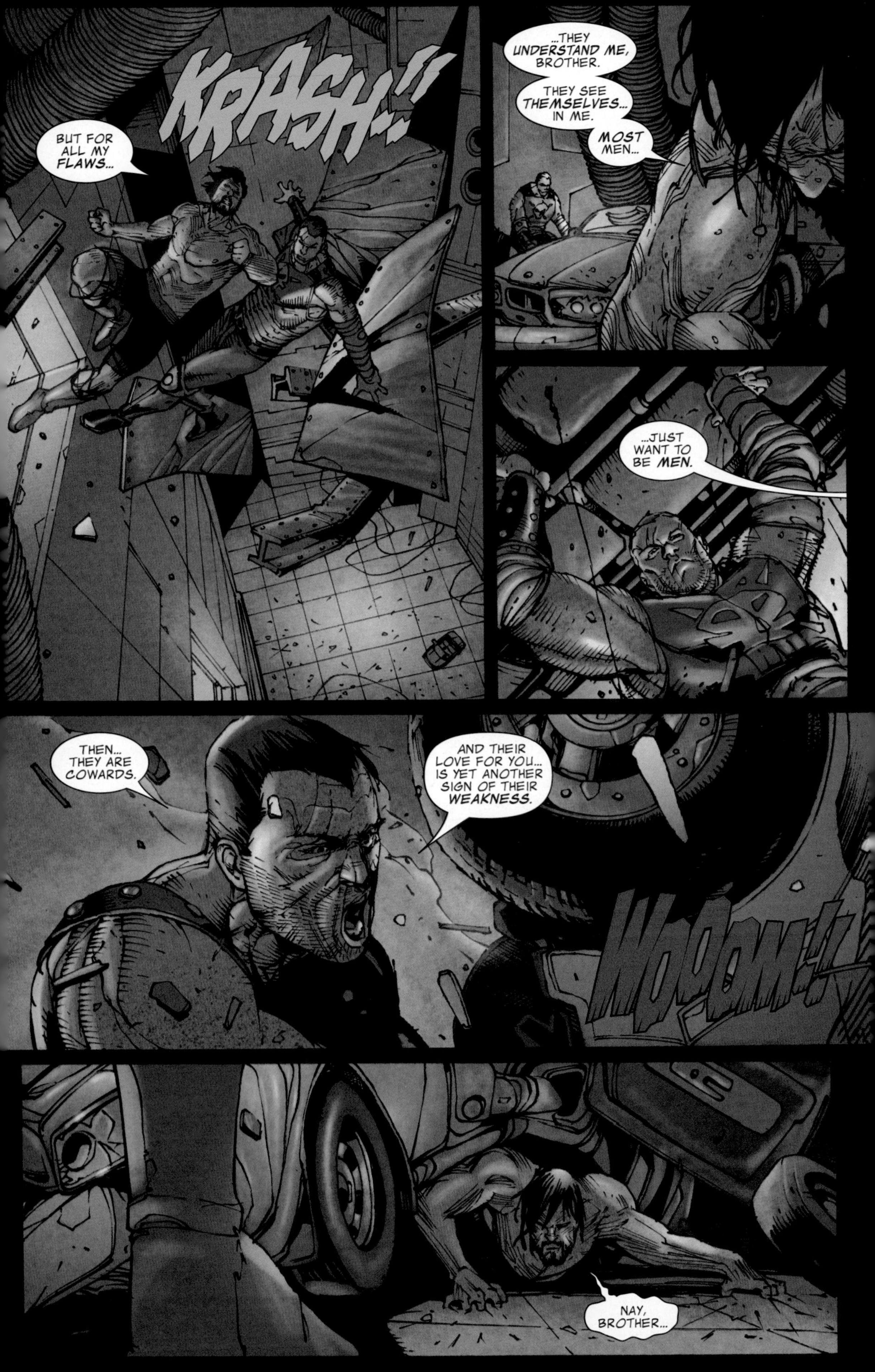
KRASH!!
BUT FOR ALL MY FLAWS...
...THEY UNDERSTAND ME, BROTHER.
THEY SEE THEMSELVES... IN ME.
MOST MEN...
...JUST WANT TO BE MEN.
THEN... THEY ARE COWARDS.
AND THEIR LOVE FOR YOU... IS YET ANOTHER SIGN OF THEIR WEAKNESS.
NAY, BROTHER...

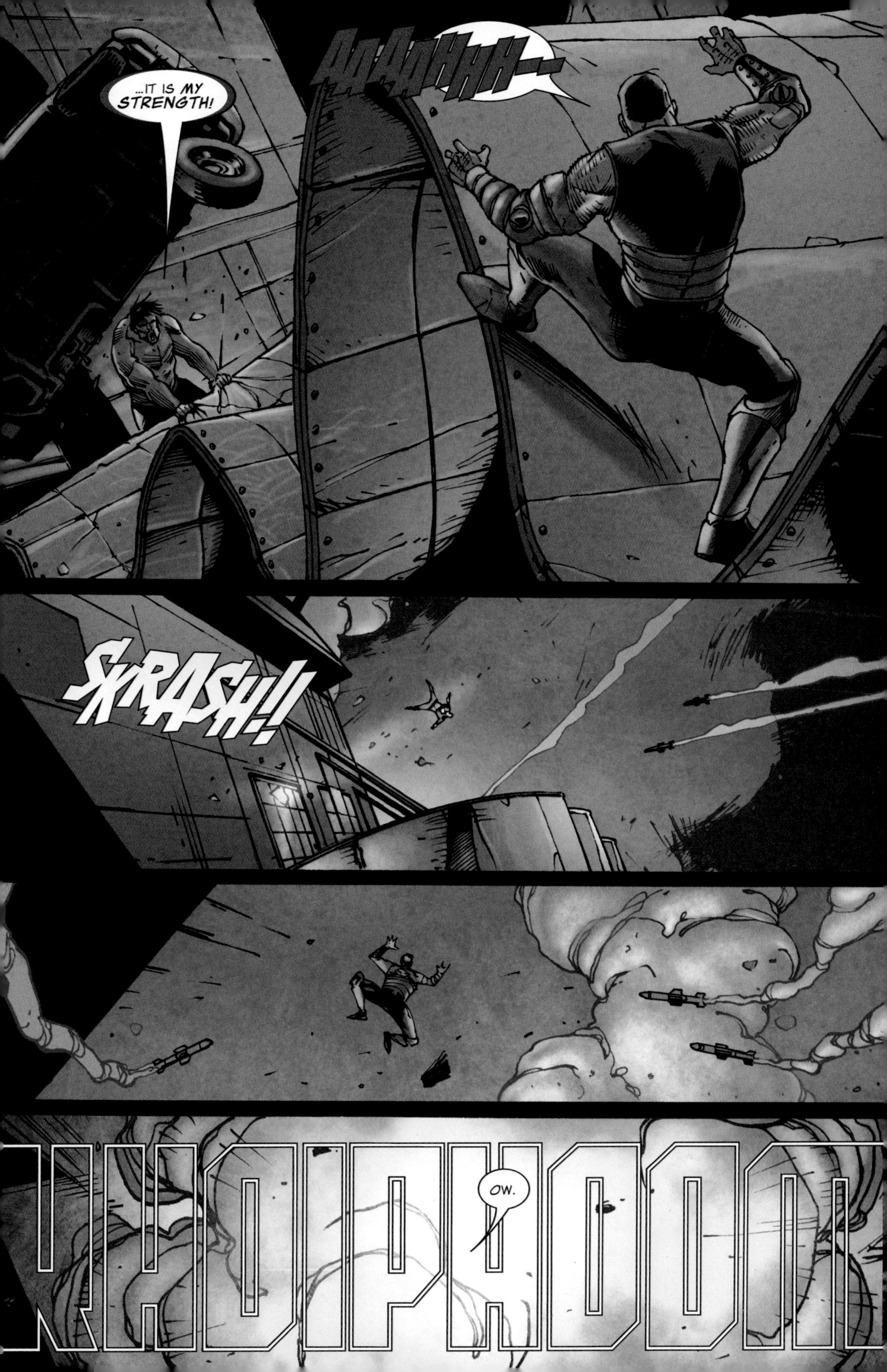
...IT IS MY STRENGTH!
AAAAHHH--
SKRASH!!
KHOIPHOOM
OW.

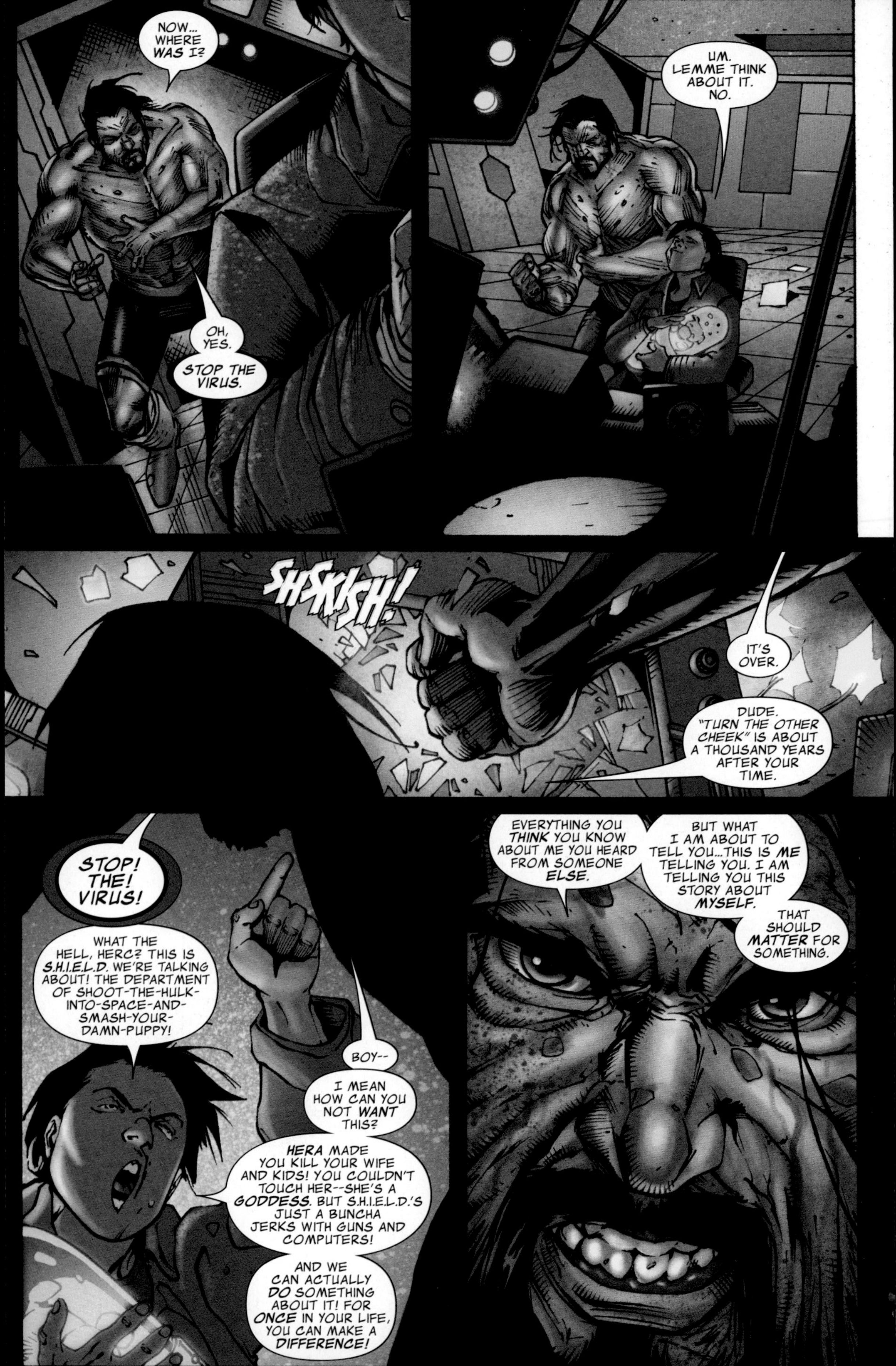
NOW... WHERE WAS I?
OH, YES.
STOP THE VIRUS.
UM. LEMME THINK ABOUT IT. NO.
SH-SKISH!
IT'S OVER.
DUDE. "TURN THE OTHER CHEEK" IS ABOUT A THOUSAND YEARS AFTER YOUR TIME.
STOP! THE! VIRUS!
WHAT THE HELL, HERC? THIS IS S.H.I.E.L.D. WE'RE TALKING ABOUT! THE DEPARTMENT OF SHOOT-THE-HULK-INTO-SPACE-AND-SMASH-YOUR-DAMN-PUPPY!
BOY--
I MEAN HOW CAN YOU NOT WANT THIS?
HERA MADE YOU KILL YOUR WIFE AND KIDS! YOU COULDN'T TOUCH HER--SHE'S A GODDESS. BUT S.H.I.E.L.D.'S JUST A BUNCHA JERKS WITH GUNS AND COMPUTERS!
AND WE CAN ACTUALLY DO SOMETHING ABOUT IT! FOR ONCE IN YOUR LIFE, YOU CAN MAKE A DIFFERENCE!
EVERYTHING YOU THINK YOU KNOW ABOUT ME YOU HEARD FROM SOMEONE ELSE.
BUT WHAT I AM ABOUT TO TELL YOU...THIS IS ME TELLING YOU. I AM TELLING YOU THIS STORY ABOUT MYSELF.
THAT SHOULD MATTER FOR SOMETHING.

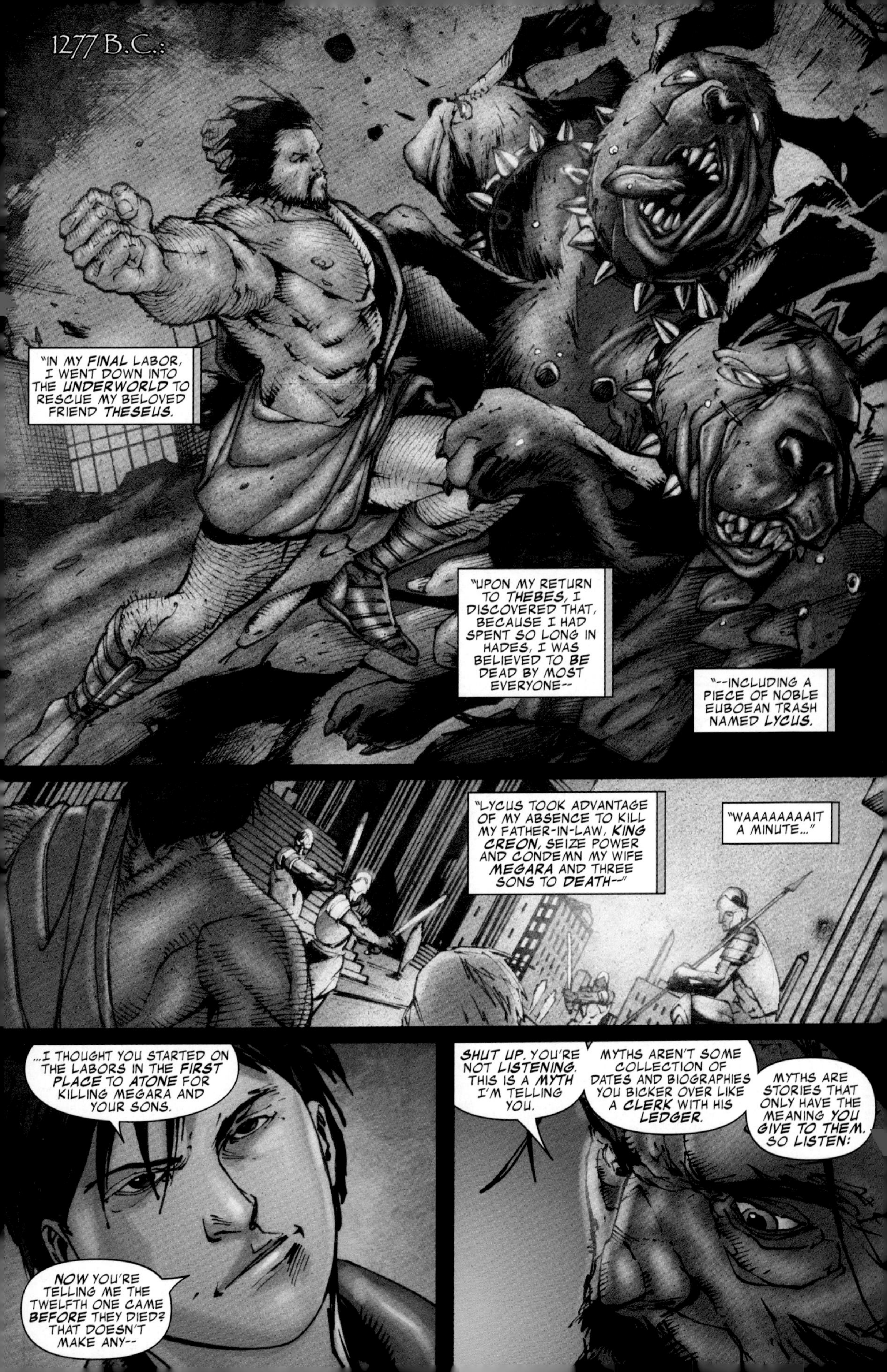

1277 B.C.:
"IN MY FINAL LABOR, I WENT DOWN INTO THE UNDERWORLD TO RESCUE MY BELOVED FRIEND THESEUS.
"UPON MY RETURN TO THEBES, I DISCOVERED THAT, BECAUSE I HAD SPENT SO LONG IN HADES, I WAS BELIEVED TO BE DEAD BY MOST EVERYONE--
"--INCLUDING A PIECE OF NOBLE EUBOEAN TRASH NAMED LYCUS.
"LYCUS TOOK ADVANTAGE OF MY ABSENCE TO KILL MY FATHER-IN-LAW, KING CREON, SEIZE POWER AND CONDEMN MY WIFE MEGARA AND THREE SONS TO DEATH--"
"WAAAAAAAAIT A MINUTE..."
...I THOUGHT YOU STARTED ON THE LABORS IN THE FIRST PLACE TO ATONE FOR KILLING MEGARA AND YOUR SONS.
NOW YOU'RE TELLING ME THE TWELFTH ONE CAME BEFORE THEY DIED? THAT DOESN'T MAKE ANY--
SHUT UP. YOU'RE NOT LISTENING. THIS IS A MYTH I'M TELLING YOU.
MYTHS AREN'T SOME COLLECTION OF DATES AND BIOGRAPHIES YOU BICKER OVER LIKE A CLERK WITH HIS LEDGER.
MYTHS ARE STORIES THAT ONLY HAVE THE MEANING YOU GIVE TO THEM. SO LISTEN:

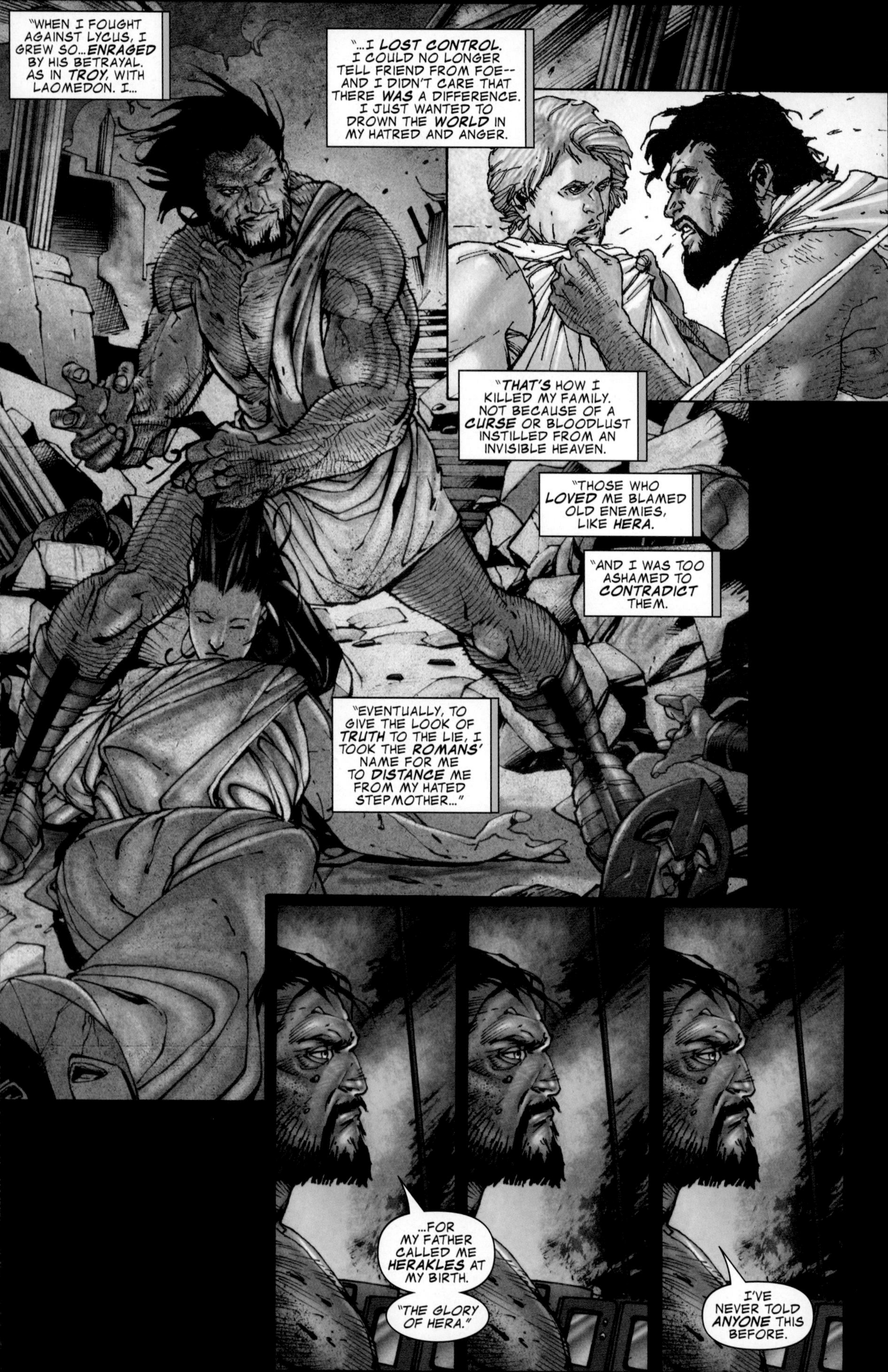
"WHEN I FOUGHT AGAINST LYCUS, I GREW SO...ENRAGED BY HIS BETRAYAL. AS IN TROY, WITH LAOMEDON. I...
"...I LOST CONTROL. I COULD NO LONGER TELL FRIEND FROM FOE--AND I DIDN'T CARE THAT THERE WAS A DIFFERENCE. I JUST WANTED TO DROWN THE WORLD IN MY HATRED AND ANGER.
"THAT'S HOW I KILLED MY FAMILY. NOT BECAUSE OF A CURSE OR BLOODLUST INSTILLED FROM AN INVISIBLE HEAVEN.
"THOSE WHO LOVED ME BLAMED OLD ENEMIES, LIKE HERA.
"AND I WAS TOO ASHAMED TO CONTRADICT THEM.
"EVENTUALLY, TO GIVE THE LOOK OF TRUTH TO THE LIE, I TOOK THE ROMANS' NAME FOR ME TO DISTANCE ME FROM MY HATED STEPMOTHER..."
...FOR MY FATHER CALLED ME HERAKLES AT MY BIRTH.
"THE GLORY OF HERA."
I'VE NEVER TOLD ANYONE THIS BEFORE.

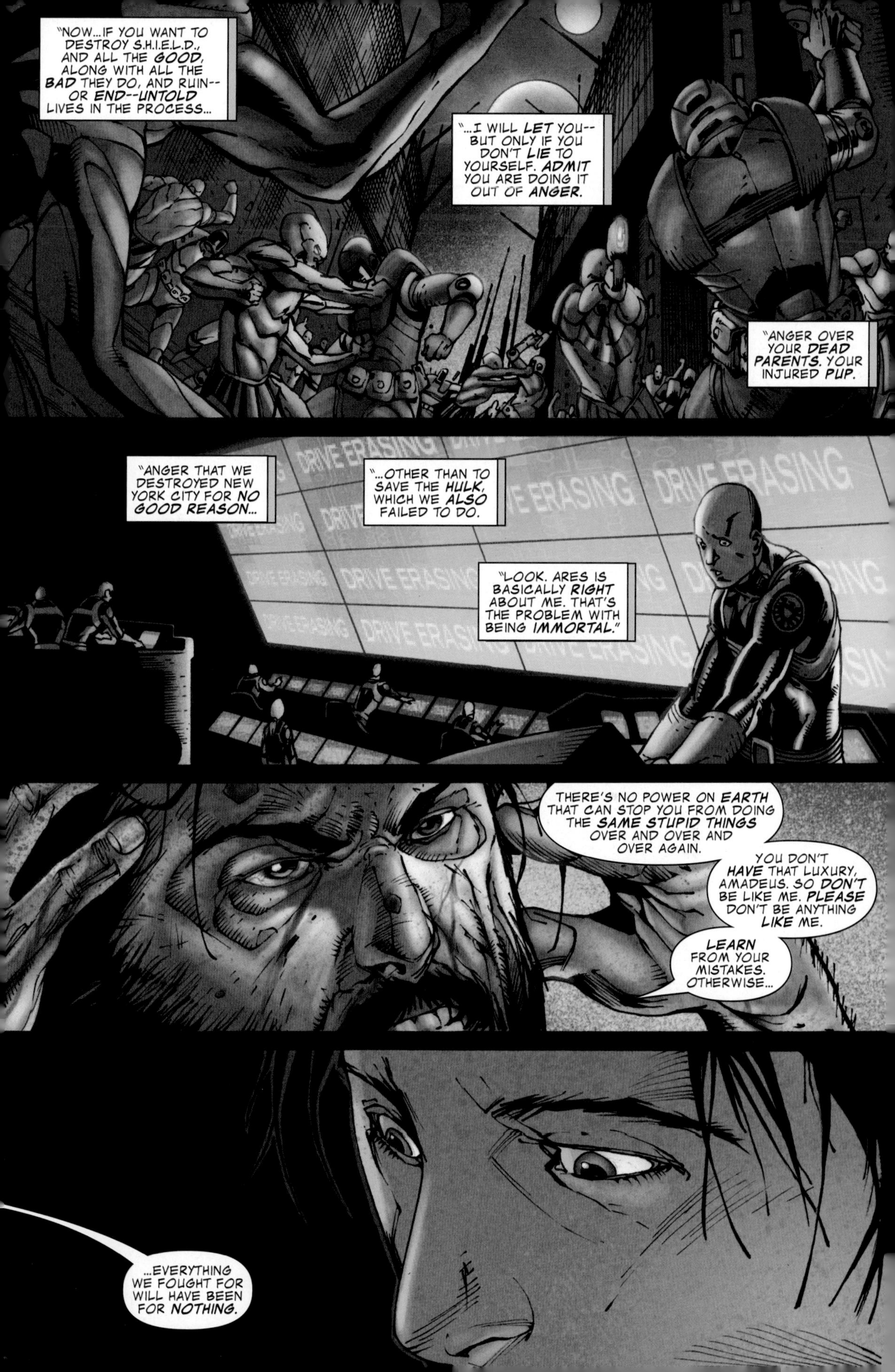
"NOW...IF YOU WANT TO DESTROY S.H.I.E.L.D., AND ALL THE GOOD, ALONG WITH ALL THE BAD THEY DO, AND RUIN-- OR END--UNTOLD LIVES IN THE PROCESS...
"...I WILL LET YOU-- BUT ONLY IF YOU DON'T LIE TO YOURSELF. ADMIT YOU ARE DOING IT OUT OF ANGER.
"ANGER OVER YOUR DEAD PARENTS. YOUR INJURED PUP.
DRIVE ERASING
"ANGER THAT WE DESTROYED NEW YORK CITY FOR NO GOOD REASON...
"...OTHER THAN TO SAVE THE HULK, WHICH WE ALSO FAILED TO DO.
"LOOK. ARES IS BASICALLY RIGHT ABOUT ME. THAT'S THE PROBLEM WITH BEING IMMORTAL."
THERE'S NO POWER ON EARTH THAT CAN STOP YOU FROM DOING THE SAME STUPID THINGS OVER AND OVER AND OVER AGAIN.
YOU DON'T HAVE THAT LUXURY, AMADEUS. SO DON'T BE LIKE ME. PLEASE DON'T BE ANYTHING LIKE ME.
LEARN FROM YOUR MISTAKES. OTHERWISE...
...EVERYTHING WE FOUGHT FOR WILL HAVE BEEN FOR NOTHING.

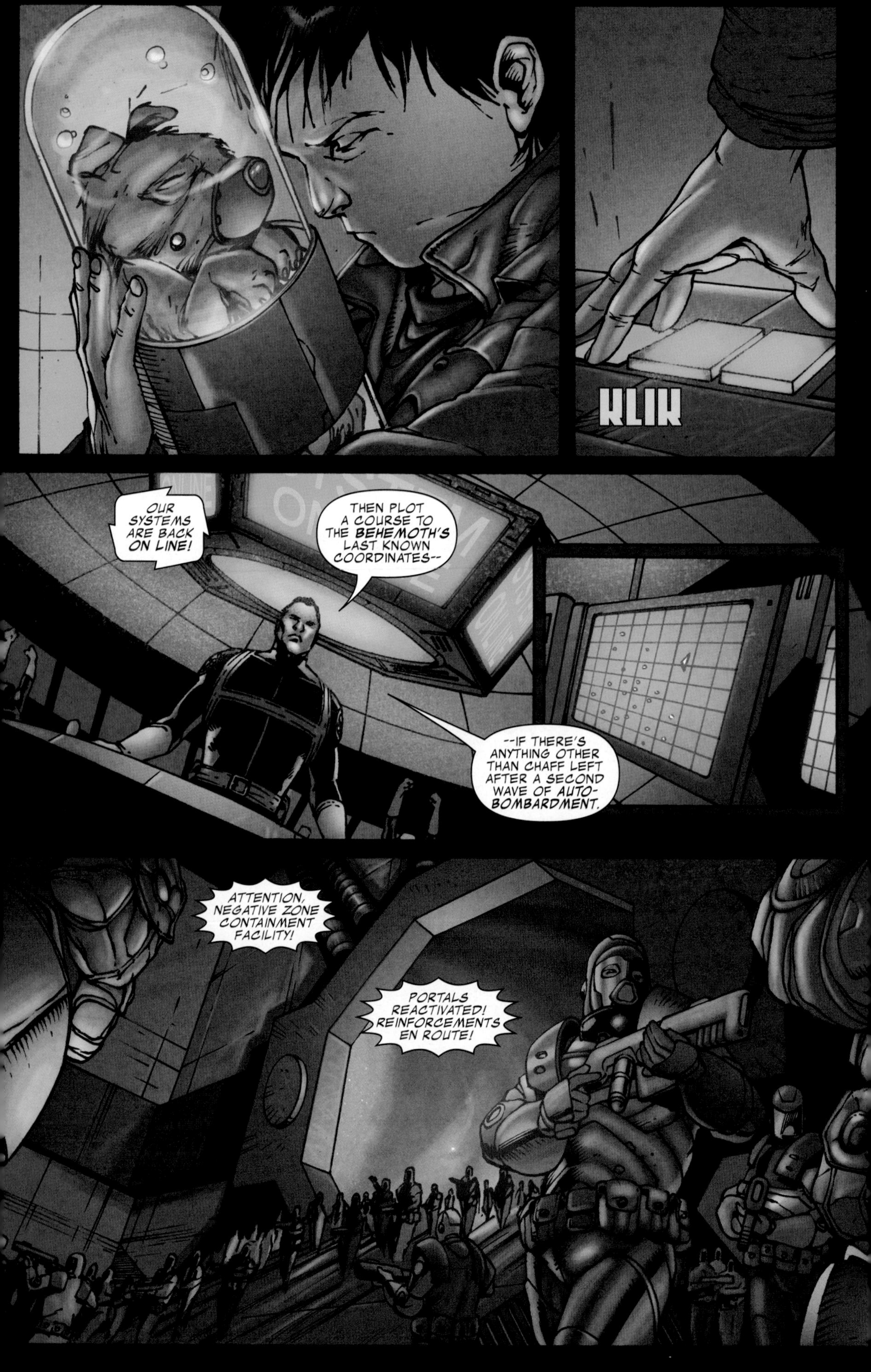
KLIK
OUR SYSTEMS ARE BACK ON LINE!
THEN PLOT A COURSE TO THE BEHEMOTH'S LAST KNOWN COORDINATES--
--IF THERE'S ANYTHING OTHER THAN CHAFF LEFT AFTER A SECOND WAVE OF AUTO-BOMBARDMENT.
ATTENTION, NEGATIVE ZONE CONTAINMENT FACILITY!
PORTALS REACTIVATED! REINFORCEMENTS EN ROUTE!

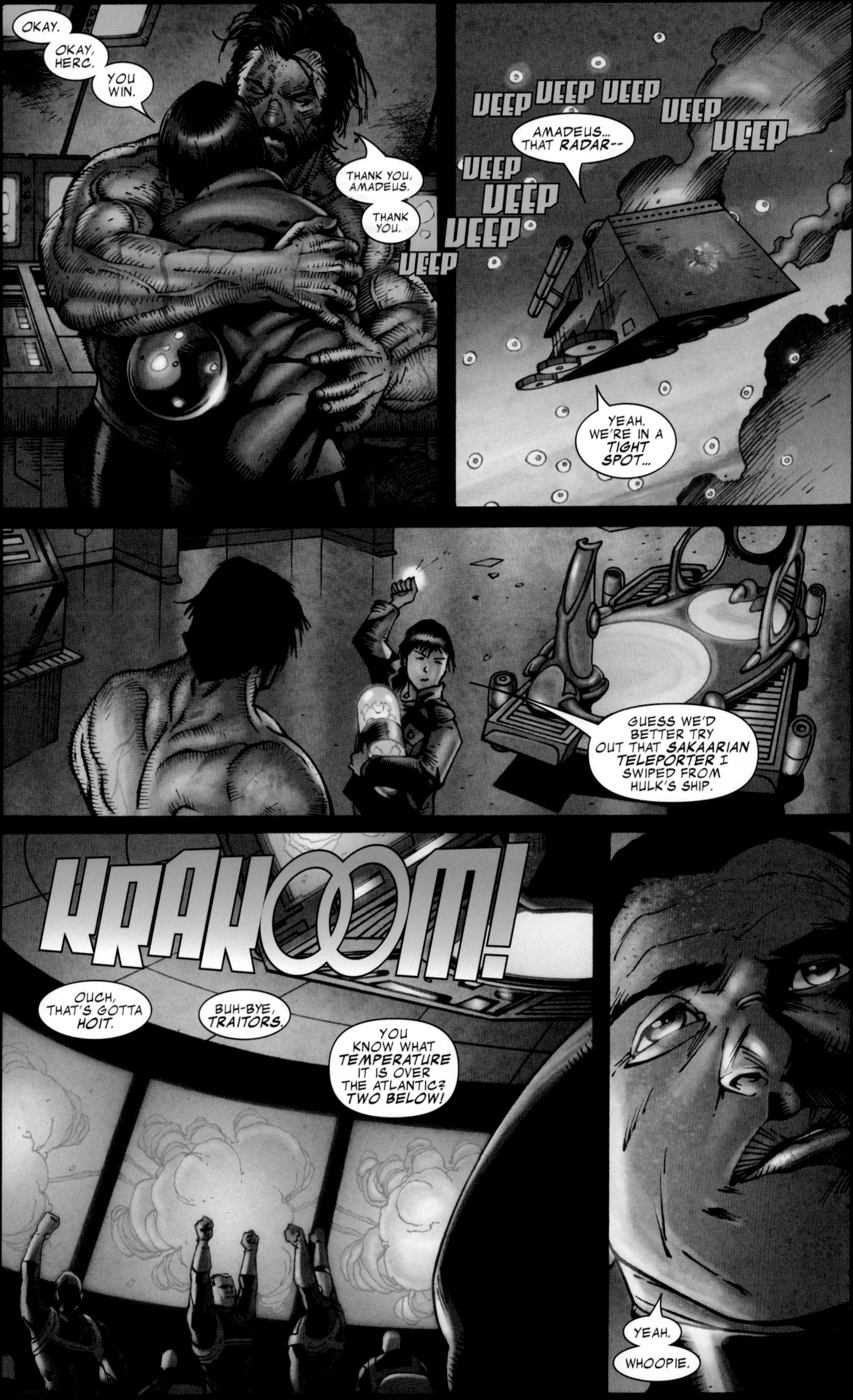
OKAY.
OKAY, HERC.
YOU WIN.
THANK YOU, AMADEUS.
THANK YOU.
VEEP VEEP VEEP VEEP VEEP VEEP VEEP VEEP VEEP
AMADEUS... THAT RADAR--
YEAH. WE'RE IN A TIGHT SPOT...
GUESS WE'D BETTER TRY OUT THAT SAKAARIAN TELEPORTER I SWIPED FROM HULK'S SHIP.
KRAKOOM!
OUCH, THAT'S GOTTA HOIT.
BUH-BYE, TRAITORS.
YOU KNOW WHAT TEMPERATURE IT IS OVER THE ATLANTIC? TWO BELOW!
YEAH.
WHOOPIE.

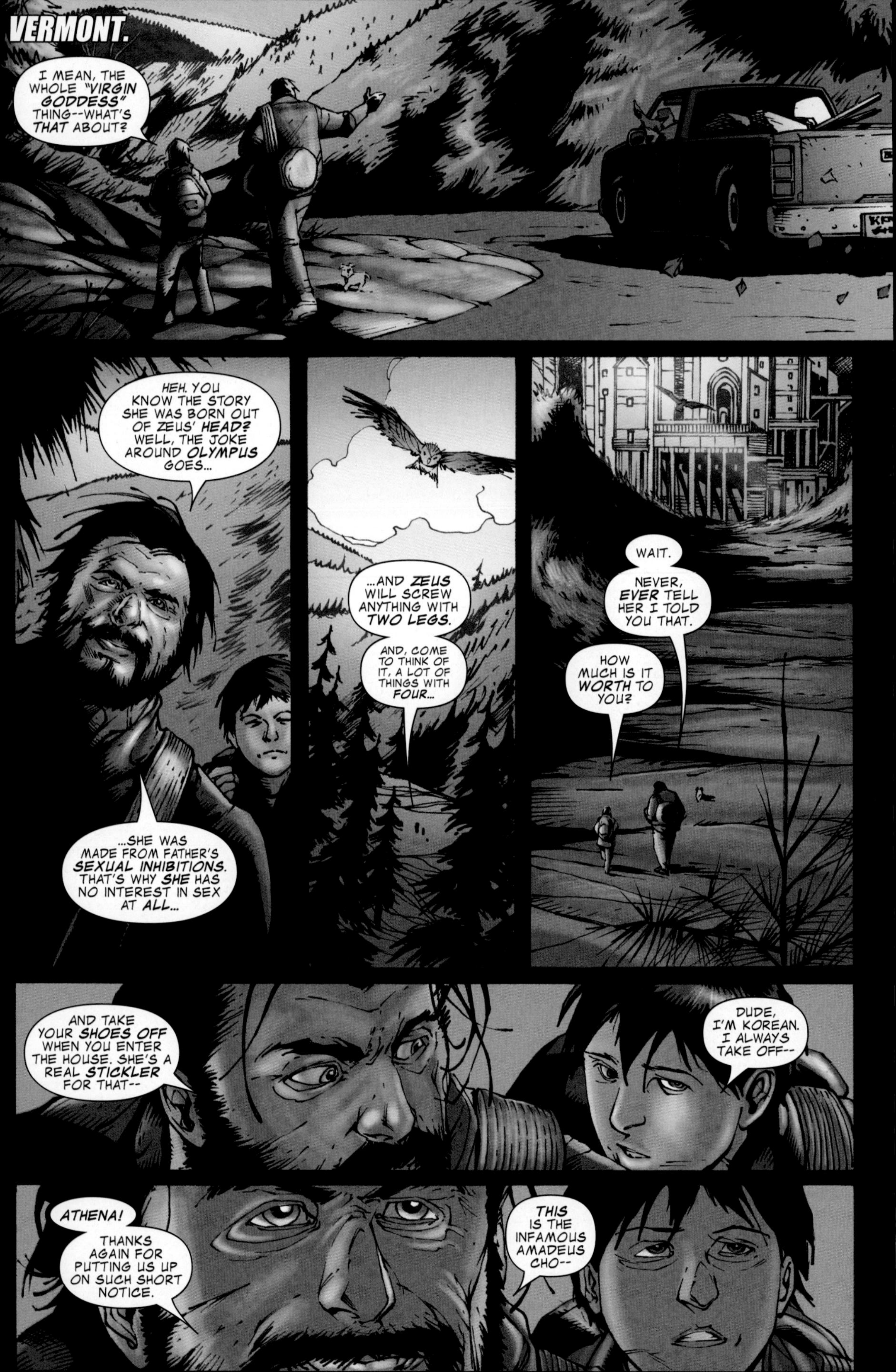
VERMONT.
I MEAN, THE WHOLE "VIRGIN GODDESS" THING--WHAT'S THAT ABOUT?
HEH. YOU KNOW THE STORY SHE WAS BORN OUT OF ZEUS' HEAD? WELL, THE JOKE AROUND OLYMPUS GOES...
...SHE WAS MADE FROM FATHER'S SEXUAL INHIBITIONS. THAT'S WHY SHE HAS NO INTEREST IN SEX AT ALL...
...AND ZEUS WILL SCREW ANYTHING WITH TWO LEGS.
AND, COME TO THINK OF IT, A LOT OF THINGS WITH FOUR...
WAIT.
NEVER, EVER TELL HER I TOLD YOU THAT.
HOW MUCH IS IT WORTH TO YOU?
AND TAKE YOUR SHOES OFF WHEN YOU ENTER THE HOUSE. SHE'S A REAL STICKLER FOR THAT--
DUDE, I'M KOREAN. I ALWAYS TAKE OFF--
ATHENA!
THANKS AGAIN FOR PUTTING US UP ON SUCH SHORT NOTICE.
THIS IS THE INFAMOUS AMADEUS CHO--

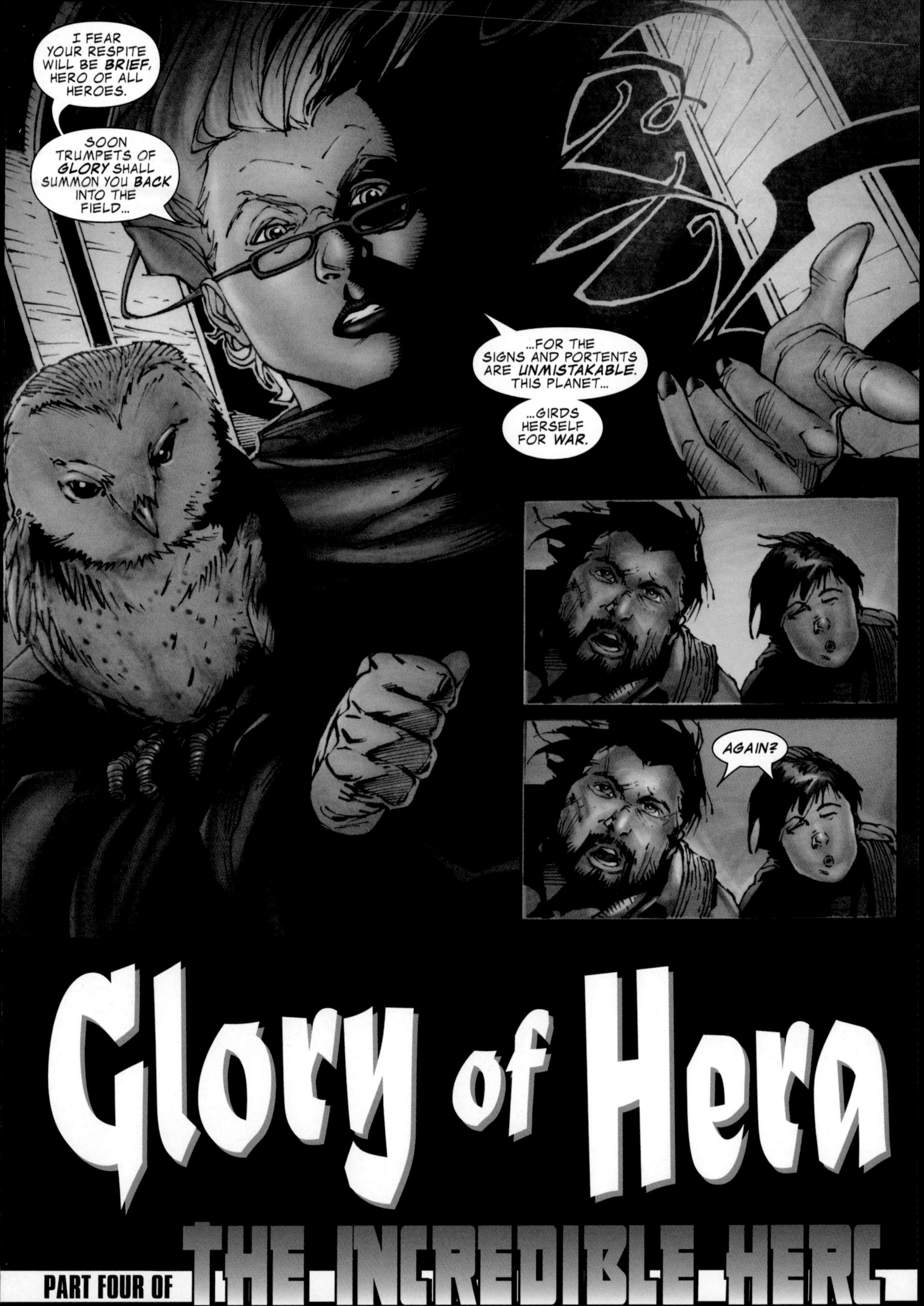
I FEAR YOUR RESPITE WILL BE BRIEF, HERO OF ALL HEROES.
SOON TRUMPETS OF GLORY SHALL SUMMON YOU BACK INTO THE FIELD...
...FOR THE SIGNS AND PORTENTS ARE UNMISTAKABLE. THIS PLANET...
...GIRDS HERSELF FOR WAR.
AGAIN?

Glory of Hera

PART FOUR OF THE INCREDIBLE HERC

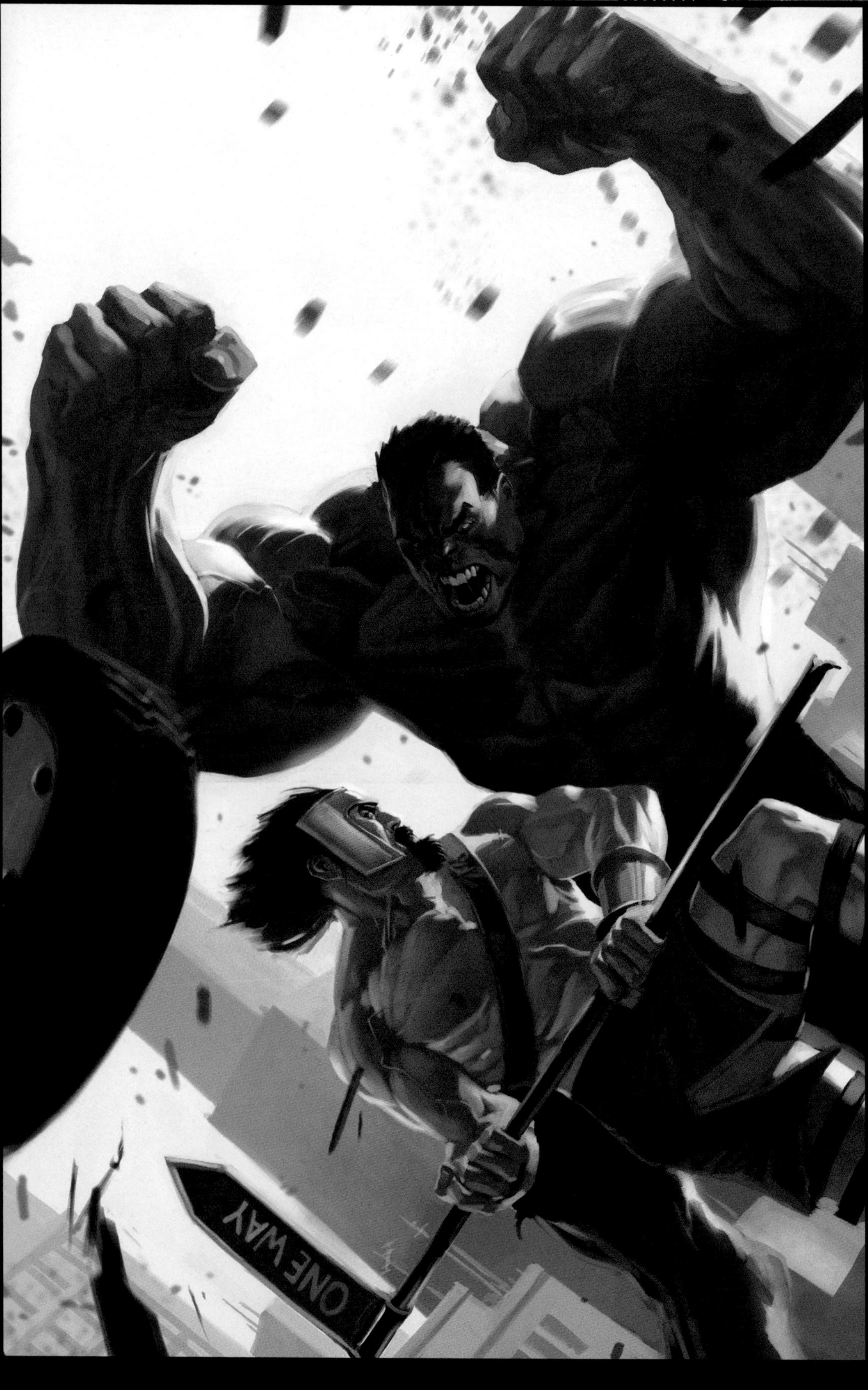
ONE WAY

HULK VS. HERCULES: WHEN TITANS COLLIDE

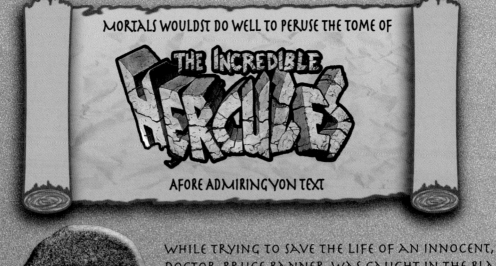

MORTALS WOULDST DO WELL TO PERUSE THE TOME OF

THE INCREDIBLE HERCULES

AFORE ADMIRING YON TEXT

WHILE TRYING TO SAVE THE LIFE OF AN INNOCENT, DOCTOR BRUCE BANNER WAS CAUGHT IN THE BLAST OF A GAMMA BOMB AND BECAME A RAMPAGING MONSTER WITH NEAR-LIMITLESS POWER:

THE INCREDIBLE HULK

FATHERED BY ZEUS, HERCULES IS A GOD AMONGST MEN, RIGHTING WRONGS AND DISPELLING EVILS. AND HE DRINKS BEER. CURRENTLY, HE IS ON THE RUN FROM THE MORTAL ENFORCEMENT AGENCY, S.H.I.E.L.D., ALONG WITH HIS SISTER, ATHENA, AND BOY GENIUS, AMADEUS CHO (WITH PUP IN TOW).

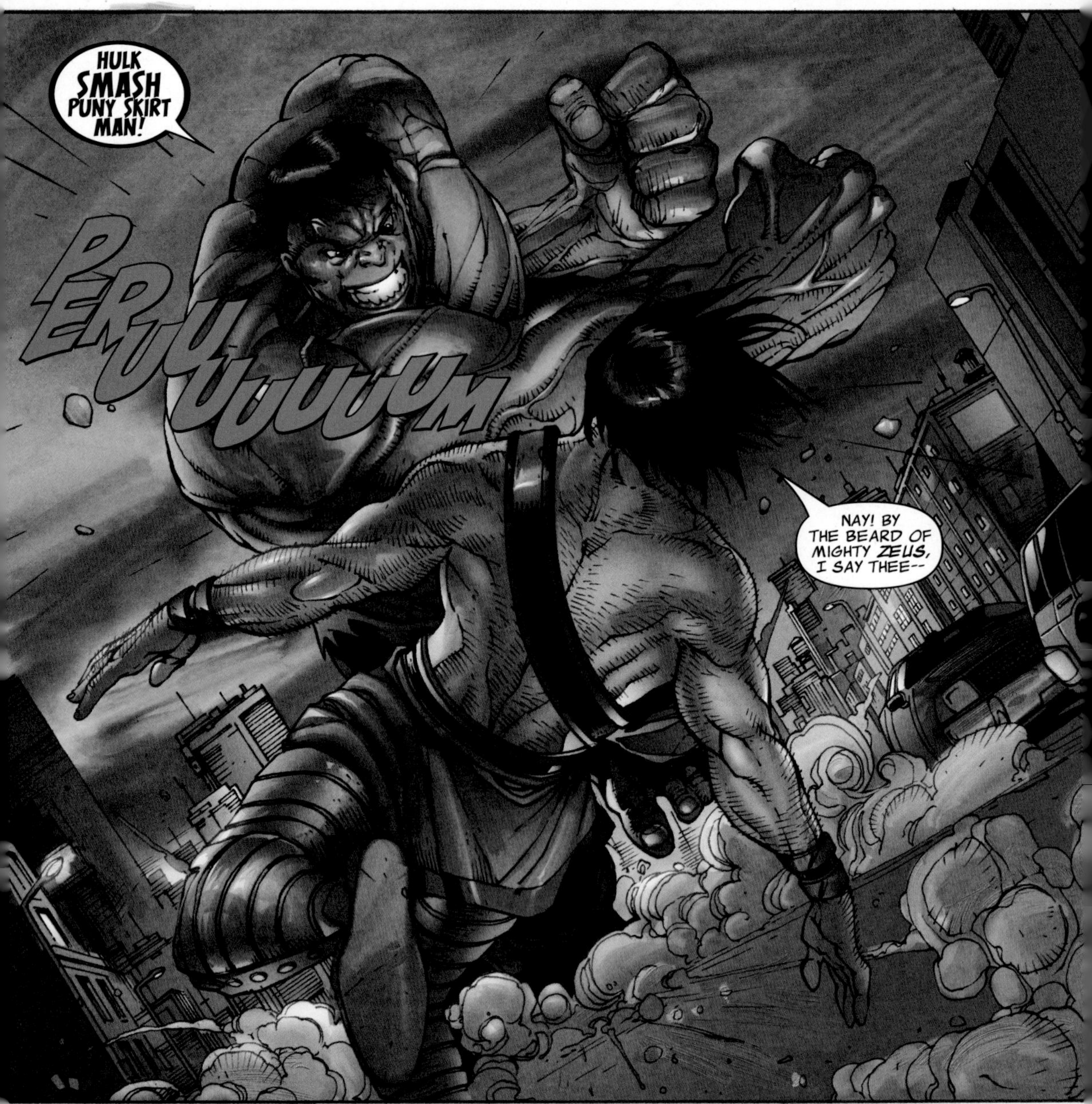
HULK SMASH PUNY SKIRT MAN!
PERUUUUUUUM
NAY! BY THE BEARD OF MIGHTY ZEUS, I SAY THEE--

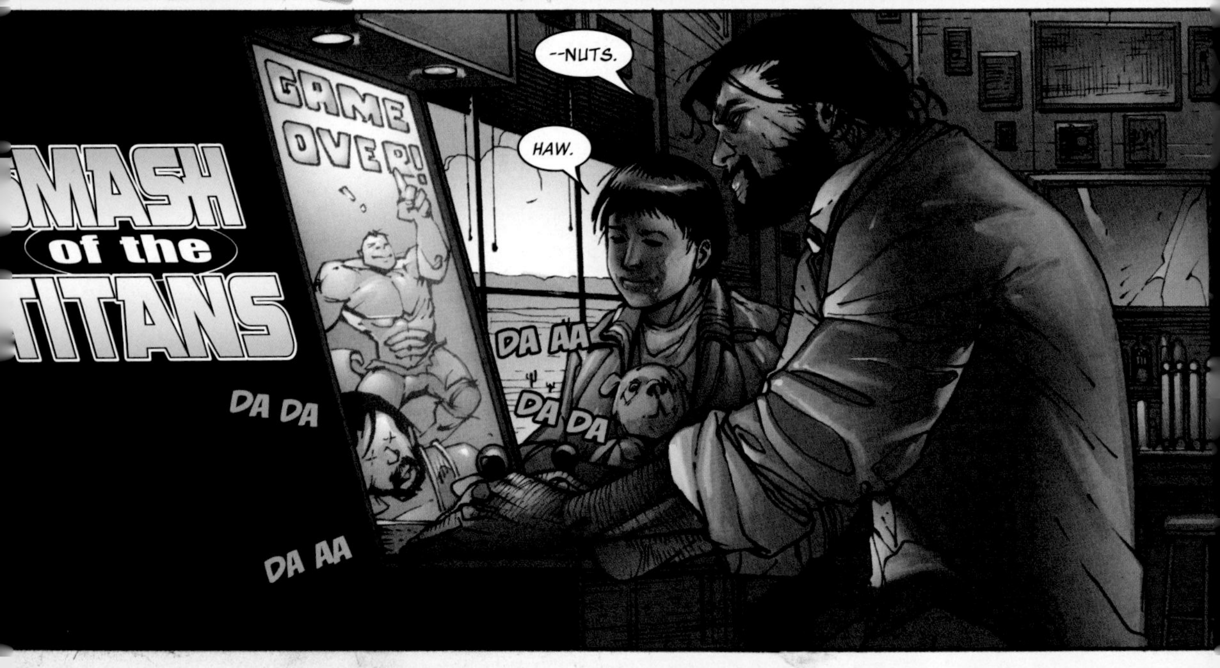
--NUTS.
HAW.
GAME OVER!
SMASH of the TITANS
DA AA
DA DA
DA DA
DA AA

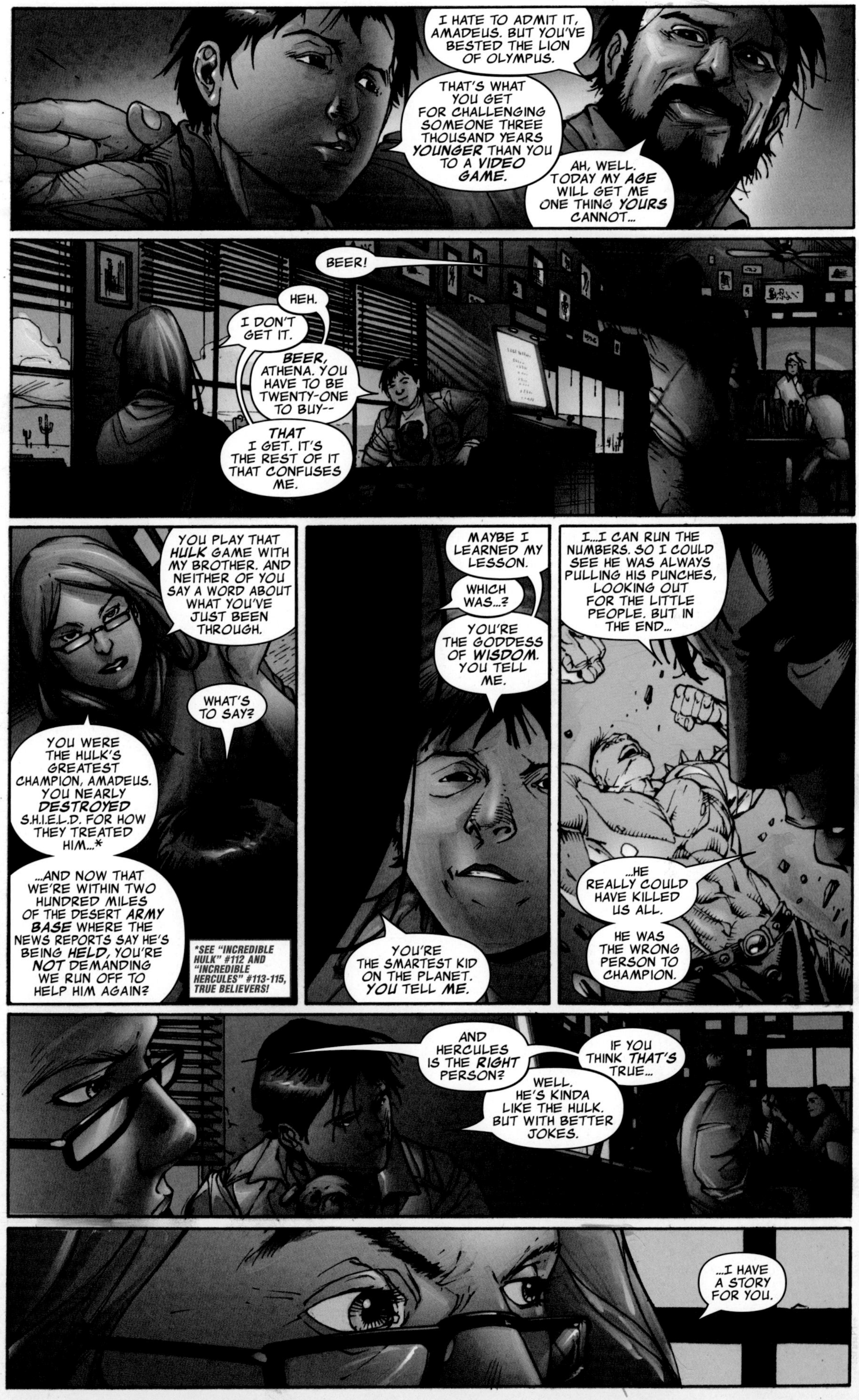
I HATE TO ADMIT IT, AMADEUS. BUT YOU'VE BESTED THE LION OF OLYMPUS.
THAT'S WHAT YOU GET FOR CHALLENGING SOMEONE THREE THOUSAND YEARS YOUNGER THAN YOU TO A VIDEO GAME.
AH, WELL. TODAY MY AGE WILL GET ME ONE THING YOURS CANNOT...
BEER!
HEH.
I DON'T GET IT.
BEER, ATHENA. YOU HAVE TO BE TWENTY-ONE TO BUY--
THAT I GET. IT'S THE REST OF IT THAT CONFUSES ME.
YOU PLAY THAT HULK GAME WITH MY BROTHER. AND NEITHER OF YOU SAY A WORD ABOUT WHAT YOU'VE JUST BEEN THROUGH.
WHAT'S TO SAY?
YOU WERE THE HULK'S GREATEST CHAMPION, AMADEUS. YOU NEARLY DESTROYED S.H.I.E.L.D. FOR HOW THEY TREATED HIM...*
...AND NOW THAT WE'RE WITHIN TWO HUNDRED MILES OF THE DESERT ARMY BASE WHERE THE NEWS REPORTS SAY HE'S BEING HELD, YOU'RE NOT DEMANDING WE RUN OFF TO HELP HIM AGAIN?
*SEE "INCREDIBLE HULK" #112 AND "INCREDIBLE HERCULES" #113-115, TRUE BELIEVERS!
MAYBE I LEARNED MY LESSON.
WHICH WAS...?
YOU'RE THE GODDESS OF WISDOM. YOU TELL ME.
YOU'RE THE SMARTEST KID ON THE PLANET. YOU TELL ME.
I...I CAN RUN THE NUMBERS. SO I COULD SEE HE WAS ALWAYS PULLING HIS PUNCHES, LOOKING OUT FOR THE LITTLE PEOPLE. BUT IN THE END...
...HE REALLY COULD HAVE KILLED US ALL.
HE WAS THE WRONG PERSON TO CHAMPION.
AND HERCULES IS THE RIGHT PERSON?
IF YOU THINK THAT'S TRUE...
WELL. HE'S KINDA LIKE THE HULK. BUT WITH BETTER JOKES.
...I HAVE A STORY FOR YOU.

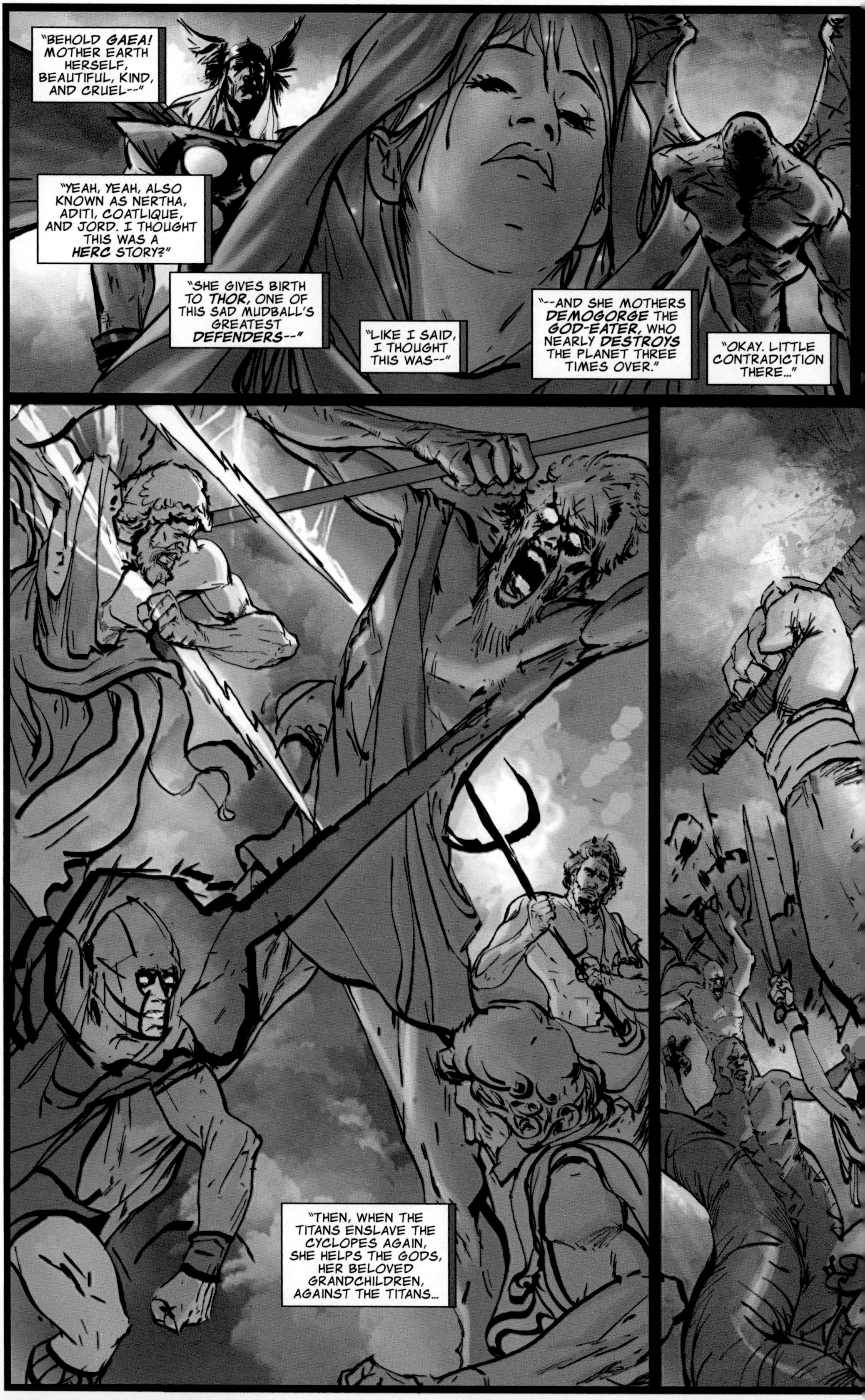
"BEHOLD GAEA! MOTHER EARTH HERSELF, BEAUTIFUL, KIND, AND CRUEL--"
"YEAH, YEAH, ALSO KNOWN AS NERTHA, ADITI, COATLIQUE, AND JORD. I THOUGHT THIS WAS A HERC STORY?"
"SHE GIVES BIRTH TO THOR, ONE OF THIS SAD MUDBALL'S GREATEST DEFENDERS--"
"LIKE I SAID, I THOUGHT THIS WAS--"
"--AND SHE MOTHERS DEMOGORGE THE GOD-EATER, WHO NEARLY DESTROYS THE PLANET THREE TIMES OVER."
"OKAY. LITTLE CONTRADICTION THERE..."
"THEN, WHEN THE TITANS ENSLAVE THE CYCLOPES AGAIN, SHE HELPS THE GODS, HER BELOVED GRANDCHILDREN, AGAINST THE TITANS...

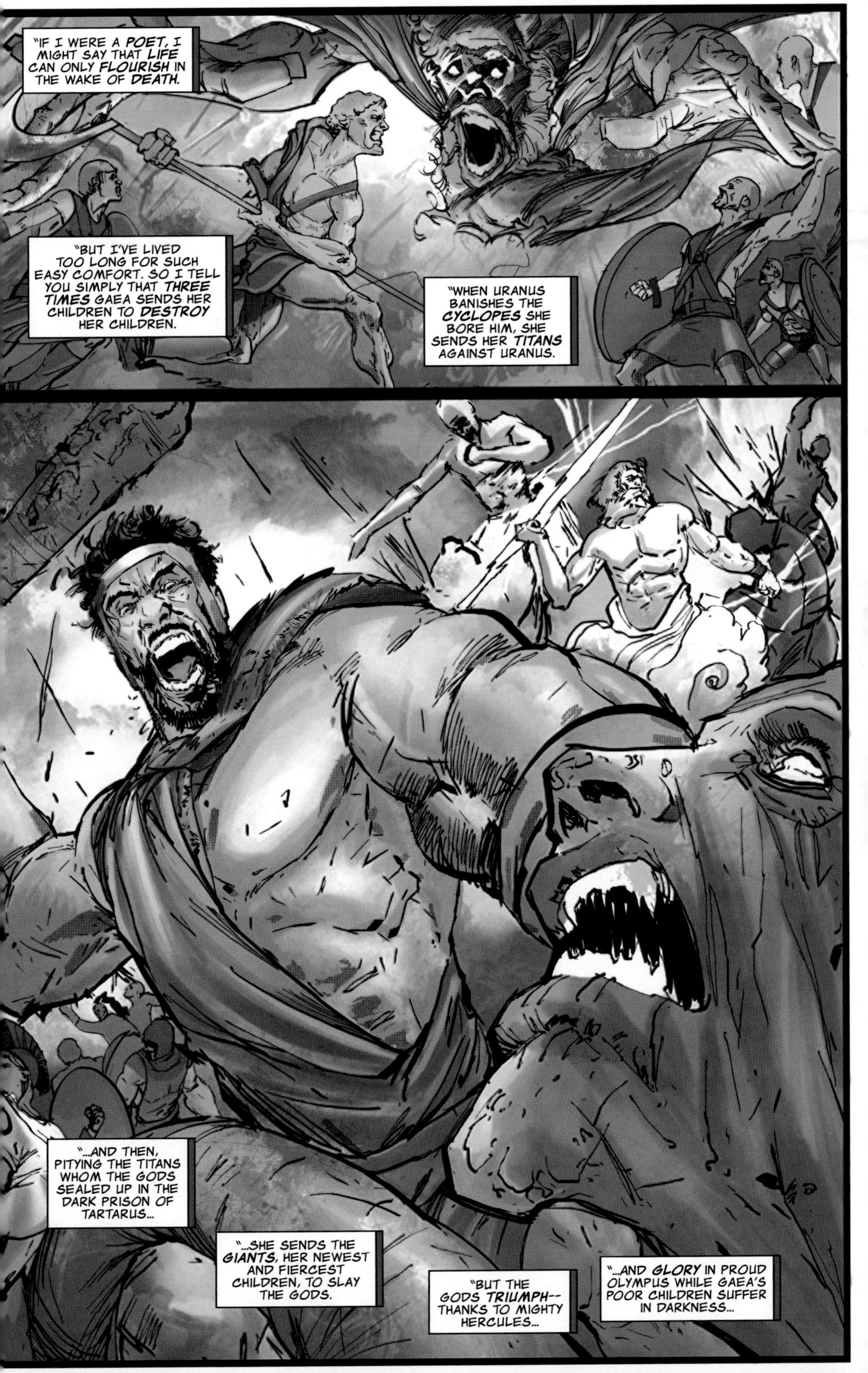
"IF I WERE A POET, I MIGHT SAY THAT LIFE CAN ONLY FLOURISH IN THE WAKE OF DEATH.
"BUT I'VE LIVED TOO LONG FOR SUCH EASY COMFORT. SO I TELL YOU SIMPLY THAT THREE TIMES GAEA SENDS HER CHILDREN TO DESTROY HER CHILDREN.
"WHEN URANUS BANISHES THE CYCLOPES SHE BORE HIM, SHE SENDS HER TITANS AGAINST URANUS.
"...AND THEN, PITYING THE TITANS WHOM THE GODS SEALED UP IN THE DARK PRISON OF TARTARUS...
"...SHE SENDS THE GIANTS, HER NEWEST AND FIERCEST CHILDREN, TO SLAY THE GODS.
"BUT THE GODS TRIUMPH-- THANKS TO MIGHTY HERCULES...
"...AND GLORY IN PROUD OLYMPUS WHILE GAEA'S POOR CHILDREN SUFFER IN DARKNESS...

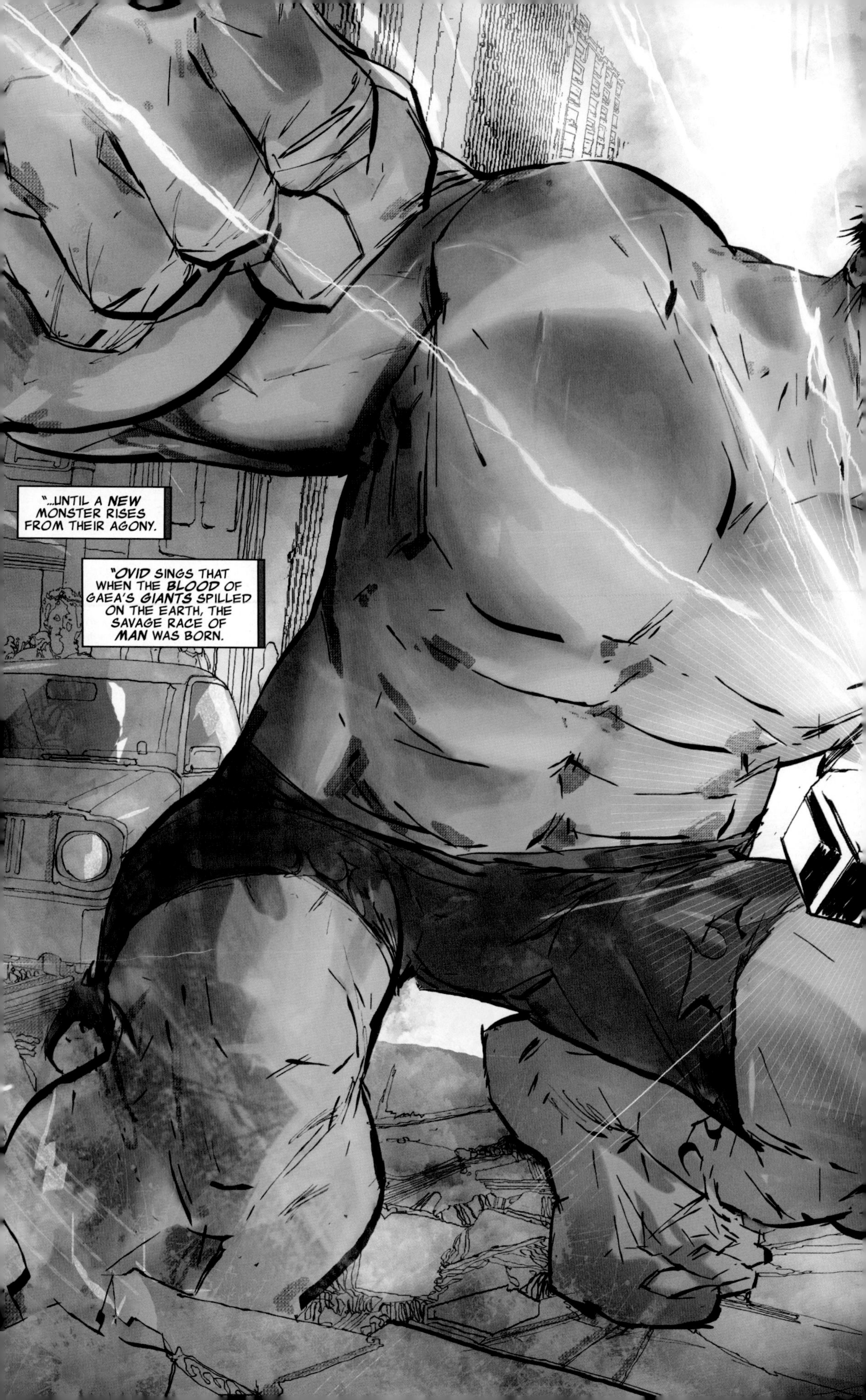

"...UNTIL A NEW MONSTER RISES FROM THEIR AGONY.
"OVID SINGS THAT WHEN THE BLOOD OF GAEA'S GIANTS SPILLED ON THE EARTH, THE SAVAGE RACE OF MAN WAS BORN.

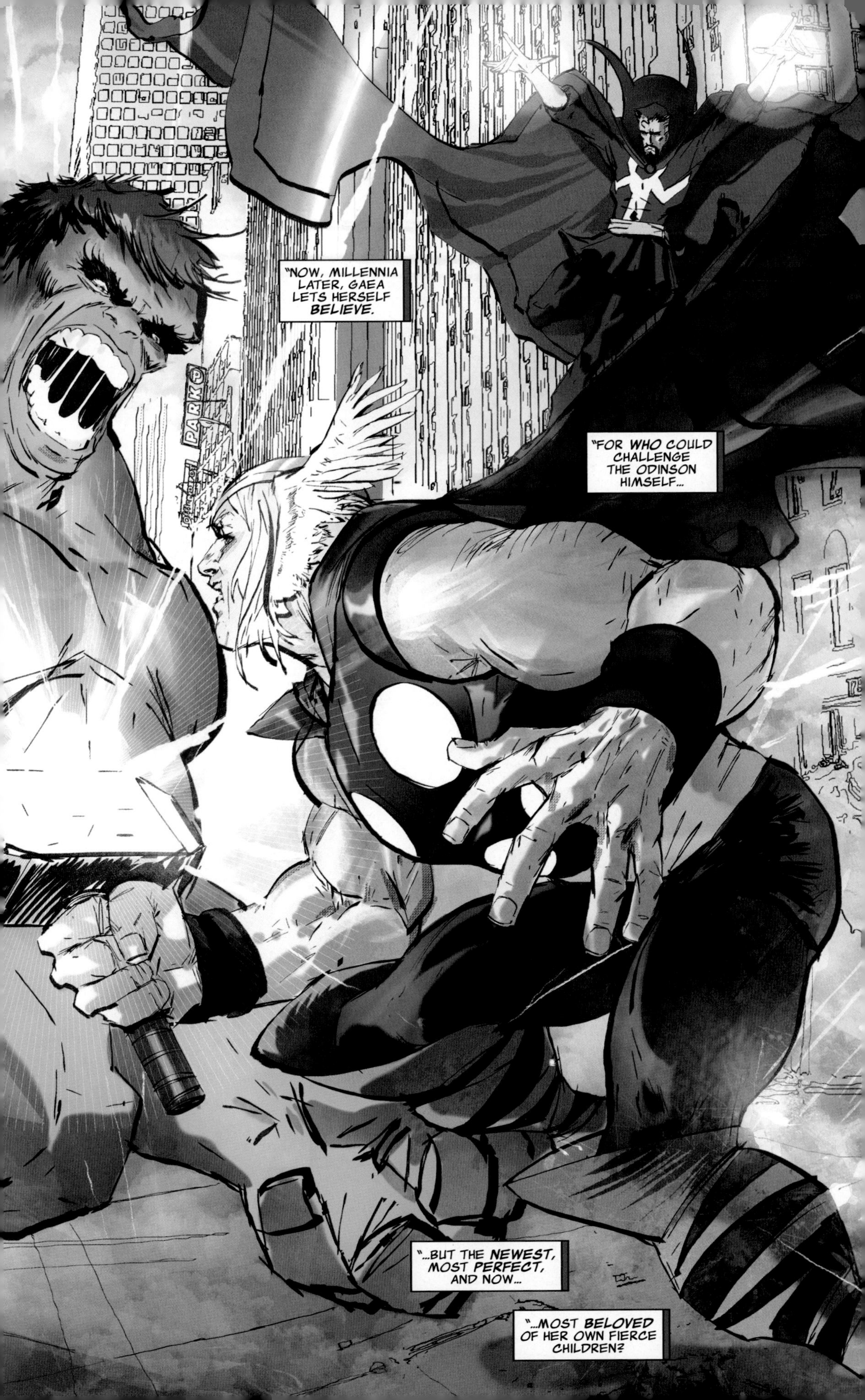
"NOW, MILLENNIA LATER, GAEA LETS HERSELF BELIEVE.
PARK
"FOR WHO COULD CHALLENGE THE ODINSON HIMSELF...
"...BUT THE NEWEST, MOST PERFECT, AND NOW...
"...MOST BELOVED OF HER OWN FIERCE CHILDREN?

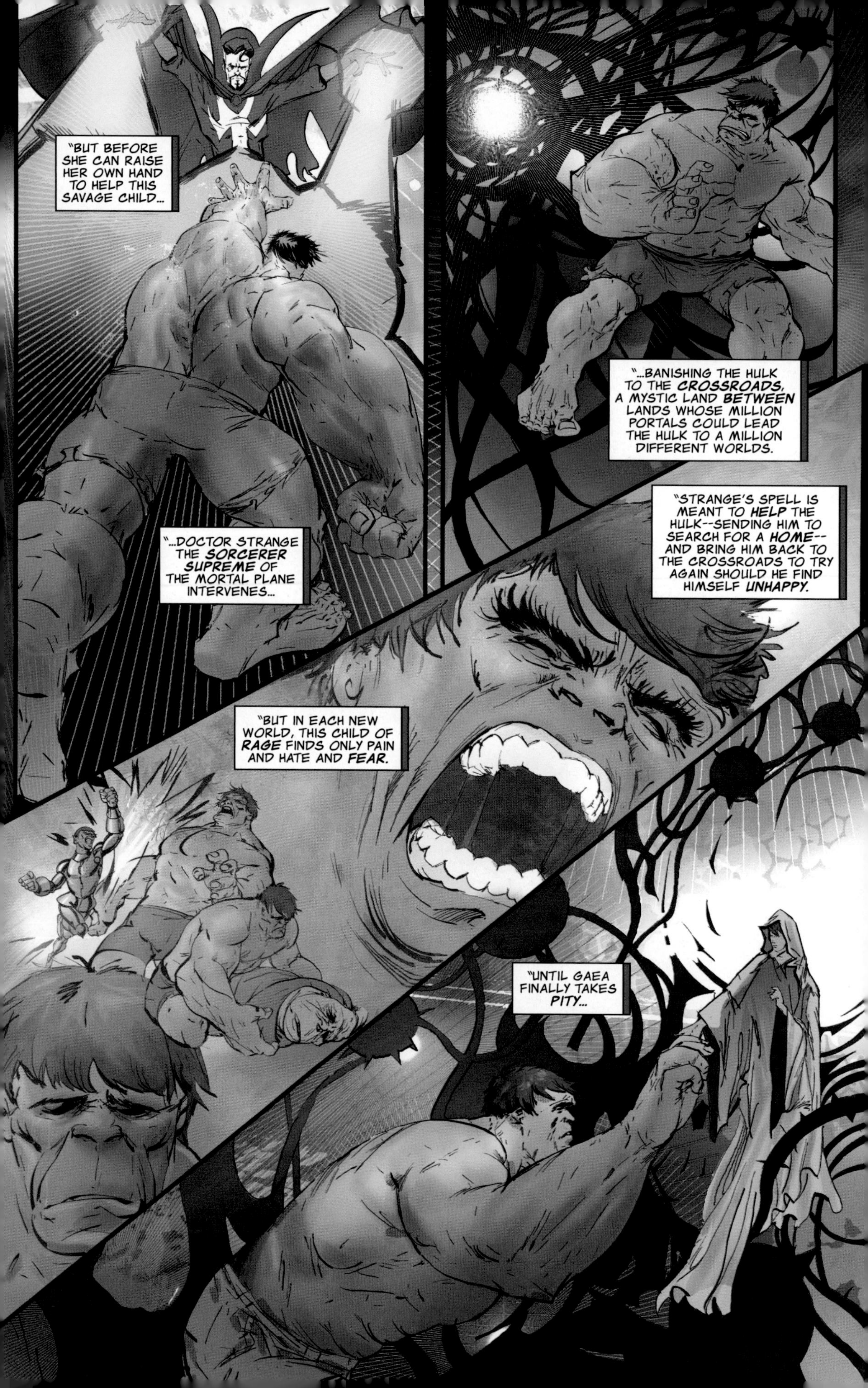
"BUT BEFORE SHE CAN RAISE HER OWN HAND TO HELP THIS SAVAGE CHILD...
"...DOCTOR STRANGE THE SORCERER SUPREME OF THE MORTAL PLANE INTERVENES...
"...BANISHING THE HULK TO THE CROSSROADS, A MYSTIC LAND BETWEEN LANDS WHOSE MILLION PORTALS COULD LEAD THE HULK TO A MILLION DIFFERENT WORLDS.
"STRANGE'S SPELL IS MEANT TO HELP THE HULK--SENDING HIM TO SEARCH FOR A HOME--AND BRING HIM BACK TO THE CROSSROADS TO TRY AGAIN SHOULD HE FIND HIMSELF UNHAPPY.
"BUT IN EACH NEW WORLD, THIS CHILD OF RAGE FINDS ONLY PAIN AND HATE AND FEAR.
"UNTIL GAEA FINALLY TAKES PITY...

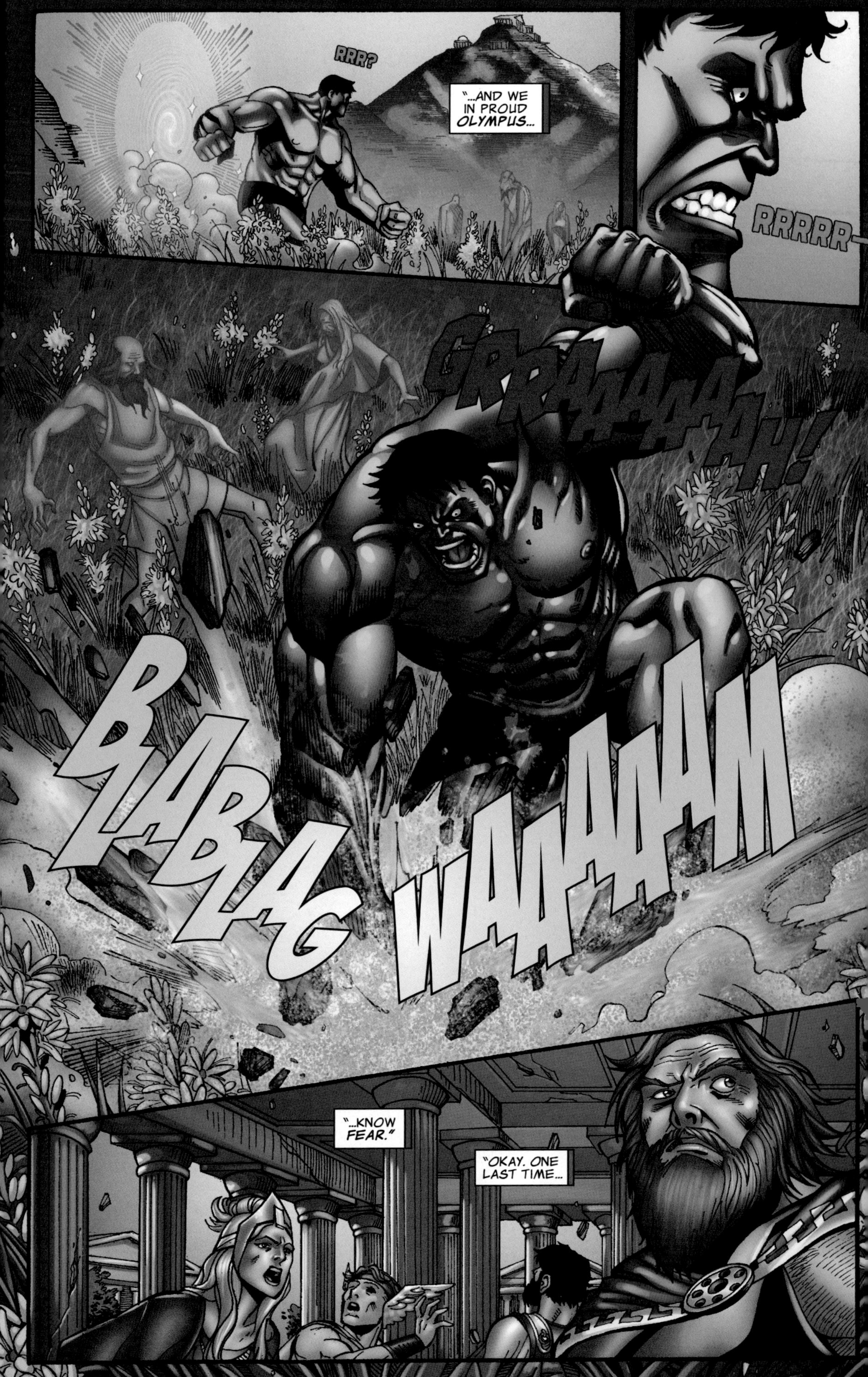
RRR?
"...AND WE IN PROUD OLYMPUS...
RRRRR—
GRRAAAAAAAH!
BLABLAG
WAAAAAM
"...KNOW FEAR."
"OKAY. ONE LAST TIME...

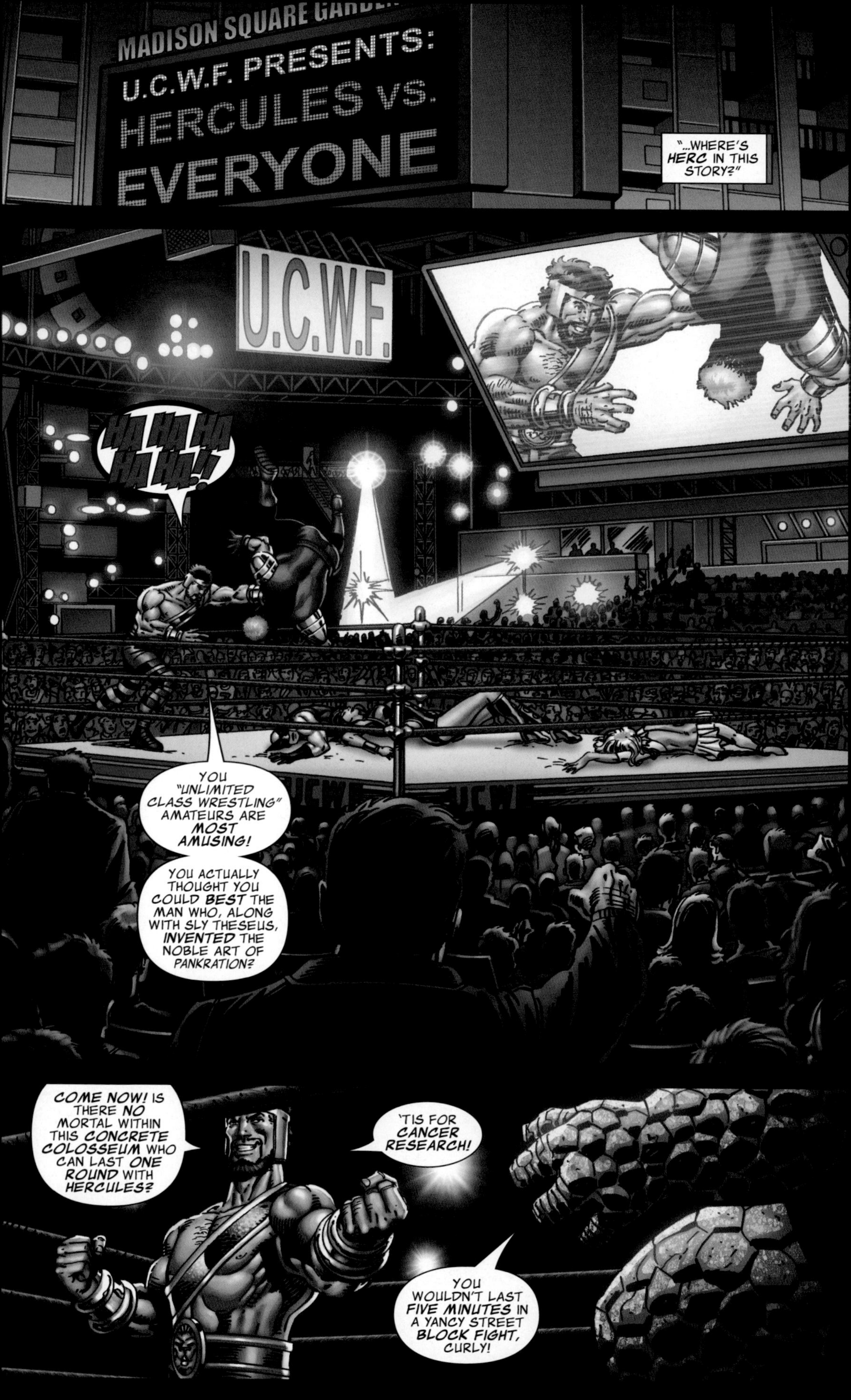
MADISON SQUARE GARDEN
U.C.W.F. PRESENTS: HERCULES VS. EVERYONE
"...WHERE'S HERC IN THIS STORY?"
U.C.W.F.
HA HA HA HA HA!!
YOU "UNLIMITED CLASS WRESTLING" AMATEURS ARE MOST AMUSING!
YOU ACTUALLY THOUGHT YOU COULD BEST THE MAN WHO, ALONG WITH SLY THESEUS, INVENTED THE NOBLE ART OF PANKRATION?
COME NOW! IS THERE NO MORTAL WITHIN THIS CONCRETE COLOSSEUM WHO CAN LAST ONE ROUND WITH HERCULES?
'TIS FOR CANCER RESEARCH!
YOU WOULDN'T LAST FIVE MINUTES IN A YANCY STREET BLOCK FIGHT, CURLY!

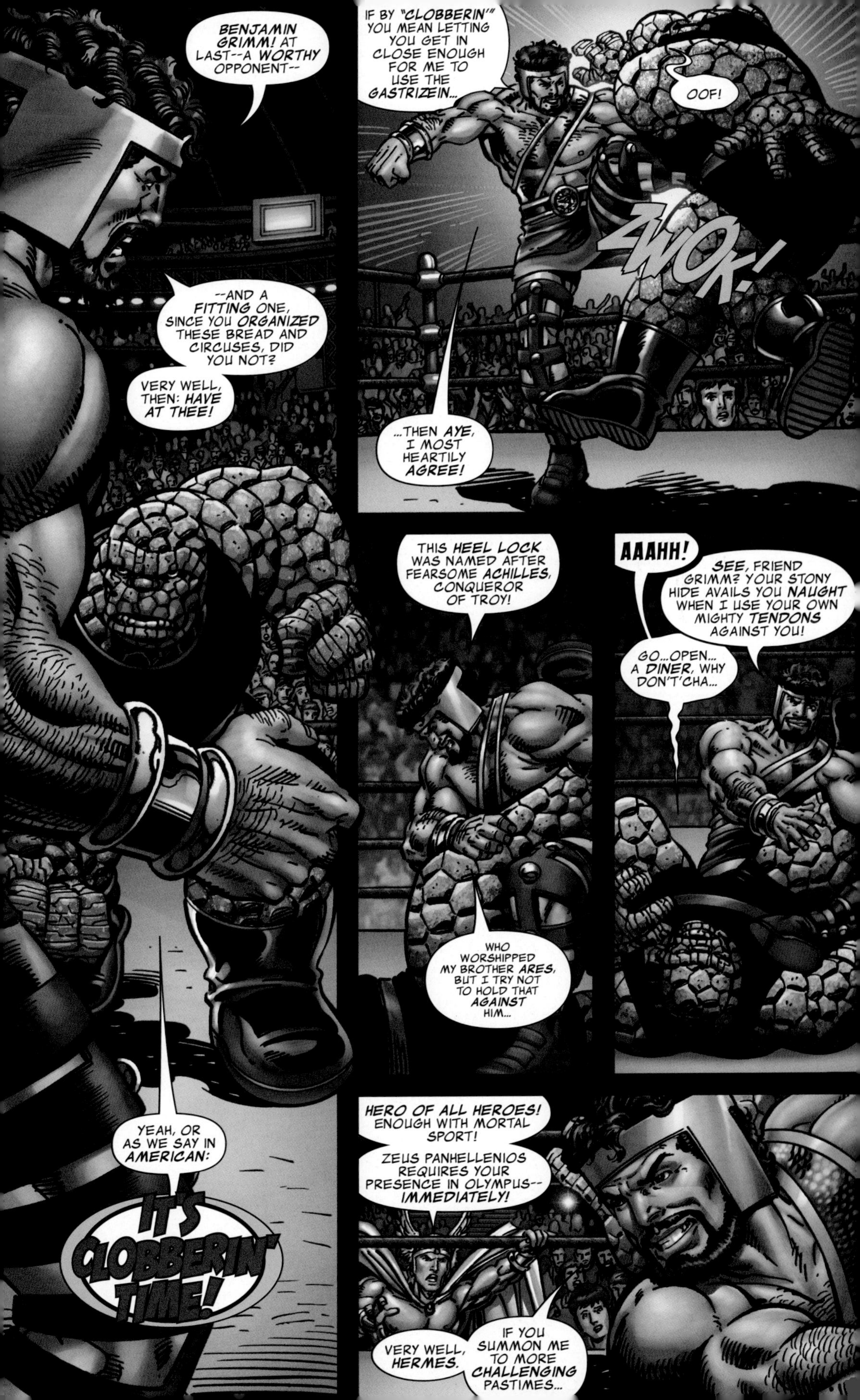

BENJAMIN GRIMM! AT LAST--A WORTHY OPPONENT--
--AND A FITTING ONE, SINCE YOU ORGANIZED THESE BREAD AND CIRCUSES, DID YOU NOT?
VERY WELL, THEN: HAVE AT THEE!
YEAH, OR AS WE SAY IN AMERICAN:
IT'S CLOBBERIN' TIME!
IF BY "CLOBBERIN'" YOU MEAN LETTING YOU GET IN CLOSE ENOUGH FOR ME TO USE THE GASTRIZEIN...
OOF!
ZWOK!
...THEN AYE, I MOST HEARTILY AGREE!
THIS HEEL LOCK WAS NAMED AFTER FEARSOME ACHILLES, CONQUEROR OF TROY!
WHO WORSHIPPED MY BROTHER ARES, BUT I TRY NOT TO HOLD THAT AGAINST HIM...
AAAHH!
SEE, FRIEND GRIMM? YOUR STONY HIDE AVAILS YOU NAUGHT WHEN I USE YOUR OWN MIGHTY TENDONS AGAINST YOU!
GO...OPEN... A DINER, WHY DON'T'CHA...
HERO OF ALL HEROES! ENOUGH WITH MORTAL SPORT!
ZEUS PANHELLENIOS REQUIRES YOUR PRESENCE IN OLYMPUS--IMMEDIATELY!
VERY WELL, HERMES.
IF YOU SUMMON ME TO MORE CHALLENGING PASTIMES...

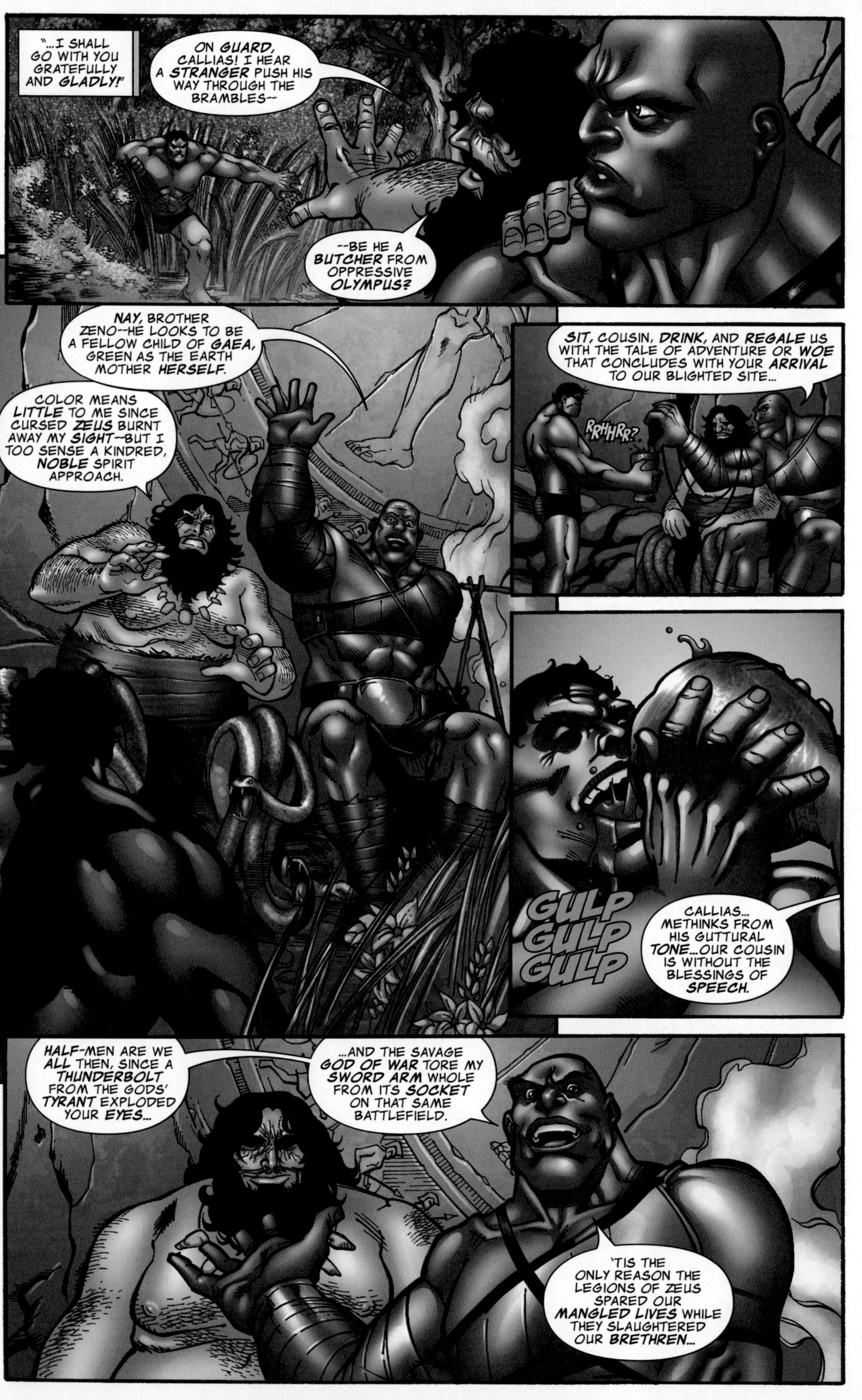
"...I SHALL GO WITH YOU GRATEFULLY AND GLADLY!"
ON GUARD, CALLIAS! I HEAR A STRANGER PUSH HIS WAY THROUGH THE BRAMBLES--
--BE HE A BUTCHER FROM OPPRESSIVE OLYMPUS?
NAY, BROTHER ZENO--HE LOOKS TO BE A FELLOW CHILD OF GAEA, GREEN AS THE EARTH MOTHER HERSELF.
COLOR MEANS LITTLE TO ME SINCE CURSED ZEUS BURNT AWAY MY SIGHT--BUT I TOO SENSE A KINDRED, NOBLE SPIRIT APPROACH.
SIT, COUSIN, DRINK, AND REGALE US WITH THE TALE OF ADVENTURE OR WOE THAT CONCLUDES WITH YOUR ARRIVAL TO OUR BLIGHTED SITE...
RRHHRR?
GULP GULP GULP
CALLIAS... METHINKS FROM HIS GUTTURAL TONE...OUR COUSIN IS WITHOUT THE BLESSINGS OF SPEECH.
HALF-MEN ARE WE ALL THEN, SINCE A THUNDERBOLT FROM THE GODS' TYRANT EXPLODED YOUR EYES...
...AND THE SAVAGE GOD OF WAR TORE MY SWORD ARM WHOLE FROM ITS SOCKET ON THAT SAME BATTLEFIELD.
'TIS THE ONLY REASON THE LEGIONS OF ZEUS SPARED OUR MANGLED LIVES WHILE THEY SLAUGHTERED OUR BRETHREN...

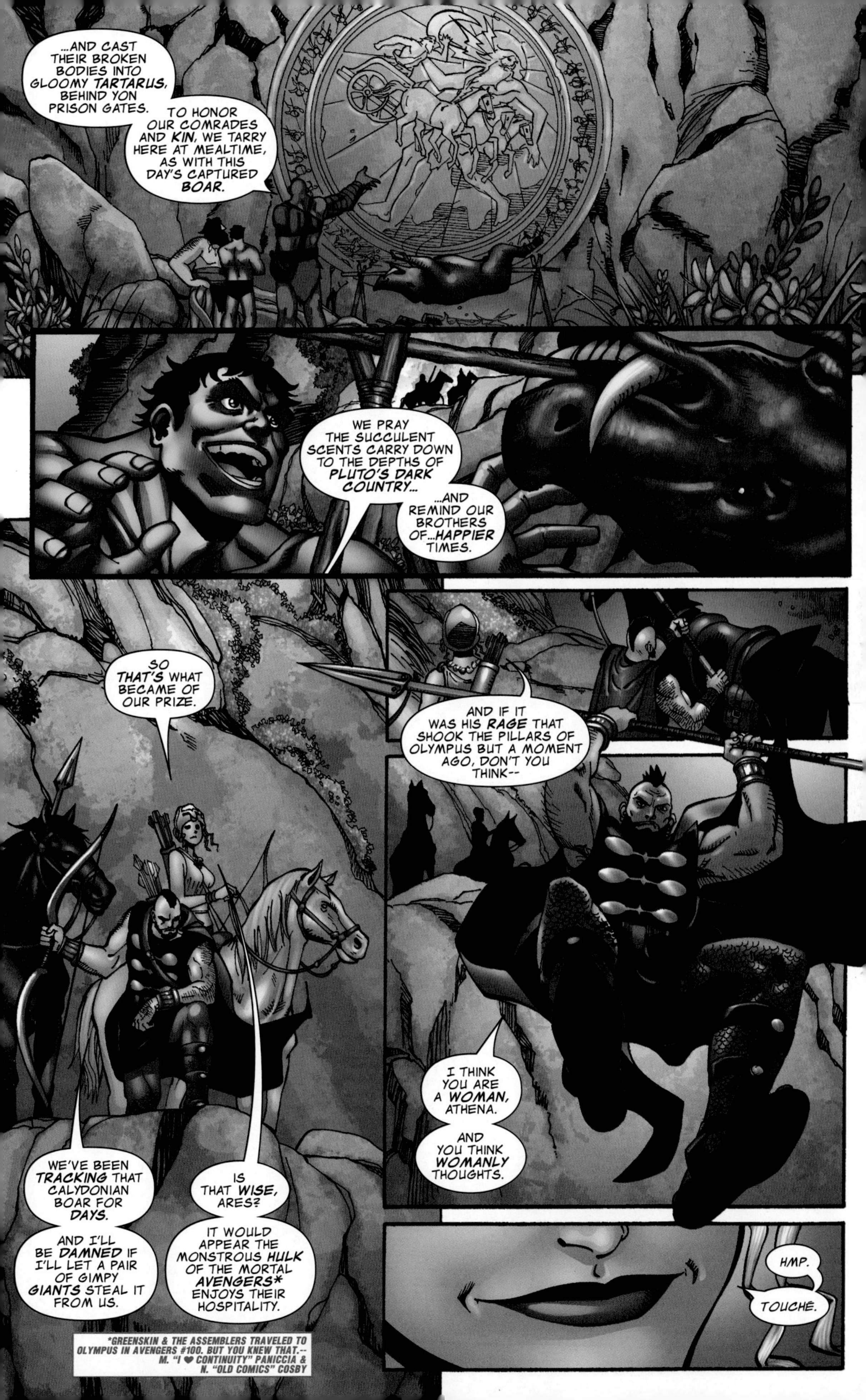

...AND CAST THEIR BROKEN BODIES INTO GLOOMY TARTARUS, BEHIND YON PRISON GATES.
TO HONOR OUR COMRADES AND KIN, WE TARRY HERE AT MEALTIME, AS WITH THIS DAY'S CAPTURED BOAR.
WE PRAY THE SUCCULENT SCENTS CARRY DOWN TO THE DEPTHS OF PLUTO'S DARK COUNTRY...
...AND REMIND OUR BROTHERS OF...HAPPIER TIMES.
SO THAT'S WHAT BECAME OF OUR PRIZE.
WE'VE BEEN TRACKING THAT CALYDONIAN BOAR FOR DAYS.
AND I'LL BE DAMNED IF I'LL LET A PAIR OF GIMPY GIANTS STEAL IT FROM US.
IS THAT WISE, ARES?
IT WOULD APPEAR THE MONSTROUS HULK OF THE MORTAL AVENGERS* ENJOYS THEIR HOSPITALITY.
AND IF IT WAS HIS RAGE THAT SHOOK THE PILLARS OF OLYMPUS BUT A MOMENT AGO, DON'T YOU THINK--
I THINK YOU ARE A WOMAN, ATHENA.
AND YOU THINK WOMANLY THOUGHTS.
HMP.
TOUCHÉ.
*GREENSKIN & THE ASSEMBLERS TRAVELED TO OLYMPUS IN AVENGERS #100. BUT YOU KNEW THAT.-- M. "I ♥ CONTINUITY" PANICCIA & N. "OLD COMICS" COSBY

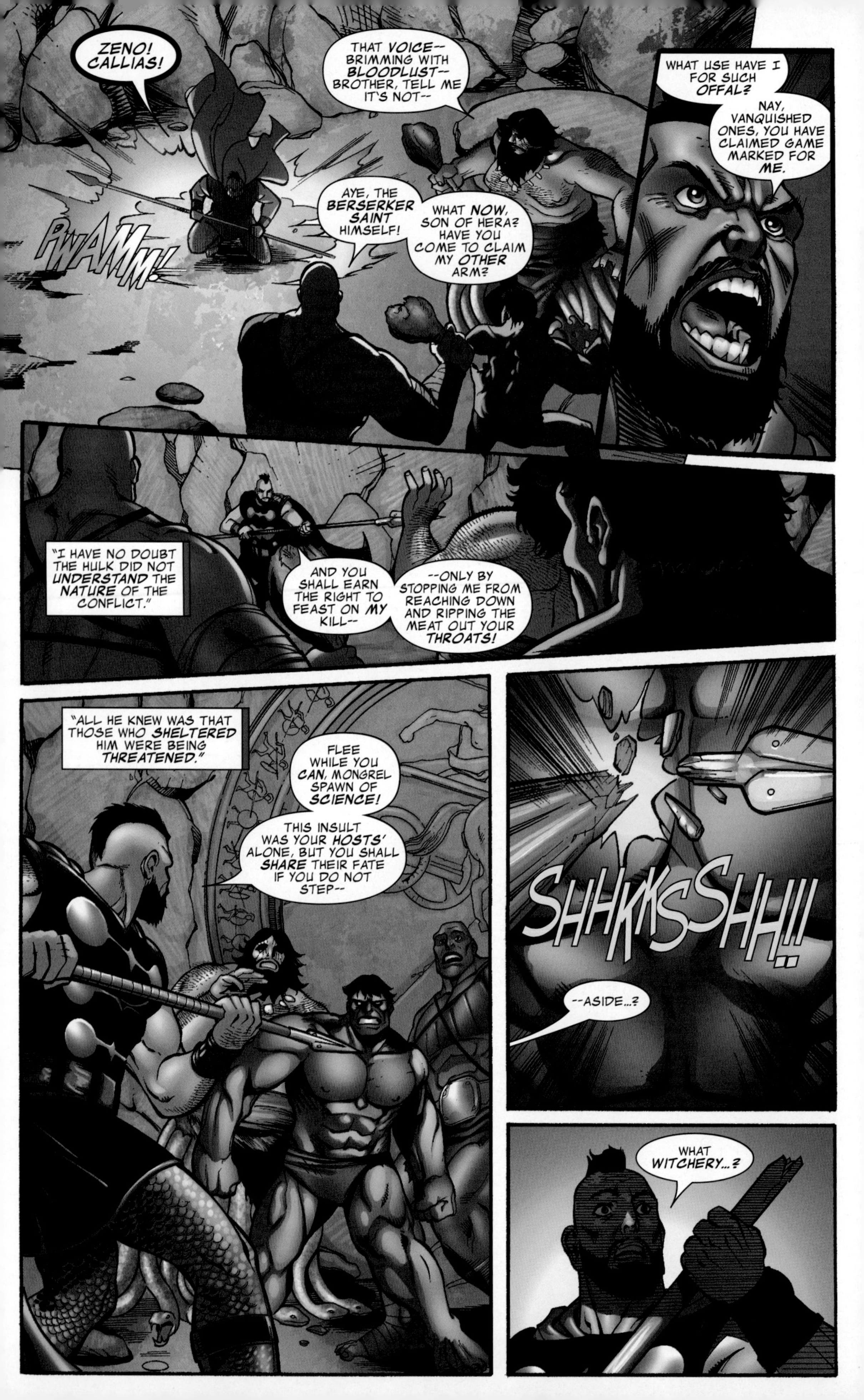
ZENO! CALLIAS!
THAT VOICE-- BRIMMING WITH BLOODLUST-- BROTHER, TELL ME IT'S NOT--
PWAMM!
AYE, THE BERSERKER SAINT HIMSELF!
WHAT NOW, SON OF HERA? HAVE YOU COME TO CLAIM MY OTHER ARM?
WHAT USE HAVE I FOR SUCH OFFAL?
NAY, VANQUISHED ONES, YOU HAVE CLAIMED GAME MARKED FOR ME.
"I HAVE NO DOUBT THE HULK DID NOT UNDERSTAND THE NATURE OF THE CONFLICT."
AND YOU SHALL EARN THE RIGHT TO FEAST ON MY KILL--
--ONLY BY STOPPING ME FROM REACHING DOWN AND RIPPING THE MEAT OUT YOUR THROATS!
"ALL HE KNEW WAS THAT THOSE WHO SHELTERED HIM WERE BEING THREATENED."
FLEE WHILE YOU CAN, MONGREL SPAWN OF SCIENCE!
THIS INSULT WAS YOUR HOSTS' ALONE, BUT YOU SHALL SHARE THEIR FATE IF YOU DO NOT STEP--
SHHKKSSHH!!
--ASIDE...?
WHAT WITCHERY...?

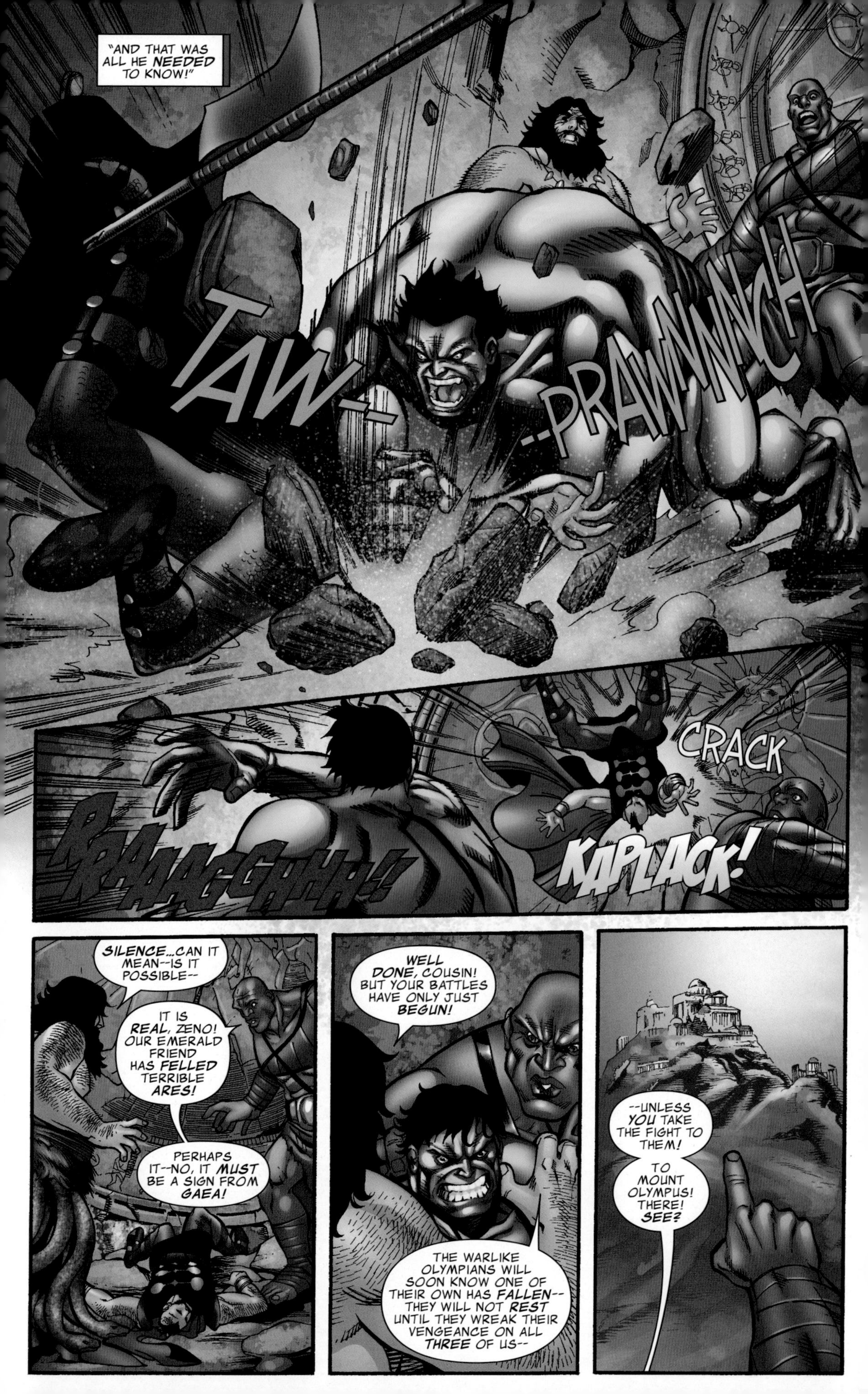
"AND THAT WAS ALL HE NEEDED TO KNOW!"
TAW--
--PRAWNNNCH
RRAAAGHHH!
CRACK
KAPLACK!
SILENCE...CAN IT MEAN--IS IT POSSIBLE--
IT IS REAL, ZENO! OUR EMERALD FRIEND HAS FELLED TERRIBLE ARES!
PERHAPS IT--NO, IT MUST BE A SIGN FROM GAEA!
WELL DONE, COUSIN! BUT YOUR BATTLES HAVE ONLY JUST BEGUN!
THE WARLIKE OLYMPIANS WILL SOON KNOW ONE OF THEIR OWN HAS FALLEN-- THEY WILL NOT REST UNTIL THEY WREAK THEIR VENGEANCE ON ALL THREE OF US--
--UNLESS YOU TAKE THE FIGHT TO THEM!
TO MOUNT OLYMPUS! THERE! SEE?

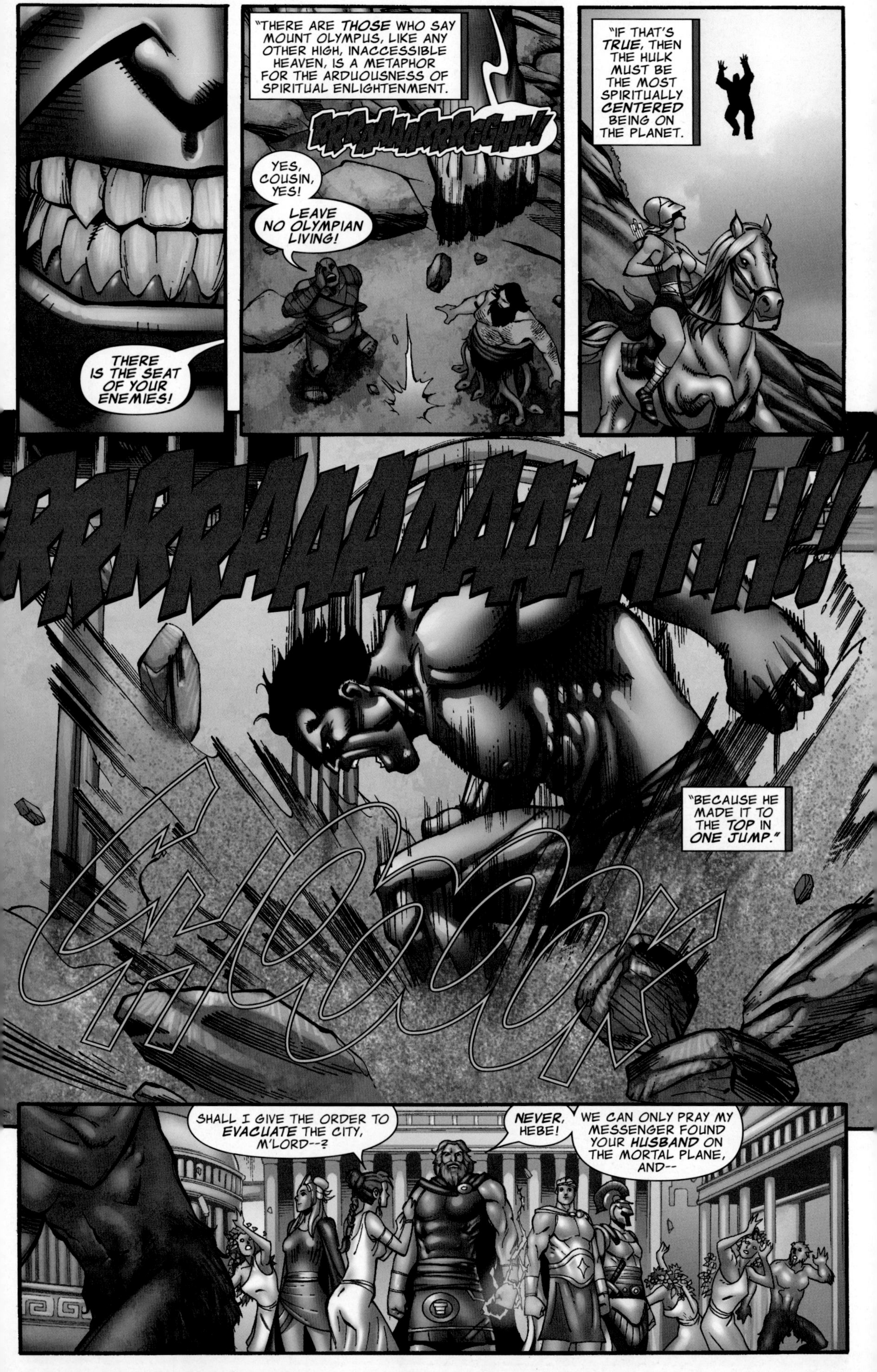
THERE IS THE SEAT OF YOUR ENEMIES!
"THERE ARE THOSE WHO SAY MOUNT OLYMPUS, LIKE ANY OTHER HIGH, INACCESSIBLE HEAVEN, IS A METAPHOR FOR THE ARDUOUSNESS OF SPIRITUAL ENLIGHTENMENT.
RRRAAARRRGGHH!!
YES, COUSIN, YES!
LEAVE NO OLYMPIAN LIVING!
"IF THAT'S TRUE, THEN THE HULK MUST BE THE MOST SPIRITUALLY CENTERED BEING ON THE PLANET.
RRRRAAAAAAAAAAHHHH!!
"BECAUSE HE MADE IT TO THE TOP IN ONE JUMP."
SHALL I GIVE THE ORDER TO EVACUATE THE CITY, M'LORD--?
NEVER, HEBE!
WE CAN ONLY PRAY MY MESSENGER FOUND YOUR HUSBAND ON THE MORTAL PLANE, AND--

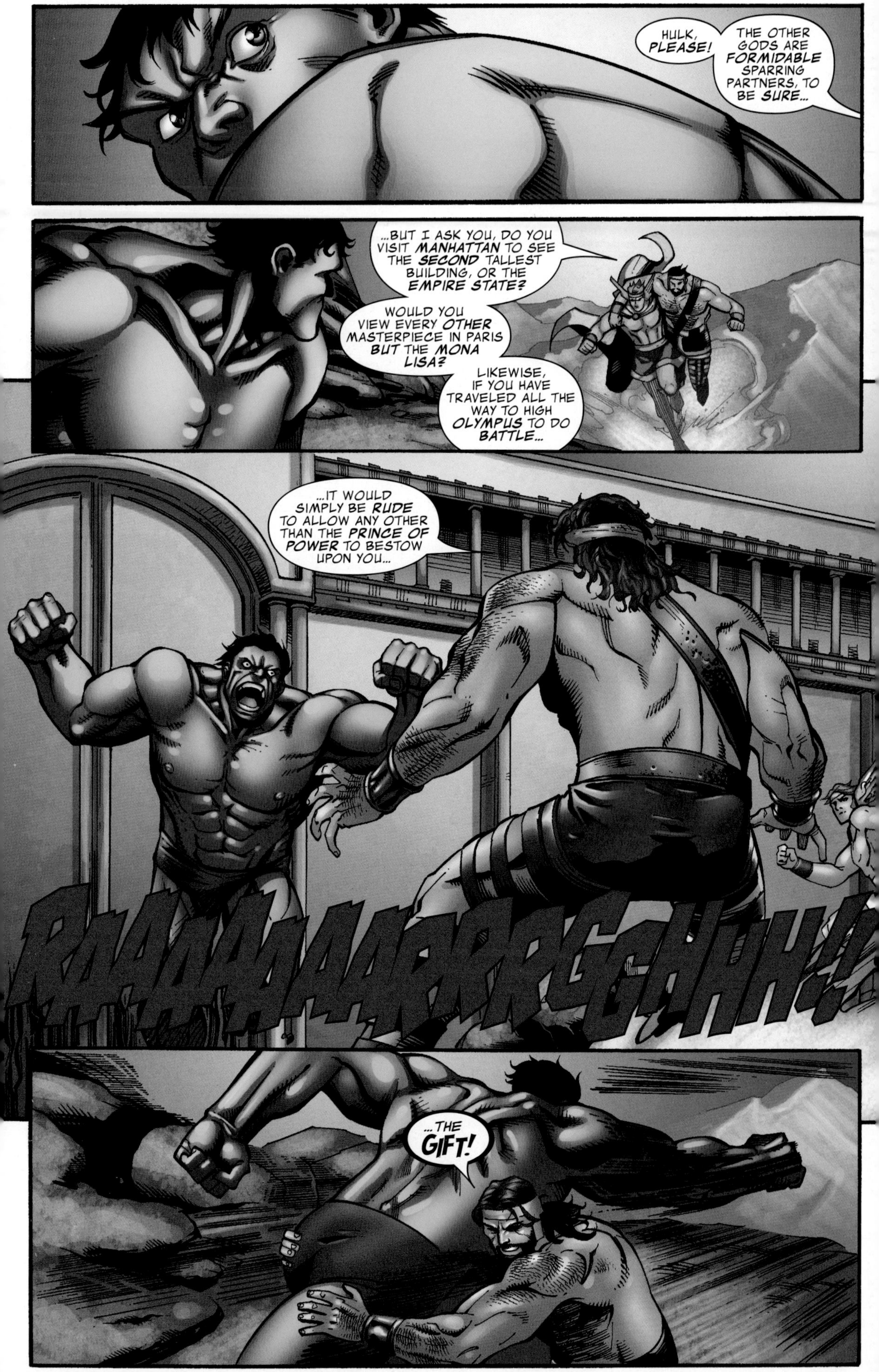
HULK, PLEASE!
THE OTHER GODS ARE FORMIDABLE SPARRING PARTNERS, TO BE SURE...
...BUT I ASK YOU, DO YOU VISIT MANHATTAN TO SEE THE SECOND TALLEST BUILDING, OR THE EMPIRE STATE?
WOULD YOU VIEW EVERY OTHER MASTERPIECE IN PARIS BUT THE MONA LISA?
LIKEWISE, IF YOU HAVE TRAVELED ALL THE WAY TO HIGH OLYMPUS TO DO BATTLE...
...IT WOULD SIMPLY BE RUDE TO ALLOW ANY OTHER THAN THE PRINCE OF POWER TO BESTOW UPON YOU...
RAAAAAAARRRGHHH!!
...THE GIFT!

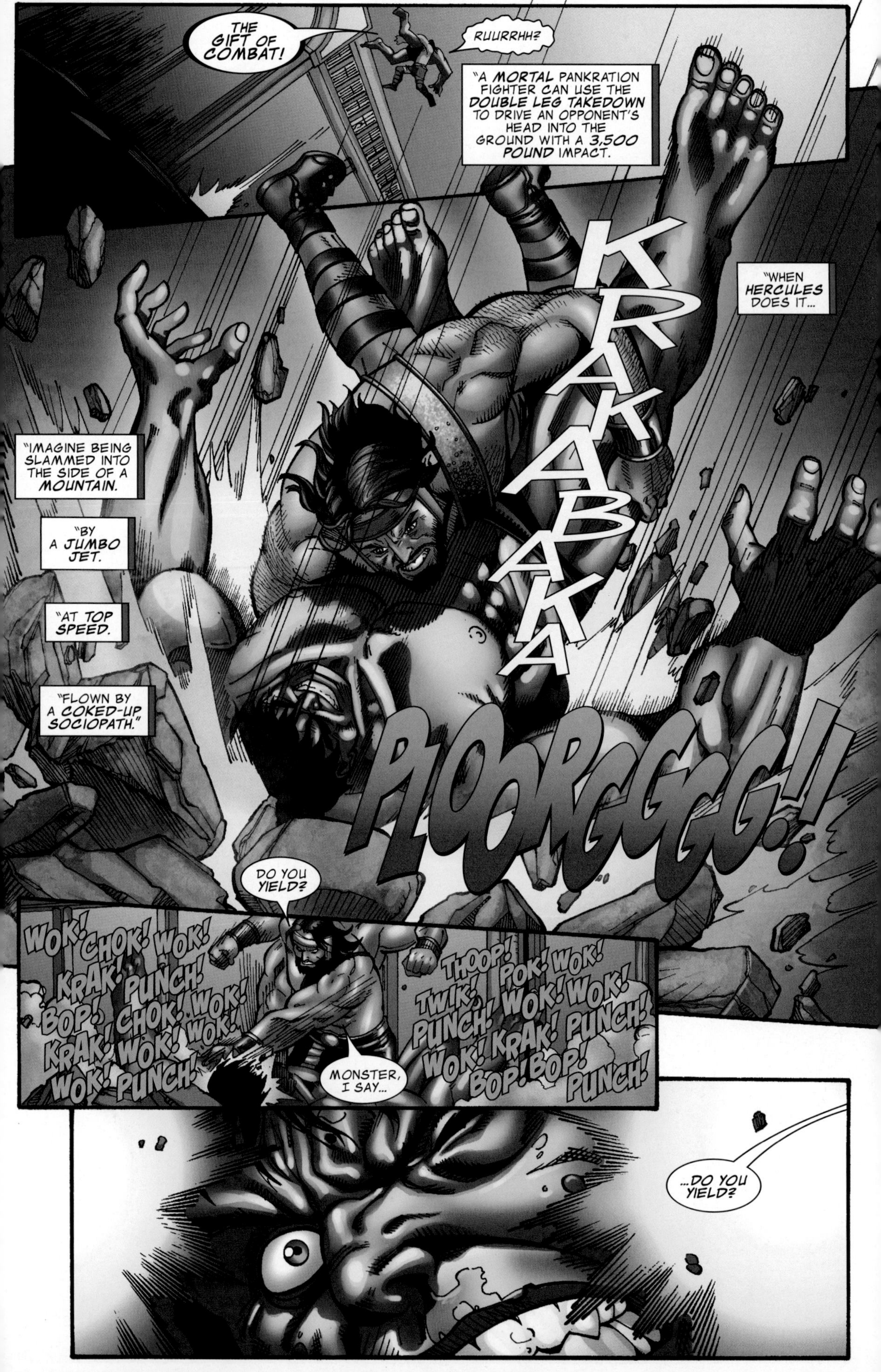
THE GIFT OF COMBAT!
RUURRHH?
"A MORTAL PANKRATION FIGHTER CAN USE THE DOUBLE LEG TAKEDOWN TO DRIVE AN OPPONENT'S HEAD INTO THE GROUND WITH A 3,500 POUND IMPACT.
"WHEN HERCULES DOES IT...
KRAKABAKAKA
"IMAGINE BEING SLAMMED INTO THE SIDE OF A MOUNTAIN.
"BY A JUMBO JET.
"AT TOP SPEED.
"FLOWN BY A COKED-UP SOCIOPATH."
PLOORGGGG!!
DO YOU YIELD?
WOK! CHOK! WOK! KRAK! PUNCH! BOP! KRAK! CHOK! WOK! WOK! WOK! WOK! PUNCH!
THOOP! POK! WOK! TWIK! PUNCH! WOK! WOK! WOK! KRAK! PUNCH! BOP! BOP! PUNCH!
MONSTER, I SAY...
...DO YOU YIELD?

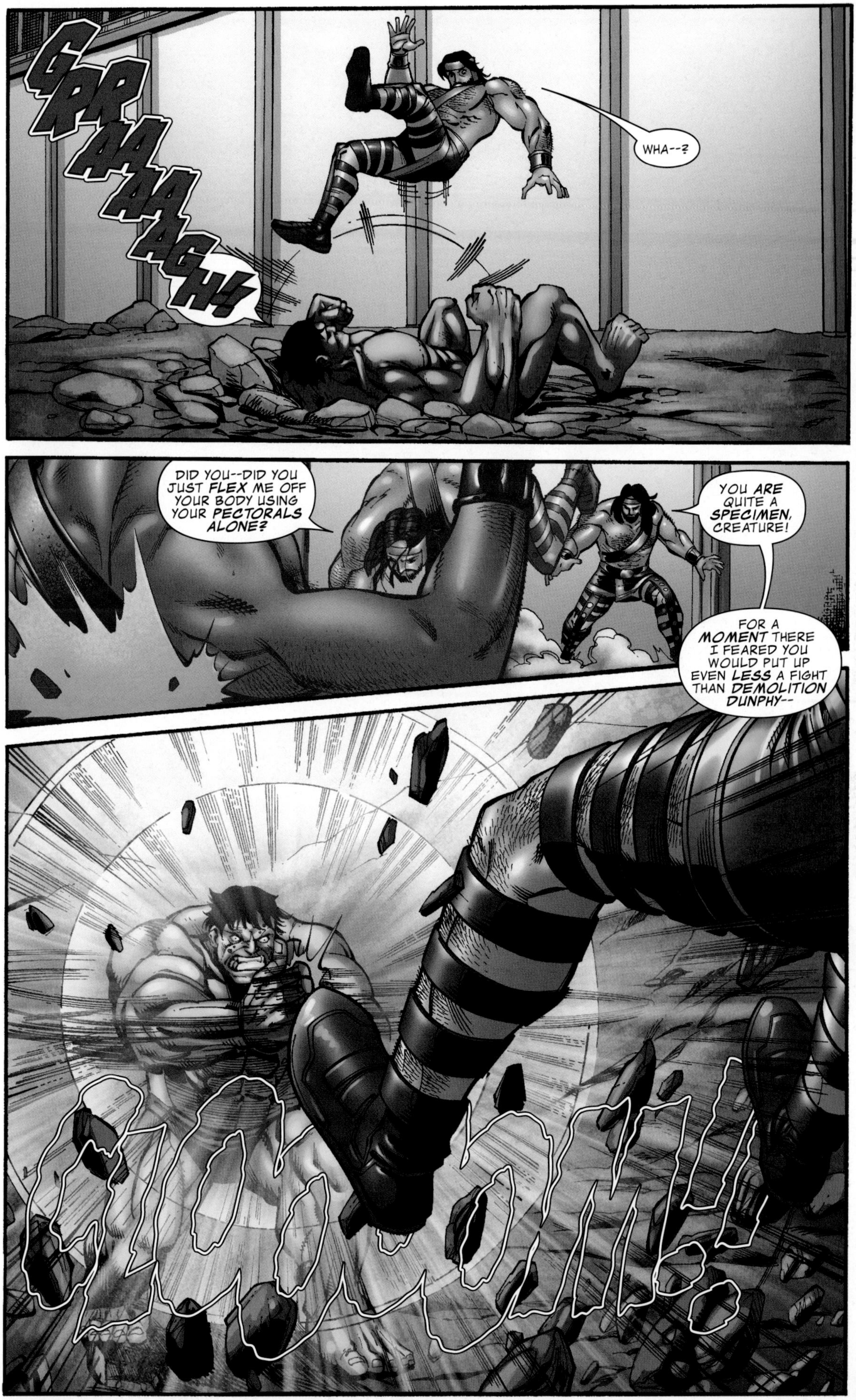
GRRAAAAAGH!!
WHA--?
DID YOU--DID YOU JUST FLEX ME OFF YOUR BODY USING YOUR PECTORALS ALONE?
YOU ARE QUITE A SPECIMEN, CREATURE!
FOR A MOMENT THERE I FEARED YOU WOULD PUT UP EVEN LESS A FIGHT THAN DEMOLITION DUNPHY--

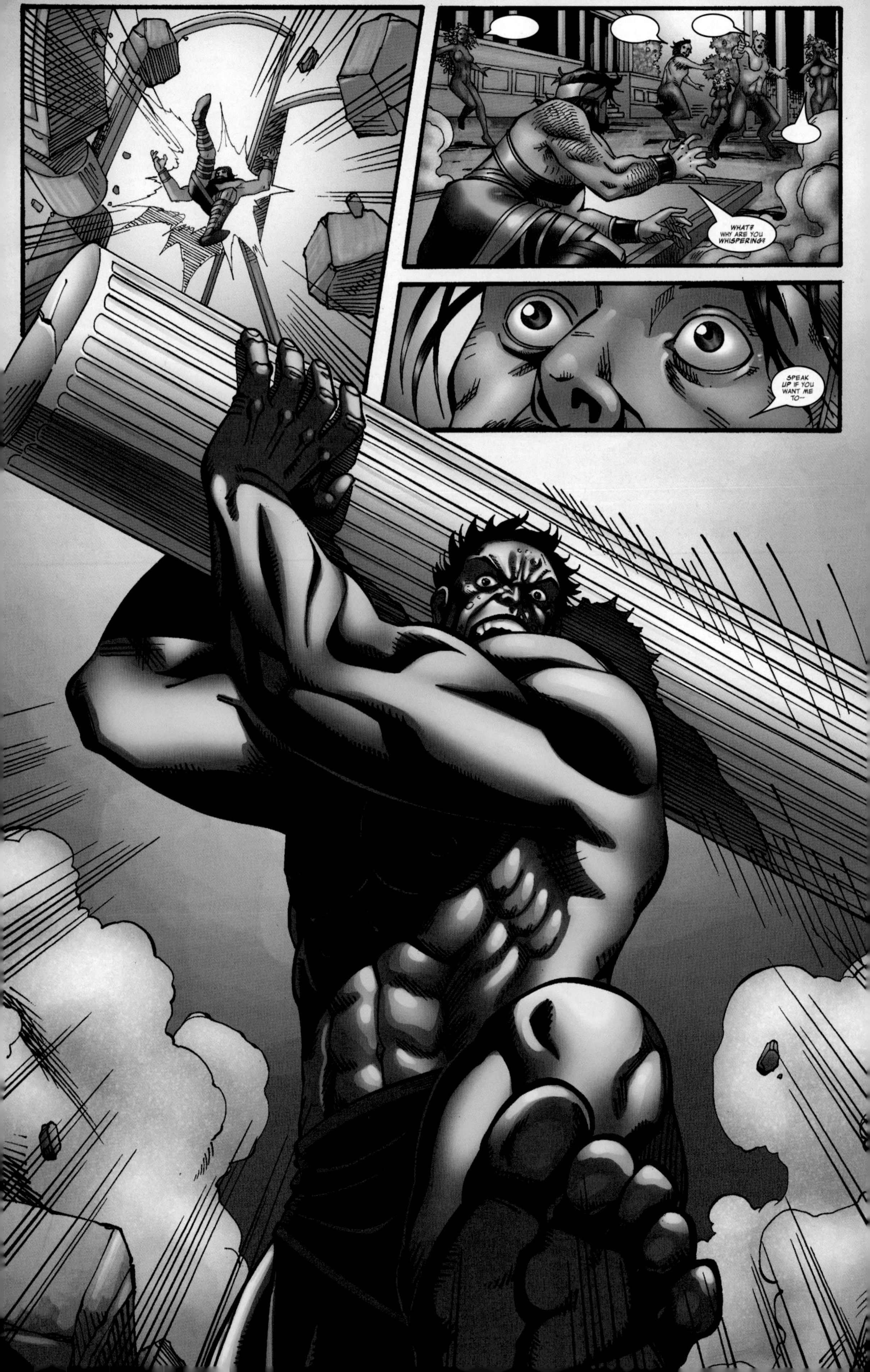
WHAT? WHY ARE YOU WHISPERING?
SPEAK UP IF YOU WANT ME TO--

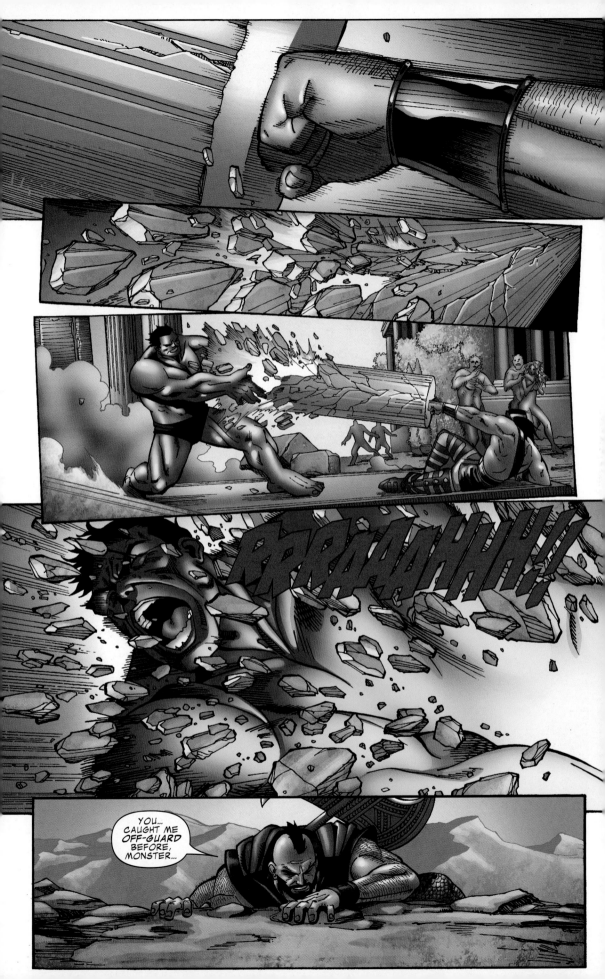

RRROAAHHH!

YOU... CAUGHT ME OFF-GUARD BEFORE, MONSTER...

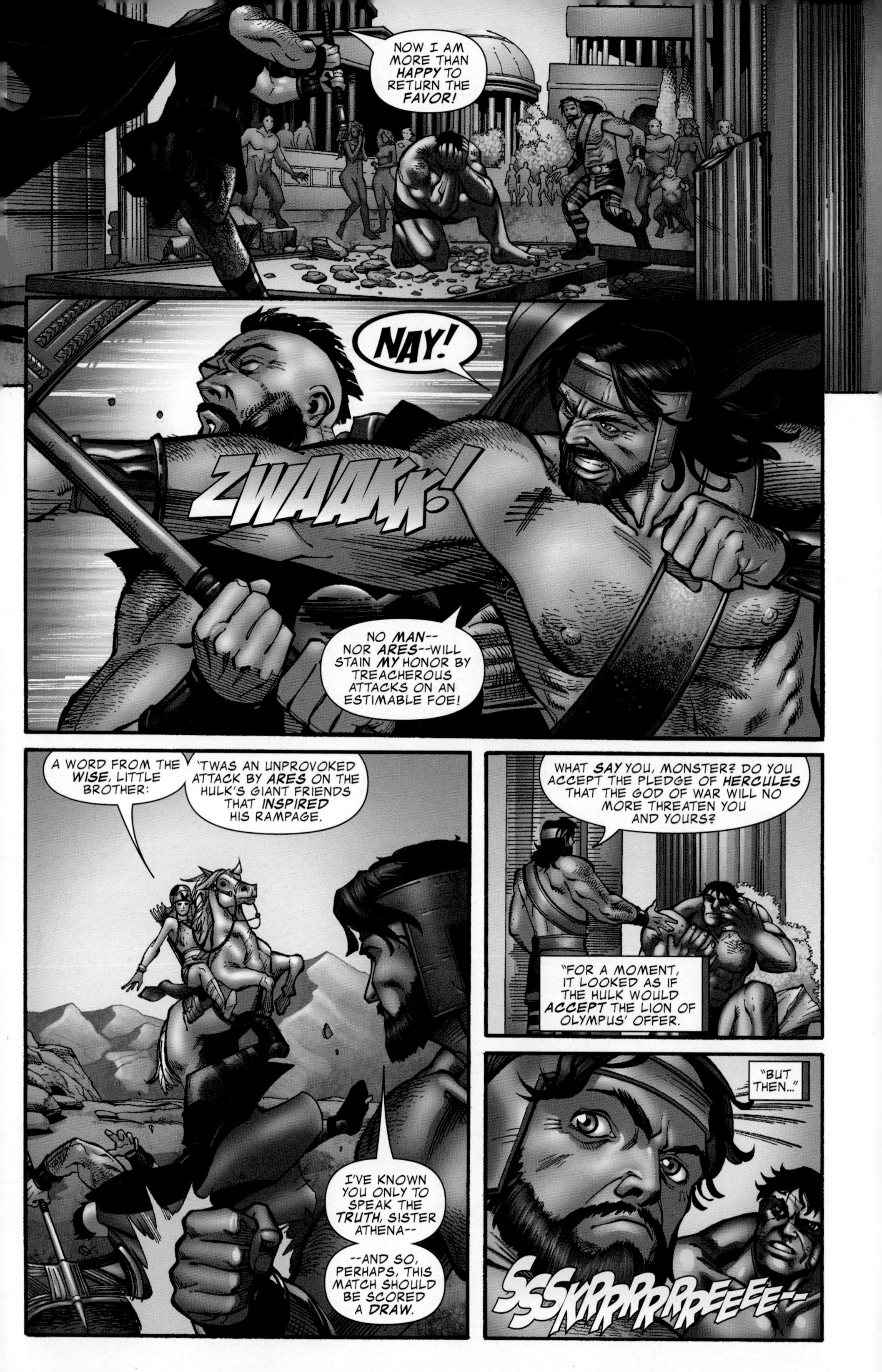
NOW I AM MORE THAN HAPPY TO RETURN THE FAVOR!
NAY!
ZWAAKK!
NO MAN-- NOR ARES--WILL STAIN MY HONOR BY TREACHEROUS ATTACKS ON AN ESTIMABLE FOE!
A WORD FROM THE WISE, LITTLE BROTHER:
'TWAS AN UNPROVOKED ATTACK BY ARES ON THE HULK'S GIANT FRIENDS THAT INSPIRED HIS RAMPAGE.
I'VE KNOWN YOU ONLY TO SPEAK THE TRUTH, SISTER ATHENA--
--AND SO, PERHAPS, THIS MATCH SHOULD BE SCORED A DRAW.
WHAT SAY YOU, MONSTER? DO YOU ACCEPT THE PLEDGE OF HERCULES THAT THE GOD OF WAR WILL NO MORE THREATEN YOU AND YOURS?
"FOR A MOMENT, IT LOOKED AS IF THE HULK WOULD ACCEPT THE LION OF OLYMPUS' OFFER.
"BUT THEN..."
SSSKRRRRRREEEE--

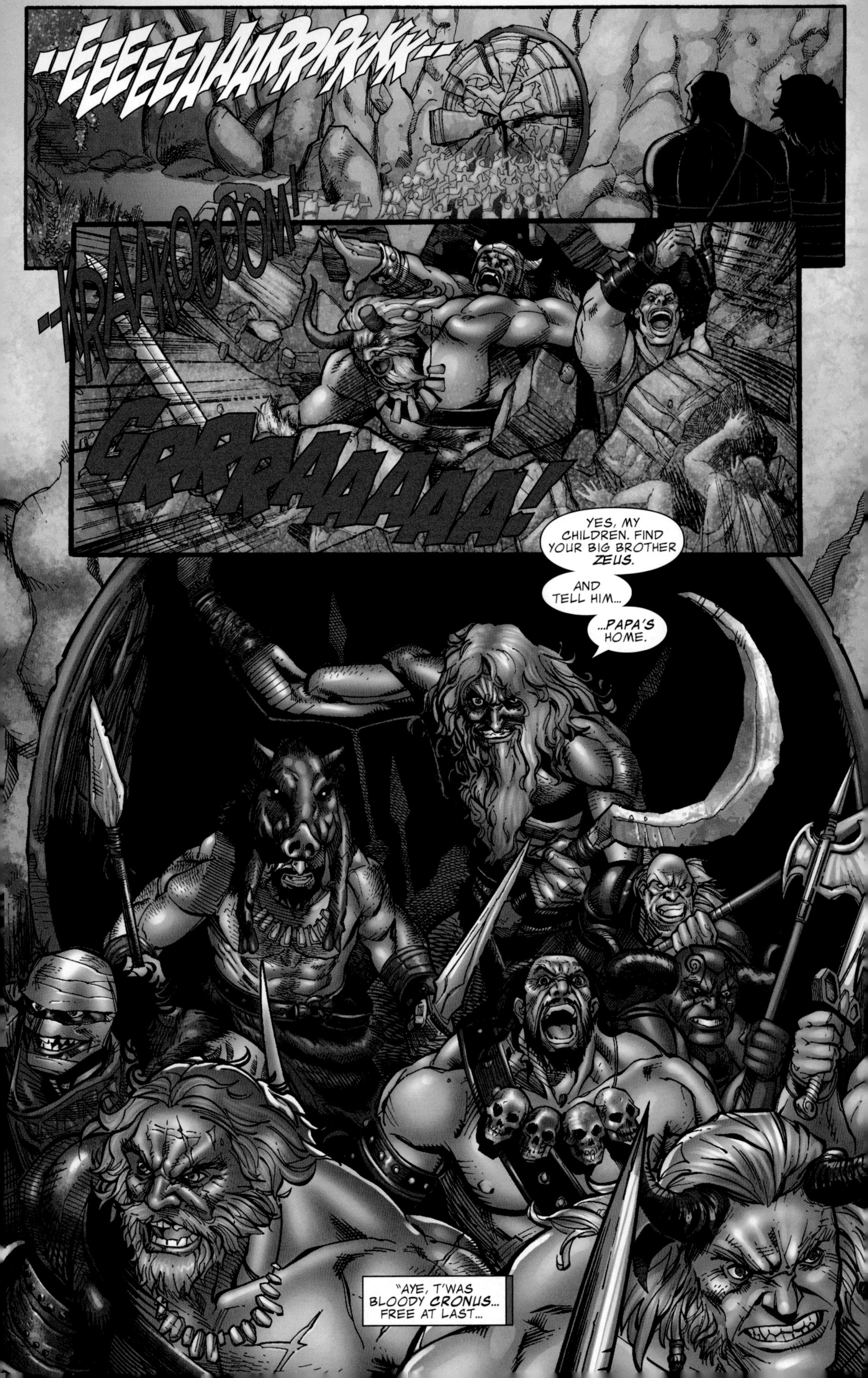
--EEEEEAAARRRKKK--
--KRAAKOOOOM!
GRRRAAAAAA!
YES, MY CHILDREN. FIND YOUR BIG BROTHER ZEUS.
AND TELL HIM...
...PAPA'S HOME.
"AYE, T'WAS BLOODY CRONUS... FREE AT LAST...

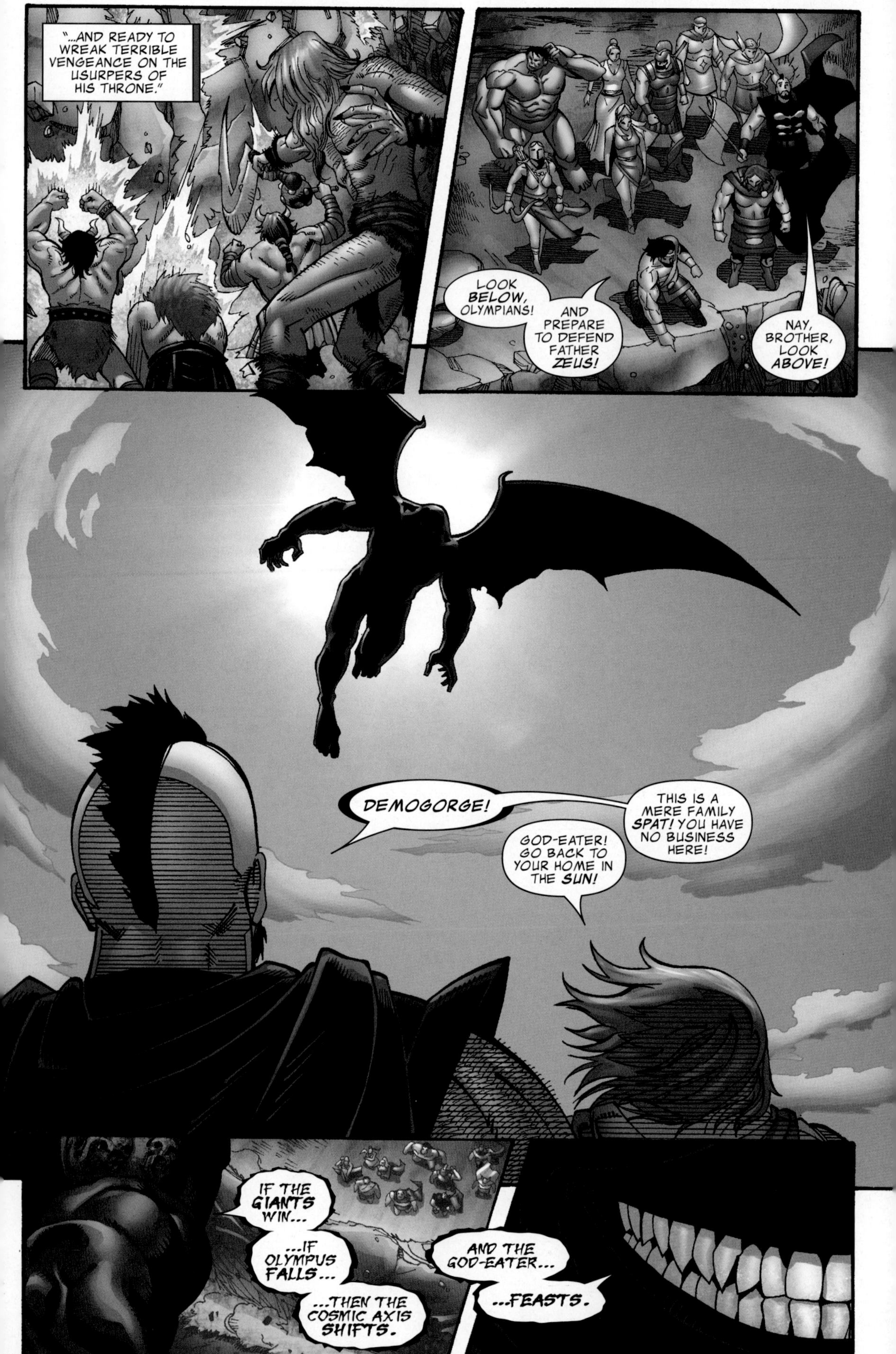
"...AND READY TO WREAK TERRIBLE VENGEANCE ON THE USURPERS OF HIS THRONE."
LOOK BELOW, OLYMPIANS!
AND PREPARE TO DEFEND FATHER ZEUS!
NAY, BROTHER, LOOK ABOVE!
DEMOGORGE!
THIS IS A MERE FAMILY SPAT! YOU HAVE NO BUSINESS HERE!
GOD-EATER! GO BACK TO YOUR HOME IN THE SUN!
IF THE GIANTS WIN...
...IF OLYMPUS FALLS...
...THEN THE COSMIC AXIS SHIFTS.
AND THE GOD-EATER...
...FEASTS.

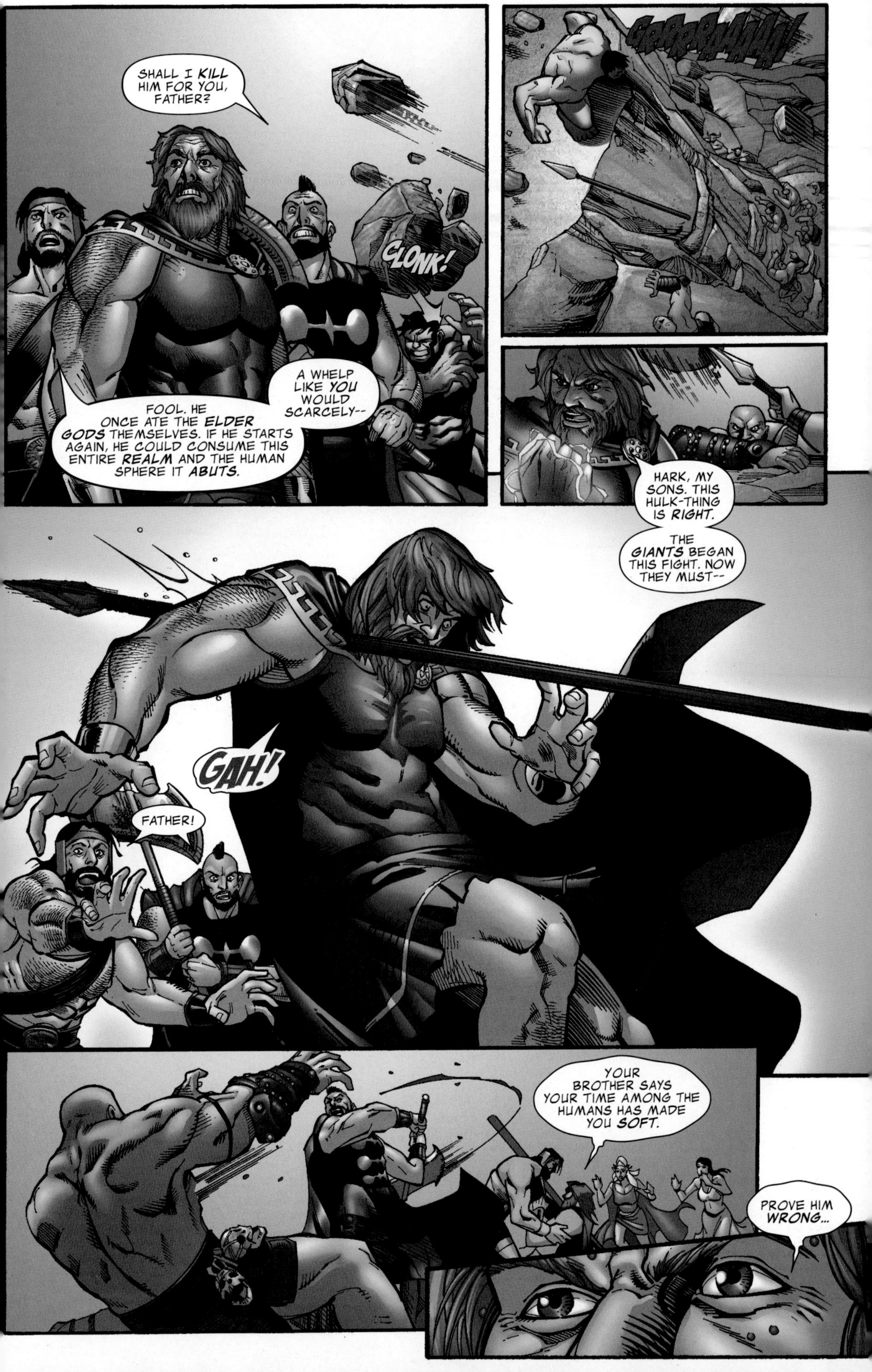
SHALL I KILL HIM FOR YOU, FATHER?
CLONK!
A WHELP LIKE YOU WOULD SCARCELY--
FOOL. HE ONCE ATE THE ELDER GODS THEMSELVES. IF HE STARTS AGAIN, HE COULD CONSUME THIS ENTIRE REALM AND THE HUMAN SPHERE IT ABUTS.
GRRRRAAAAH!
HARK, MY SONS. THIS HULK-THING IS RIGHT.
THE GIANTS BEGAN THIS FIGHT. NOW THEY MUST--
GAH!
FATHER!
YOUR BROTHER SAYS YOUR TIME AMONG THE HUMANS HAS MADE YOU SOFT.
PROVE HIM WRONG...

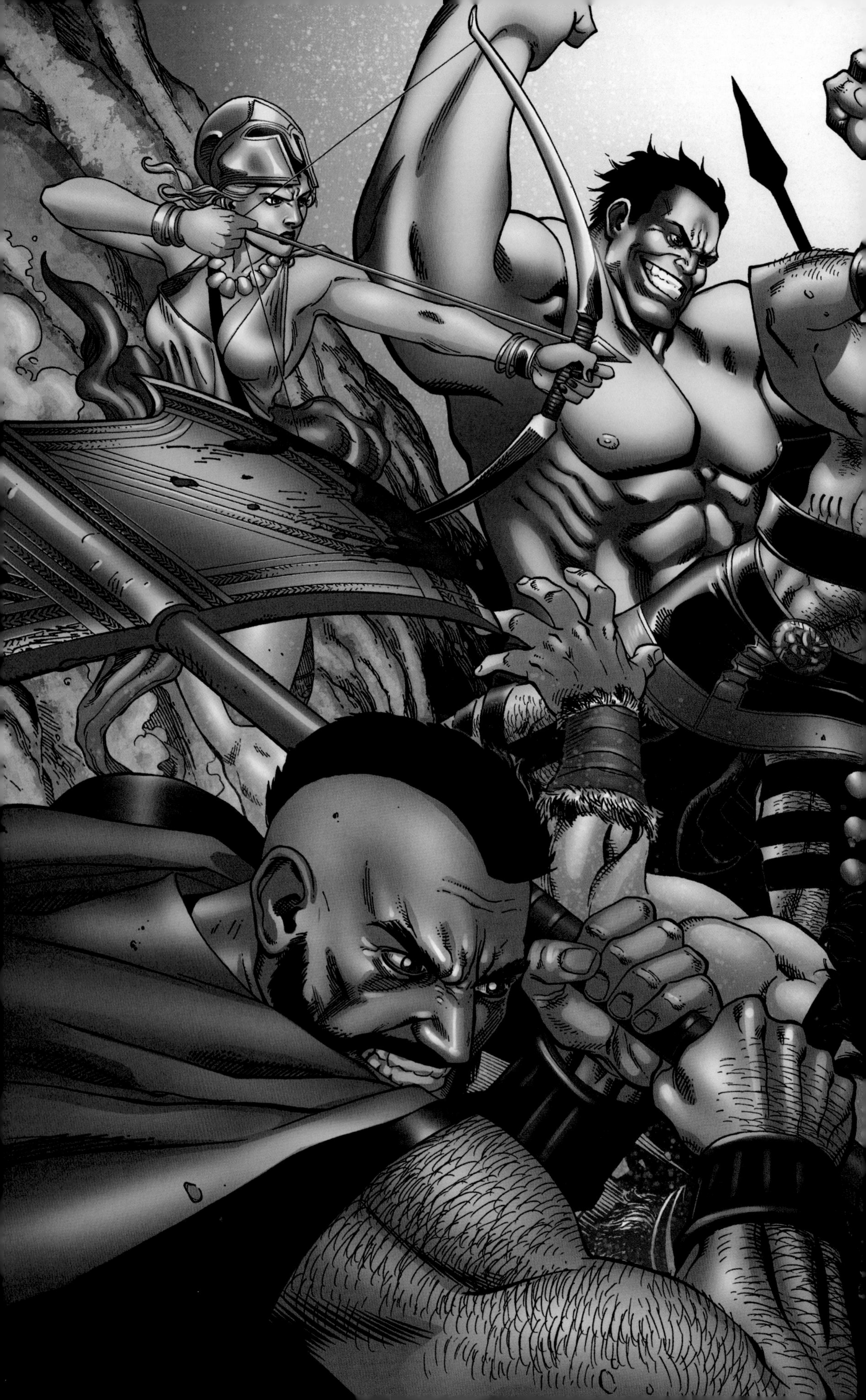

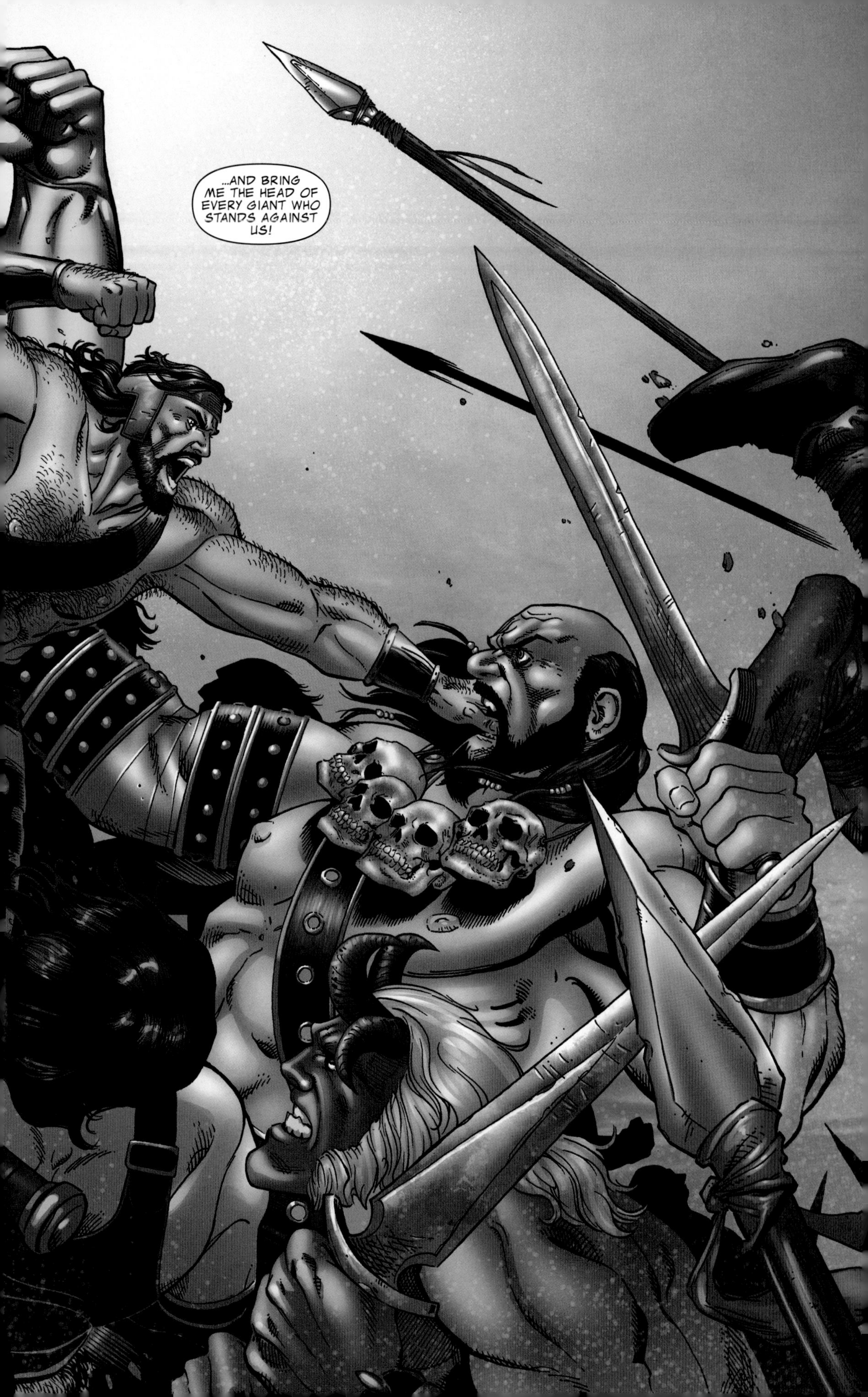
...AND BRING ME THE HEAD OF EVERY GIANT WHO STANDS AGAINST US!

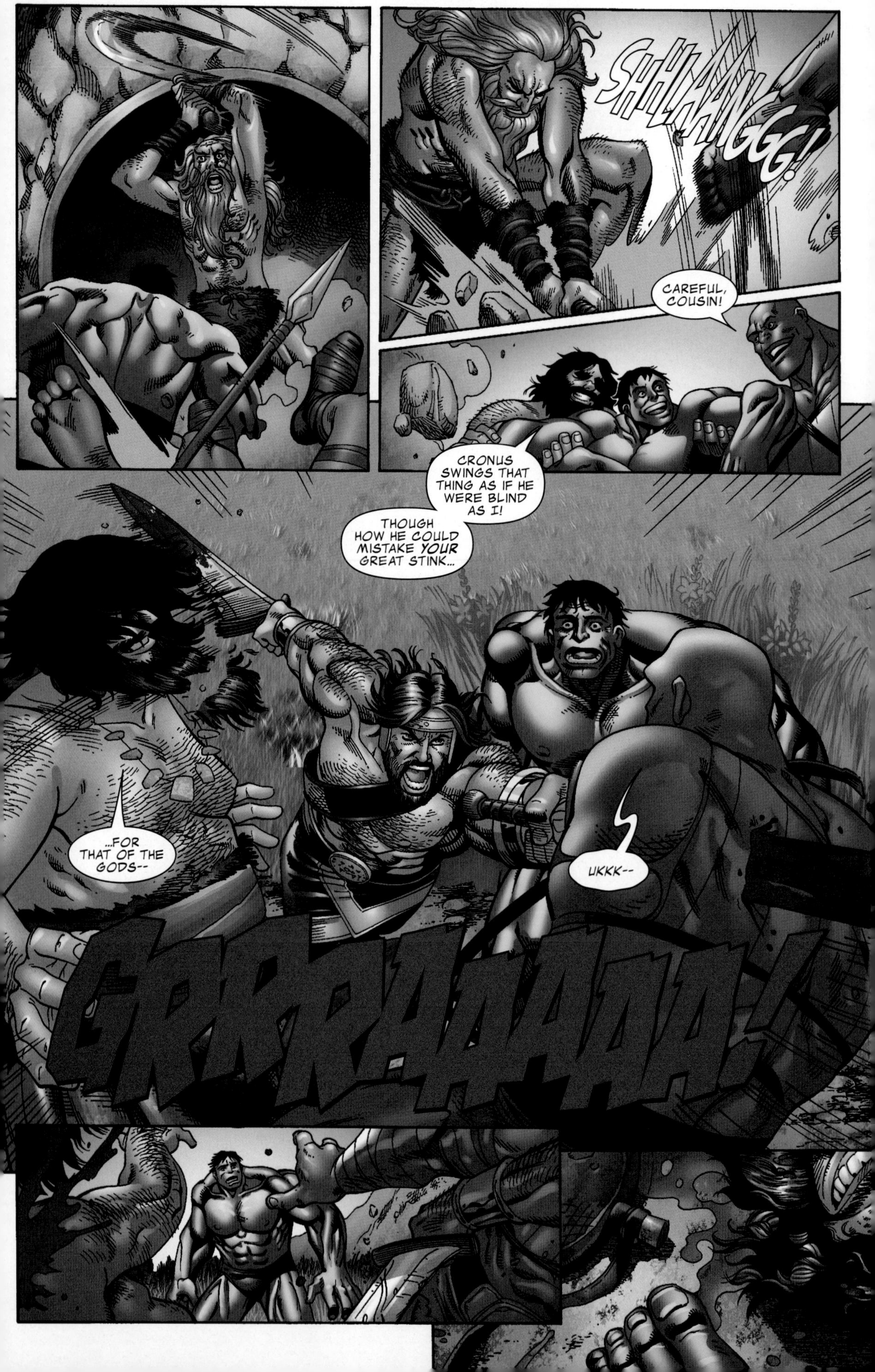
SHHHANGGG!
CAREFUL, COUSIN!
CRONUS SWINGS THAT THING AS IF HE WERE BLIND AS I!
THOUGH HOW HE COULD MISTAKE YOUR GREAT STINK...
...FOR THAT OF THE GODS--
UKKK--
CRRAAAAK!

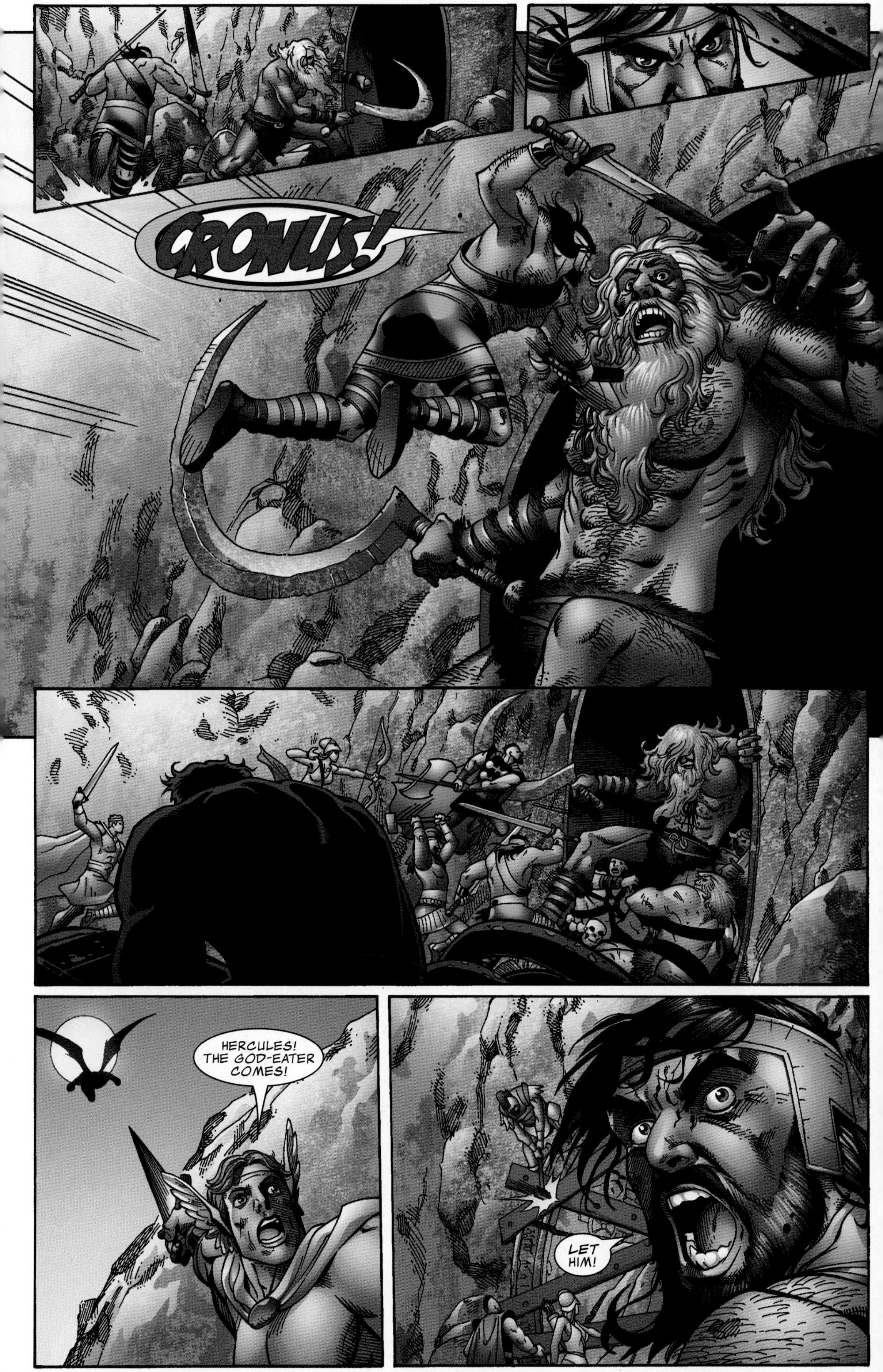
CRONUS!
HERCULES! THE GOD-EATER COMES!
LET HIM!

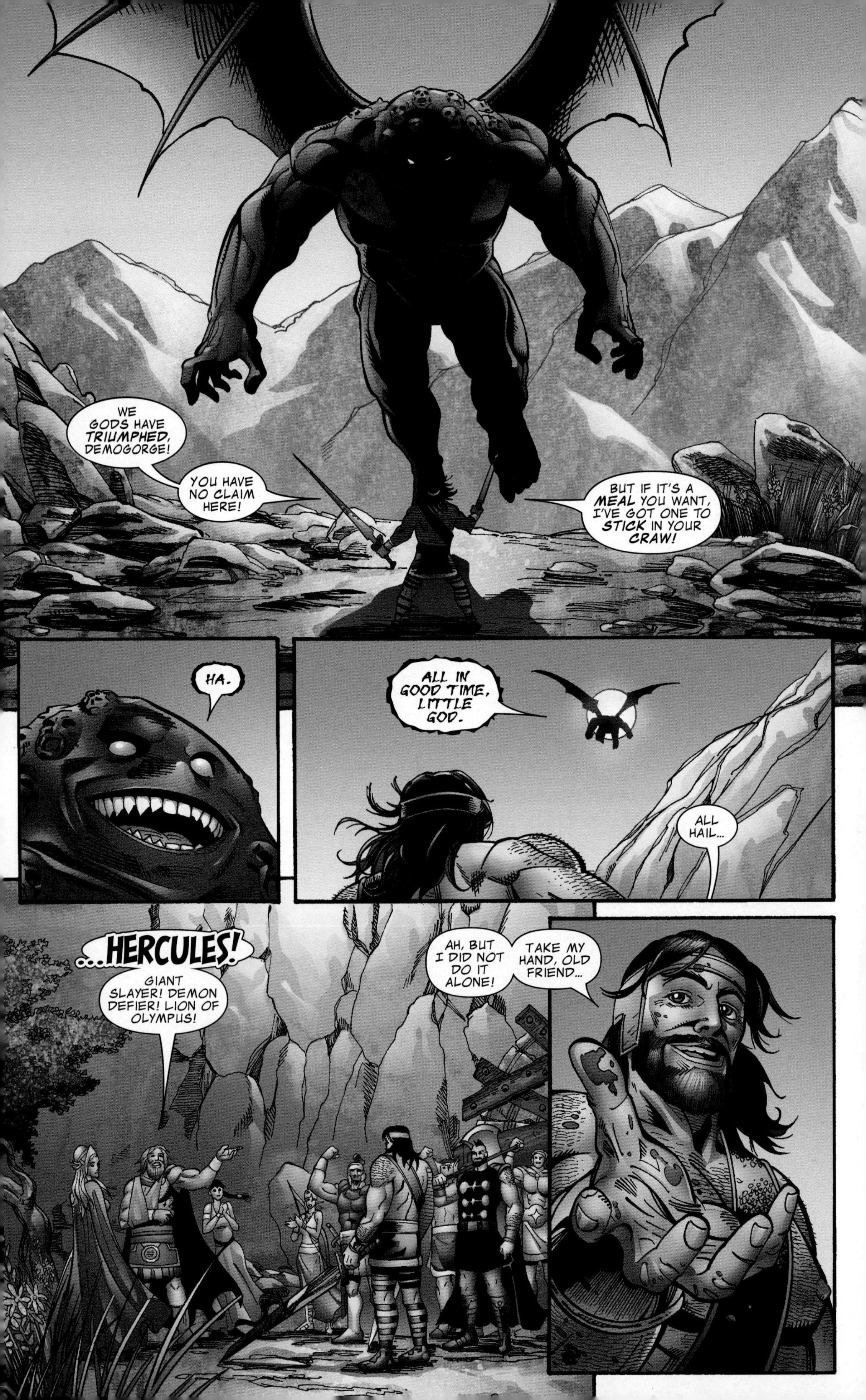

WE GODS HAVE TRIUMPHED, DEMOGORGE!
YOU HAVE NO CLAIM HERE!
BUT IF IT'S A MEAL YOU WANT, I'VE GOT ONE TO STICK IN YOUR CRAW!
HA.
ALL IN GOOD TIME, LITTLE GOD.
ALL HAIL...
...HERCULES!
GIANT SLAYER! DEMON DEFIER! LION OF OLYMPUS!
AH, BUT I DID NOT DO IT ALONE!
TAKE MY HAND, OLD FRIEND...

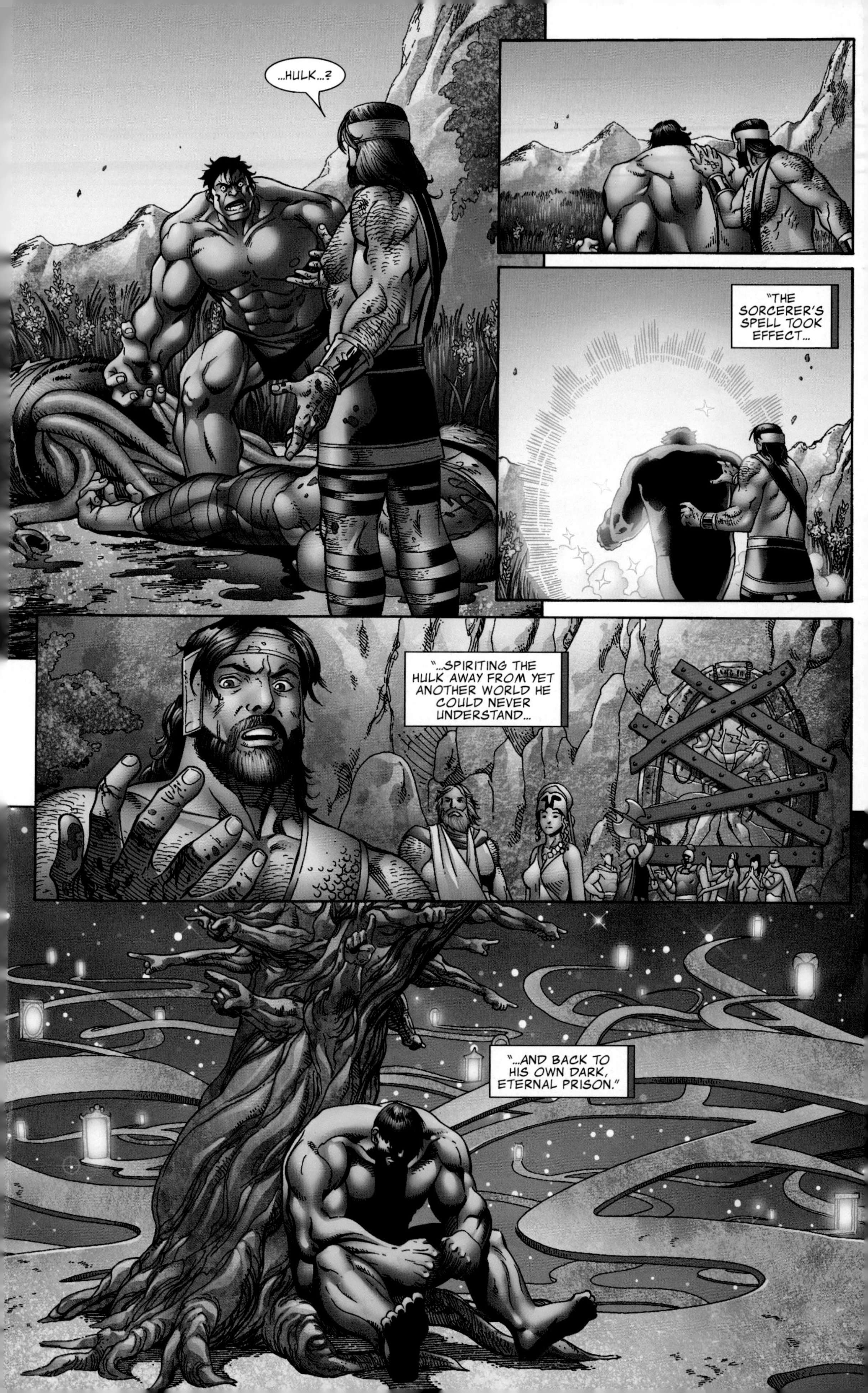
...HULK...?
"THE SORCERER'S SPELL TOOK EFFECT...
"...SPIRITING THE HULK AWAY FROM YET ANOTHER WORLD HE COULD NEVER UNDERSTAND...
"...AND BACK TO HIS OWN DARK, ETERNAL PRISON."

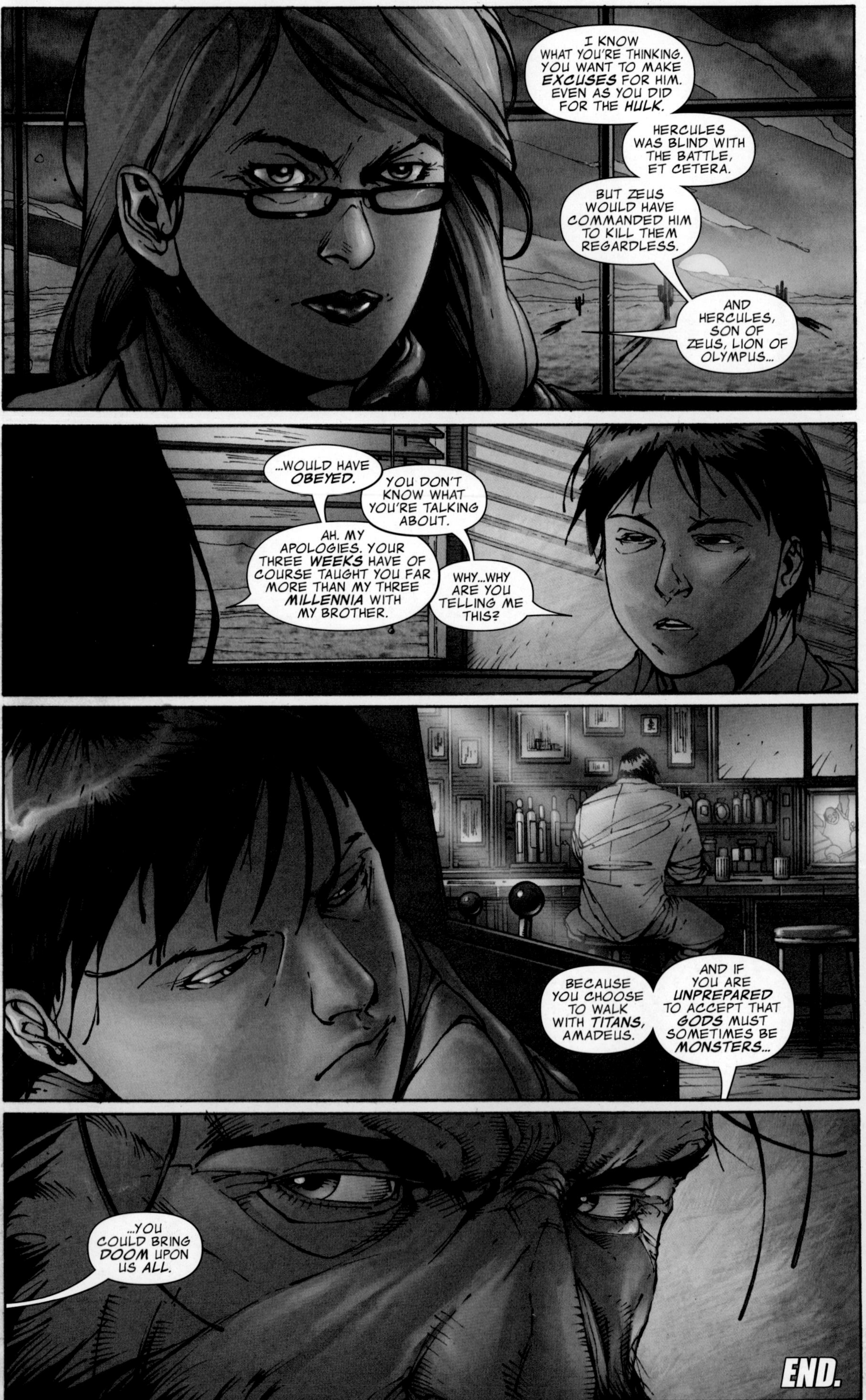
I KNOW WHAT YOU'RE THINKING. YOU WANT TO MAKE EXCUSES FOR HIM. EVEN AS YOU DID FOR THE HULK.
HERCULES WAS BLIND WITH THE BATTLE, ET CETERA.
BUT ZEUS WOULD HAVE COMMANDED HIM TO KILL THEM REGARDLESS.
AND HERCULES, SON OF ZEUS, LION OF OLYMPUS...
...WOULD HAVE OBEYED.
YOU DON'T KNOW WHAT YOU'RE TALKING ABOUT.
AH. MY APOLOGIES. YOUR THREE WEEKS HAVE OF COURSE TAUGHT YOU FAR MORE THAN MY THREE MILLENNIA WITH MY BROTHER.
WHY...WHY ARE YOU TELLING ME THIS?
BECAUSE YOU CHOOSE TO WALK WITH TITANS, AMADEUS.
AND IF YOU ARE UNPREPARED TO ACCEPT THAT GODS MUST SOMETIMES BE MONSTERS...
...YOU COULD BRING DOOM UPON US ALL.
END.